PRAISE FOR ASBO 1

Filled with truth, *ASBO Teacher* illuminates the reality of modern-day teaching with vivid and visceral clarity. At times shocking and at others downright hilarious, Samuel's revelations are always insightful and carefully disseminated, taking in both the bigger picture and the finer details of education theory.

This is not just an enthralling account of one young teacher navigating his way through the comprehensive system; it is also filled with invaluable advice for others who are attempting to do the same.

CHARLIE CARROLL, AUTHOR OF *ON THE EDGE*

ASBO Teacher is the educational equivalent of a Bear Grylls survival guide, with particularly insightful tips on effective classroom management. It offers an informative view that details why pupils often misbehave and provides a fantastic array of practical strategies and approaches that any teacher can pick up and run with. The anecdotes and stories embedded into the book also give the issues at hand true relevance and are easy to relate to.

A cracking read and a must-have book for any classroom teacher.

SAM STRICKLAND, PRINCIPAL, THE DUSTON SCHOOL, AND AUTHOR OF
EDUCATION EXPOSED AND *EDUCATION EXPOSED 2*

Samuel Elliott's *ASBO Teacher* takes us on a whirlwind tour of the modern British education system that is hair-raising, eye-opening, and hugely entertaining.

For those embarking on a career in the inner-city classroom this book is surely an invaluable resource, an essential guide, and a compendium of 'everything you need to learn about teaching that the establishment may never teach you'. I hope many new teachers educate and entertain themselves by reading it.

MELISSA KITE, CONTRIBUTING EDITOR, *THE SPECTATOR*

The subtitle of this book calls it irreverent, but to label it wholly as this does it a disservice. It is crammed full of brilliant behaviour management strategies that are rooted in research, psychology and Samuel's own experience, giving teachers a unique insight into why kids might misbehave and what they can do about it.

This book won't help you turn kids into robots, but its useful realism will genuinely help improve your behaviour management skills. What is more, it is written by someone who is still in the classroom, walking the walk. I will be recommending *ASBO Teacher* to everyone.

HAILI HUGHES, TEACHER, CONSULTANT, JOURNALIST AND AUTHOR OF *MENTORING IN SCHOOLS*

ASBO
Teacher

AN IRREVERENT GUIDE TO SURVIVING
IN CHALLENGING CLASSROOMS

SAMUEL ELLIOTT

Crown House Publishing Limited
www.crownhouse.co.uk

First published by
Crown House Publishing Ltd
Crown Buildings, Bancyfelin, Carmarthen, Wales, SA33 5ND, UK
www.crownhouse.co.uk
and
Crown House Publishing Company LLC
PO Box 2223, Williston, VT 05495, USA
www.crownhousepublishing.com

British Library of Cataloguing-in-Publication Data
A catalogue entry for this book is available from the British Library.

Print ISBN 978-178583522-3
Mobi ISBN 978-178583536-0
ePub ISBN 978-178583537-7
ePDF ISBN 978-178583538-4

LCCN 2020950265

Printed and bound in the UK by
Charlesworth Press, Wakefield, West Yorkshire

FOREWORD

I was something of a toerag when I was at school. (Some might tell you I still am, but they didn't meet me back then.) I skived almost all of what is now referred to as Year 9 and, when I did put in an appearance, I was lazy, uncooperative and a royal pain in the arse. That said, I was more of a class clown than a thoroughgoing ne'er-do-well. In my favour, I was very good at seeming contrite. My head teacher once told me that, of all the boys he'd had to sanction, I was always the sorriest. I left school with three substandard GCSEs and a determination never to set foot in a school again.

My naughtiness pales into laughable insignificance when contrasted with the tales of terror Sam Elliott tells of himself. Sam's story is utterly compelling. His journey from ASBO to teacher, and thence to ASBO Teacher, is very different to my own. Unlike Sam, who seems to have turned himself around in remarkably short order, I spent many long, rather pathetic years in a wilderness of heroin addiction and petty crime before eventually cleaning up in my mid-twenties. I would like to say that I took to teaching like a duck to water, but that would be a lie. It would be closer to the truth to say that my relation to my chosen career was more that of an abandoned shopping trolley dumped in a fetid pond. Like many new teachers, I experienced much of the ritual harrowing that Sam describes in this book and, through a long and bitter struggle, I carved out a stern teacher persona that meant I could begin to teach in a way that meant a precious few of my students got at least something worthwhile from their education.

It is utterly depressing to think that this trial by terror is still a routine occurrence for too many teachers. Some time ago, I described successful teachers surviving – occasionally thriving – in broken schools as warlords in a failed state. Despite the chaos raging around them, their classrooms are bastions against barbarism and oases of sweetness and light. As you will see, Sam has taken on this mantle with pride. His stories of classroom life are both an inspiration and a source of despair.

The fact that so many schools continue to be such unwholesome places in which to work or learn is very much a cause for despair. After a break of eight years gallivanting around the country as a Z-list edu-celebrity, I am now back in the classroom teaching English part-time in three different schools. Each of the schools in which I am fortunate enough to work have committed to eliminating low-level disruption. Each school has challenging intakes and, in each, teachers have been forced to tolerate appalling levels of defiance and disrespect because those responsible for setting the school culture shrugged their collective shoulders, sheepishly shook their heads and asked, 'Well, what can you expect from kids like these?'

But in each of these schools a quiet revolution is underway. Robust systems are now in place which ensure that teachers can teach and children can learn. There is a better way. This undiscovered country is no Shangri-La. Schools up and down the country are working out that having high expectations for students' behaviour is not just possible; it is – for all its challenges – vastly easier than the alternative.

But for those teachers condemned to work in schools where leaders have abandoned the belief that 'kids like these' are capable of behaving with even minimal levels of politeness and respect, hope is in desperately short supply. Lack of collective responsibility ensures that the system chews through bright young teachers, spitting out their desiccated husks as the twin demands of unsustainable workloads and viciously unacceptable student behaviour take their toll. *ASBO Teacher* is a survival guide for working with challenging students in challenging schools and, as such, is a beacon burning in the darkness and will provide much-needed succour and support for those who need it most.

But this book is more than a mere candle in the wind. It is a riveting read and – more than a few times – laugh-out-loud funny. The stories of the students and colleagues Sam has had the pleasure (and misfortune) to teach and work with jump from the page with ringing authenticity. You can imagine yourself in his classroom, laughing at his jokes and being desperately keen to win your very own Geography Ambassador badge. This isn't all. *ASBO Teacher* is steeped in a deep understanding of the complexity of education. Sam talks readers through many of the thorny issues confronting teachers – differentiation, classroom organisation, workload, assess-ment – and, with commendable honesty and openness, attempts to pick a way through the tangles of competing claims to arrive at workable solutions.

Bullshit is as rife as ever in schools and this book provides a much-needed tonic. As your guide and fellow traveller, Sam is a wonderfully subversive staffroom crony, muttering beautifully timed comic imprecations, just as the assistant head in charge of teaching of learning spells out what new balderdash is expected of teachers in the term to come. If you work with challenging students in a school where students are failed by inadequate leadership, you could do worse than become an ASBO Teacher yourself.

DAVID DIDAU
BACKWELL

ACKNOWLEDGEMENTS

In register order, a big thank you to Teiga Clarke-Phillips, Nathan Cornwall, James Croissant, David Didau, Rebecca Elliott, Wilson Gill, Melissa Kite, Ben McIlwaine, Jake McIlwaine, Matt Perryman, Samuel Pollard, Ben Stockton, Nathan Tyson, and Gurpreet Virdee. And, of course, Emma Tuck and everyone at Crown House Publishing.

CONTENTS

INTRODUCTION

There is too much information in the teaching profession, much of which is either flawed, contradictory, or stultifyingly boring. I don't see why this should be.

If I want to drive a car, I am taught simply and directly to apply the clutch, to change gears gently, and not to career around cyclists. By contrast, in teaching, all we are really offered are Barnum statements. Popularised by circus ringleader P. T. Barnum, these are the very general, seemingly prophetic insights offered by mystics, fortune tellers, and astrologists. An example would be, 'You are having problems with a friend or relative', which could apply to anyone. Barnum statements are also what mentors and managers will offer you in those vital few moments after asking you, 'So, how did you think that went?'

Some will tell you that you 'need more engagement', maybe observing that 'Billy is being disruptive'. Others will ask you with a wry, knowing smile, 'How could you have made that easier for yourself?' thereby hoping to invoke the spirit of group work from your lips. Other popular trivialities include: 'You'll get there', 'Try using mini whiteboards', or, if things are truly desperate, 'Have you ever tried using lollipop sticks to call names out?'[1] I'm only surprised that nobody has asked me to 'await patiently the alignment of Jupiter and Saturn', and yet I think that these bland snippets of unobjectionable advice are even less useful than that.

Now, I am convinced that while every teacher will have his or her own preferred style, there are certain dos and don'ts of the profession. And I believe that these apply universally. What I offer in this book are principles that you can choose either to adopt or discard. If you were to adopt all of them, you would become a particular kind

---

1   Daisy Christodoulou explains that the implementation of these 'surface features' of Assessment for Learning (AfL) were far from Dylan Wiliam's original intention in their side-by-side interview for Carl Hendrick and Robin Macpherson (eds), *What Does This Look Like in the Classroom? Bridging the Gap Between Research and Practice*, Kindle edn (Woodbridge: John Catt Educational, 2017), loc. 561.

of teacher – one who has high expectations, a concern for pupil well-being and a fearsome reputation. But I expect that this 'menu' will be more à la carte than that.

Why is there a need for this book? Well, you are going to be given a number of contradictory messages over the course of your career. Take seating plans: at the time of writing, the dogma has it that they should be mixed ability. However, my belief is that children should be seated so as to minimise disruption, and pupil data gives us very little indication on how disruptive a pupil can be. Maybe when psychologists invent an NQ, or naughtiness quotient, we can use data from the school information management system (SIMS) to reliably seat individual pupils. Until then, you have no choice but to go into a room and decide the plan for yourself.

There are no quick fixes, but like chess there are certain strategies you can use, such as the Spanish Opening, along with positions you will want to avoid, like checkmate and hanging pieces. This book will not tell you how, where, and why to do X, Y, and Z, but it will give you the educational version of a Spanish Opening, helping you to anticipate mistakes before making them and thus to gradually improve over time.

In Chapters 1–3, I examine effective behaviour management through the narrative lens. Inevitably, these chapters are autobiographical. The stories are all true and pupil dialogue is verbatim, although I have done the literary equivalent of putting the names and places through a blender, siphoning out extraneous fluids, while retaining the salutary pulp and fibre. In the remaining chapters, I offer the principles distilled through practice. The offerings here are more concentrated. I take counterintuitive principles from my own career and attempt to stir and shake them into the heady cocktail of contemporary educational research. Whether or not I've succeeded, I shall leave to the reader to decide.

WHY ASBO TEACHER?

The concept came to me one morning in the humanities staffroom as my 'Stone' computer whirred and clanged into fitful inactivity. A boot-up so excruciatingly slow that it was barely keeping pace with its brand name; to call the process 'geological' would be a slander on sedimentary rocks everywhere. My colleague was talking about a book he wanted to write called 'Vampire Teacher'. I'd explain the premise, but I don't have access to a campfire and the radiator doesn't quite cut it. That was when I thought of *ASBO Teacher*.

But who, or what, is an ASBO Teacher? Rewind to 2007. I was in Year 10. You would find me in the park with twenty of my mates, downing vodka like I wanted to high-score the breathalyser and chain-smoking enough to contribute appreciably to climate change. I couldn't have cared less about my education. I lived in the pub that my parents ran in one of the rougher areas of Coventry, and this gave me seemingly infinite scope for mischief. For instance, in the summer of 2007, I set up my own bootlegging enterprise, where I'd fill up one of those giant four-litre squash bottles with random squirts from various upside-down spirit bottles at the bar – no half measures here. Every time I made this concoction, it turned chalk-grey, then white, and then the kind of green that looks like it should glow in the dark but disappointingly didn't. No idea why it turned out this way; maybe something to do with the combination of Pernod and cordial. Next thing you know, kids from all over Coventry would be lining up to pay me for samples of this choice vintage, since it saved them from waiting for half an hour outside Bargain Booze.

In another of my extracurriculars, I found an old cigarette machine lying forlorn in a brambly allotment behind the pub car park, and resolved to break in and have what was inside. It wasn't quite *Ocean's Eleven*, but it did involve a blowtorch, an empty beer keg, and a steel baseball bat. Once I'd battered the front in, the machine disgorged hundreds of old cigarette packs, and I scooped them into a Tesco carrier bag. I spent the whole of Year 10 selling these for £2 each, managing to make a few hundred quid. Every little helps. It was tough at first because these cigarettes weren't in packs of twenty, but in the unusual denominations of seventeen or fifteen

– apparently so they could fit in the machine. When everyone trusted me that the cigarettes were 'legit', they paid up because, again, it cut out the caprices of whatever patron saint was currently in charge of getting served.

Ten years later, I'm a teacher. I'm reading a book called *On the Edge* by Charlie Carroll, a supply teacher who requests to be sent to Britain's toughest schools. Carroll visits Nottingham, Sheffield, and London, and has to deal with all manner of abuse. One particularly cheeky chappie named Ralph makes his feelings clear, 'I'm gonna smash that fucking posh twat's face in! Fucking following me everywhere, the gay prick!'[2] It's like *Notes from a Small Island* if Bill Bryson got told to fuck off every seven pages. Nobody ever helped Carroll, and it's a shame because there are effective strategies. You'll be told that it's all about your teaching, and that's partly true, but behaviour management is the precondition.

The moral question that Carroll's story raises is simply this: 'What is a teacher to do?' When I was at school, I remember one occasion when I had beaten somebody up for beating up one of my friends; these sorts of tortuous *casus belli* were as much a feature of teenage altercations as of the Peloponnesian War or the assassination of Archduke Franz Ferdinand. The next day, there were older cousins at the school gates ready to 'bang me out'. I needed a detention – fast. So, I shouted, 'Miss!' and tore up my friend's planner so thoroughly that many would consider me an early pioneer of GDPR.[3] Suitably detained, my teacher went to the office, and I sat there terrified, watching the clock. I was nervous; testosterone coursing through my veins like antifreeze. But, hey, at least I was in a detention, safe, with the teachers in the nearby maths office.

But at 3.25pm, the classroom door thwacked open and in poured about twenty lads, none of whom had even attended the school, many of them brandishing scooter helmets. Not a teacher in sight. I had a sneaking suspicion that at least one of the teachers in the maths office must have known about this incursion, but if they did, they prudently kept out of it. Fortunately, these lads had all been

---

2   Charlie Carroll, *On the Edge: One Teacher, A Camper Van, Britain's Toughest Schools*, Kindle edn (London: Monday Books, 2010), loc. 2407.
3   General Data Protection Regulation.

expelled from school before they could develop anything approaching even basic initiative, and their only plan had been for me to have a rematch with the kid I'd already beaten up. I said, 'Why? I'll just beat him up again.' They thought about it, a few of them nodded, and some bright spark opined that I should at least apologise. 'Sorry,' I said. That was it.[4]

I could well imagine my maths teacher walking in during this face-off between me and the Mensa Youth – and what could she have done? She could probably have given 'partial agreement', a strategy advocated by Bill Rogers.[5] 'Why, yes, you *should* beat up this pupil, but maybe let him wear one of the helmets, and only from the neck down.' She might have been in favour of that.

So, what is a teacher to do? And where does *ASBO Teacher* come in? Two words: Frank Abagnale. In *Catch Me If You Can*, Frank forges cheques, impersonates airline pilots, and makes a lot of money.[6] But it couldn't last forever. Eventually, he's captured by the FBI, imprisoned, and later recruited by the FBI's bank fraud unit. His former lifestyle gave him an invaluable insight into the psychology of scam artists and con men. As a result, he was very successful.

How I came to be a teacher, I shall never know. Fate? Or maybe the scientologists are right and it was all those negative orgones I racked up as a teenager. Either way, just like Frank could identify a counterfeit from its pigments and resins, so I know every bluff, trick, and prank in all of the unwritten Haynes Manuals of pupil disruption. Is it about poverty? No. The richer my family were, the more money I had to spend on ASBOlogical appurtenances like Bacardi Breezers and Adidas hoodies. The parents, then? Well, my mum was a striver who had worked hard to earn a scholarship to private school. She was from a background so poor that my nan, instead of buying her new joggers for PE, would crochet additional length onto the trouser cuffs. Consequently, she was always banging on about university.

---

4   Or so I thought. Ten years later I would see one of them in a presentation on why we shouldn't exclude pupils. He'd been sent to prison for putting drugs up his bum.

5   Shaun Killian, My 5 Favourite On-the-Spot Behaviour Management Strategies from Bill Rogers, *Evidence-Based Teaching* (22 November 2019). Available at: https://www.evidencebasedteaching.org.au/bill-rogers-behaviour-management.

6   *Catch Me If You Can*, dir. Steven Spielberg (DreamWorks Pictures, 2002).

'But students are wastemans,' I'd point out. 'Why the fuck would I wanna go uni?' I didn't know any Latin otherwise I could've capped it with a 'QED'. So, why are pupils badly behaved? The answer is the seemingly paradoxical answer that *there is no answer.* I could give you something specious like the Edmund Hillary rationale: 'Because it's there'.[7] But the truth isn't quite so intrepid. I was just a Cov lad who couldn't give a fuck.

To give you an idea, one Friday I had been getting drunk at the Forum – more high street and bowling alley than toga and chariot, although Caesar could just as well have been stabbed there. There had been complaints about us from the locals. I'm not surprised: there were about 200 of us hanging out along the 100-metre stretch between Bargain Booze and KFC. All in tracksuits, drinking something that looked like radioactive waste, with many parked up on mopeds and road-legal dirt bikes. Later that night, I was wrestled into a police car by two officers and delivered back to the pub. These were the days before Uber so I suppose I owed them a fiver.

On Monday, everybody at school was talking with admiration about how I'd been grappled by two police officers. 'They couldn't get him in the car,' said one. 'Trust me, my brudda's on a big man ting.' Thankfully, none of them saw the crocodile tears in the back seat that diverted the officers from their original destination of Chace Avenue Police Station.

The same scene played out every fortnight or so, until one day, two police community support officers tricked me into signing a yellow form. I thought it was some kind of well-being survey. Next thing you know, there's an 'ASBO caseworker' ringing my mum. 'What's an ASBO?' I asked, as all the bar staff fell about in crumpled postures, laughing. 'Antisocial behaviour order,' the barman said. 'Basically, the government wants you to stop being such a little knobhead.' Outside of a Mike Skinner concert or fire sale at JD Sports, ASBOs were one of the few ways of keeping the yobbos off the streets. It's why the police were so keen on chauffeuring me home every Friday night.

---

7   Technically, George Mallory first said it: *Forbes*, 'Because It's There' (29 October 2001). Available at: https://www.forbes.com/global/2001/1029/060. html#397284ad2080.

Is this anything to be proud of? Not really. It is simply my equivalent of the senior leadership team's (SLT) youthful dalliance with bell-bottoms and platform shoes with dead goldfish inside. Back in the 1970s, when Mr Blockhead was out every Saturday doing his best John Travolta impression, the only professionals he was concerned with was a television show where the young Judge John Deed runs into abandoned warehouses with a sawn-off shotgun every week. When there was an oil crisis so severe it meant people had to cut back on everyday essentials like hairstyles that didn't grow down over their ears. Then, in an unforeseeable turn of events thirty years later, a 12-year-old rapper named Little T would singlehandedly rehabilitate the perm.[8] 'His lyrics leave much to be desired, so it's hard to see why it caught on again.' With lyrics like that, it's easy to see why it caught on again. No longer the preserve of Liverpudlian carjackers from the 1980s, the cycle of idiocy has come full circle. But I am part of this cycle, and I do not pretend otherwise. I boast of my youthful antics in the same way that Mr Blockhead might reminisce about his denim shirt with the pointy collar and the satin tiger stitched on the reverse.

Thinking back over these events, I've thought of a useful rule for enforcing discipline within the comprehensive education system. I was reading a book called *The Learning Rainforest* by Tom Sherrington. He talks about 'rainforest teaching', which comprises 80% knowledge teaching and 20% opportunity for more experimental, group-based activities.[9] So far, so good. However, although he has worked in challenging schools, throughout the book he mostly refers to King Edward VI Grammar School (KEGS), and says that, 'Once you have met students with an extraordinary work ethic or students who can dazzle you with their insights and imagination … you see possibilities for learning that you can never unsee.'[10] While Sherrington makes a convincing case for rainforest teaching, he also notes that in 'more challenging contexts' there are

---

8   Also known as the 'Meet Me at McDonald's' haircut – it's the kind of hairstyle that kids who meet up outside McDonald's invariably have.

9   Tom Sherrington, *The Learning Rainforest: Great Teaching in Real Classrooms* (Woodbridge: John Catt Educational, 2017), pp. 142–143.

10 Sherrington, *The Learning Rainforest*, p. 41.

several benefits to what he calls 'plantation thinking'.[11] This is where the school environment is more strict, controlled, and authoritarian. The purpose is to provide 'a safety-net that seeks to ensure that every child gets a solid curriculum experience'.[12] I contend that in certain communities, plantation teaching is more appropriate than its rainforest counterpart. This is because of what I call the disadvantage–strictness ratio: in short, tougher areas require tougher schools.

Back when I was a pupil, the only thing I could dazzle you with was the headlamp of an unregistered moped. For me, teachers had to be strict because I didn't have any cultural capital outside of school – unless the Walsgrave Bargain Booze has recently been classified as a UNESCO World Heritage Site. In exploratory or group-based learning activities, I'd draw more blanks than a mime artist with an invisible paintbrush. And what I needed most was to be drilled with the propositional knowledge that I wasn't getting anywhere else. This is not to blame my teachers. Everything I did in Year 10 was my own fault and falls squarely on my own shoulders. But there are still kids like me in schools today, and if we're asking in a strictly logical sense, 'How do we get them from A to B?' this is how: (a) direct instruction that is knowledge-based, and (b) zero-tolerance disciplinary measures. I know that only these two in conjunction can bridge the yawning crevasse of social disadvantage.

At the moment, we have to be cautious in how we implement findings from cognitive psychology, since in some schools there is an implicit trade-off between learning and behaviour. Here's one example: 'A workable solution for individual teachers is to vary seating plans as much as possible [since] changing the physical and emotional context even to this small degree can disrupt students' ability

---

11 The term is an unfortunate one since it inspires the intellectual sloven to cries of 'slavery'. I leave the rebuttal to social psychologist Erich Fromm: teacher–pupil authority is 'the condition for helping of the person subjected', whereas slave-owner authority is 'the condition for exploitation'. This is the difference between 'rational' and 'inhibiting' authority. I argue in favour of the former: see Erich Fromm, *The Sane Society* (Abingdon and New York: Routledge, 2002 [1955]), pp. 93–94.
12 Sherrington, *The Learning Rainforest*, p. 41. This is not to say that I agree with the full definition of 'plantation' outlined on p. 39; I mean it entirely in the sense that teachers acknowledge a 'right way of doing things' and not interventions, accountability to external agencies, or the increased status of data.

to recall and transfer [information].'[13] David Didau and Nick Rose argue that disrupting certain short-term cues can boost learning over the long term. However, I can think of many classes where a high number of disruptive pupils means there's only one workable seating plan. If I were to vary my seating plan, chairs would be flung, rulers snapped, and projectile fidget-spinners embedded in the walls. To a lesser extent, the same is true of other findings such as interleaving content; it would work at KEGS, but it makes naughty kids less confident and thereby increases disruption. Currently, our expectations of pupil behaviour are lower than fracking equipment, and the only way to implement research-based ideas wholesale is for us to deal with naughty children, either by being strict, removing them from circulation, or through dedicated isolation facilities.

Why are some catchments worse than others? It has much to do with a culture of honour in what we call rough areas. According to Steven Pinker, cultures of honour 'spring up when a rapid response to a threat is essential because one's wealth can be carried away by others'.[14] Where do we find them? Typically, in 'urban underworlds or rural frontiers or in times when the state did not exist'.[15] As deprived as some areas of Coventry and Birmingham are, they're nothing compared with the blood feuds of the American West, or the Yanomamö tribesmen of Venezuela who routinely cleave each other with machetes over marriage rights. There is a continuum between honour cultures and those known as 'dignity cultures', where 'people are expected to have enough self-control to shrug off irritations, slights, and minor conflicts'.[16] Deprived urban areas exist closer

---

13 David Didau and Nick Rose, *What Every Teacher Needs to Know About Psychology* (Woodbridge: John Catt Educational, 2016), p. 67.

14 Steven Pinker, *How the Mind Works* (London: Penguin, 1999), p. 497.

15 Pinker, *How the Mind Works*, p. 497. Another theory is Robert Putnam's social capital – 'a sense of trust and cooperation and common interest' – which is lacking in these communities. Since Putnam's theory applies just as well to wealthier areas, I have chosen to ignore it. See David Goodhart, *The Road to Somewhere: The New Tribes Shaping British Politics* (London: Penguin, 2017), p. 110; and Brian Keeley, *Human Capital: How What You Know Shapes Your Life* (OECD Insights) (Paris: Organisation for Economic Co-operation and Development, 2007), p. 102. The relevant subsection of chapter 6 headed 'What is Social Capital?' is available at https://www.oecd.org/insights/37966934.pdf.

16 Jonathan Haidt, *The Coddling of the American Mind: How Good Intentions and Bad Ideas Are Setting Up a Generation for Failure* (London: Penguin, 2018), p. 209.

towards the honour end of the spectrum than areas in wealthier catchments.

How does this affect our practice? In higher socio-economic status (SES) backgrounds, parenting can be either authoritarian or permissive, but lower SES parents are 'typically authoritarian', reflecting the social reality of a childhood that is 'rife with threat'.[17] This is why telling professionals to nurture children can be damaging. In tougher areas, *Sweet Valley High* sentiments not only transform standards into limbo poles, they mark out professionals as outsiders: soppy individuals, almost foreign in their naiveté, who can be terrorised with impunity. At the moment, these teachers try desperately to 'engage' city kids with gimmicks – an egregious example being Nando's-themed 'takeaway' homeworks, where pupils are asked to try at least one 'extra-hot' task, along with whatever 'mild' and 'medium' tasks they see fit. All this shows is that you've never been to a Nando's before: when did you last ask for a medium butterfly chicken and have the waiter raise an eyebrow before telling you, 'That's a bit low on the Peri-ometer'? As Tom Bennett puts it, 'engagement is an outcome, not a process'.[18]

In this book, I'm providing a set of tips, tricks, and heuristics (rules of thumb) that I have gleaned from my ASBO apprenticeship, my close reading of the literature, and my first four years of teaching. The word 'authority' has many political connotations. Full disclosure: I am not a conservative. The appeal of Boris Johnson has always eluded me. And as for military investment, if you like looking at missiles and army helicopters so much, try Airfix. Neither is this some sergeant-major manifesto for shouting at children. My solutions are more nuanced than you might expect for an author who has already managed to hit just about every hot button going before clearing the introduction.

My final piece of advice before reading this book is to understand that if you're working in the comprehensive system, the social rules,

---

17 Robert Sapolsky, *Behave: The Biology of Humans at Our Best and Worst* (London: Penguin, 2018), p. 208.
18 Tom Bennett and Jill Berry, Behaviour. In Carl Hendrick and Robin Macpherson (eds), *What Does This Look Like in the Classroom? Bridging the Gap Between Research and Practice*, Kindle edn (Woodbridge: John Catt Educational, 2017), loc. 757.

norms, and even aspirations are starkly different from schools in wealthier areas. I'm not suggesting you rail-grind a BMX into the school reception on your first day or that you spit some bars about spits and bars, if geography is your thing. What I am saying is that if you are going to change the culture in these schools, you need to learn elements of the culture in order to understand how not to get terrorised, and the weapons that initial teaching training (ITT) currently equips you with are as useful as a KFC spork in the midst of *The Hunger Games*. Read the book, observe fellow professionals, and try these tricks for yourself. Enjoy.

Chapter 1

EMPOWERED YOUNG LEARNER

This chapter covers my formative years. I recommend taking a short sudoku break at the end of each section to recover whatever IQ points you may have lost. We begin at the foundation level, Key Stage 3, where I deploy a range of misbehaviour strategies to provide opportunities for similar miscreants. By Year 10, I make a positive contribution to the wider life and ethos of the city of Coventry through the medium of television. Finally, I use formative assessment in the form of a textbook and an IKEA desk to secure some life chances for myself.

WHY PUPILS ARE NAUGHTY (KEY STAGE 3)

It was a sunny day in July when I arrived for my transition day at Willenhall School in Coventry. I remember sitting on the hard shoulder that separated the canteen loading bay from what was then the sixth form, which consisted of two holiday homes bolted together.

I had no idea what was going on – all of us Year 6s were so dazed by the enormity of Big School. Then one boy from Year 7 came over and deliberately stood on my trainers, so I wrestled him to the ground and stomped on his head. The boy ran off and some Year 8s came over to commend me for my excellent work. 'Nice one, mate – we hate that lad. If you need anything, just ask.'

From this one situation, I learned the simple rule that when you're in school, the more outrageously you can misbehave, the better. On one of my first days in Year 7, I brought in a packet of cigarettes I'd stolen from my mum's bag. I remember standing behind the Forum Fish Bar at 8am with two mates, smoking, coughing, my lungs channelling black spirits. Game on, I thought.

I had been getting away with minor misbehaviours at first. Play-fighting. Pulling chairs out. In art, I picked up a clay sculpture of a giant hand, tucked it into my jumper sleeve and knocked my friend off a chair with it. But I was only ever sent out, spoken to pleadingly, or remonstrated with. Mum and dad were never rung, and since that was my only concern, I just kept plugging away at it.

Then, one day in Year 7 … a detention. My maths teacher saw that my work ethic consisted of drawing either small triangles with tiny numbers above, a circle with $pi = mc^2$ randomly in the middle, or x and y symbols stacking up on the page like jumping jacks. I'd watched A Beautiful Mind and was confident that maths was just a bunch of random symbols. So, I got inspired and embarked on the path of the misunderstood genius. When the teacher rang my mum and gave me a detention, I cried.

My maths teacher – Miss Moorcroft – was the only real hard-case in school, and her lesson slot seemed etched in relief on my timetable like tombstone initials: AM. My least favourite time of day, my least favourite teacher, and the two were always somehow entwined. A real mourning subject.

I misbehaved for every teacher except Miss Moorcroft. She was my form tutor and one of the few teachers with the audacity to give me a detention. Thanks to her I had to be clever about skipping lessons, or 'wagging it'. The rule was that as long as you could get away with something, you'd do it – a kind of Murphy's lawlessness. In order to wag it, I came in for registration, asked a friend to sign me in on subsequent registers, and hopped the fence with my two mates to drink a bottle of Glen's Vodka in the graveyard that abutted the school. Once, a vicar accosted us, speaking into a walkie-talkie about how he'd 'got us'. But he hadn't. Not unless the Man Upstairs was considering rolling out divine intervention from merely feeding the 5,000 to Key Stage 3 truancies. Other times, we went to KFC, sometimes 'chilling' on the roof that stood four stories above the road. My friend got bored and kicked a bucket congealed with tar off the roof. God knows where it went. We wagged for a solid month until they introduced electronic registers for every lesson.

Nevertheless, the games continued, and part of the reason I held off from entering teaching was because of the behaviours I had collaborated with as an adolescent. My science teacher was a Mr Campbell-Bannerman, and during one of his lessons someone bit a candy necklace and fired it. The next thing I remember would have defied even William Golding's imagination, since we were all up on the tables in the library, hooting like savages as we pelted this poor teacher with projectile candies. Nevertheless, I always enjoyed science, and exhaustively tested the hypothesis of shatterproof rulers. And, hey, at least nobody called him Piggy.

DANNY DYER'S DEADLIEST MANDEM (KEY STAGE 4)

Fifteen years later, I'm working at Willenhall School. I've just been on to SIMS and printed off my report from Year 11. Here it is:

Subject	MAG	TAG	AUT1	AUT2	SPR1	Expected
Business	E	D	3	3	N/A	U
English	B	A	3	3	2	B
History	C	B	3	3	3	U
IT – digital applications	C	B	2	3	2	C
Maths	D	C	3	3	3	C
PE	N/A	N/A	N/A	N/A	N/A	U
PSHE	N/A	N/A	N/A	N/A	N/A	U
Product design	A	A	N/A	1	2	N/A

Subject	MAG	TAG	AUT1	AUT2	SPR1	Expected
Additional science	D	C	2	3	3	D
Systems and control	A	A	3	3	3	G

Let's crunch the numbers, shall we? Firstly, target grades, or TAG for short. A couple of As there. Some Bs and Cs too. The boy has potential. Next up, flight path. These are the numbers specifying whether I'm reaching my target grade (1) or failing to achieve my minimum acceptable grade (MAG) (3). The number 2 means that I'm reaching my MAG but falling short of my TAG. So, is Samuel Elliott making good progress?

Well, despite what my science teacher says about needing to improve on 'skills such as displaying and analysing data', we need to understand that data analysis is not a skill.[1] Understanding these numbers requires an understanding of what a 15-year-old 'badman' is up to. No number of spreadsheets will tell you this, so I will.

Around the time of the report, I wandered into school. It was 11am. I wore my tracksuit because it was a Friday, and I always wore non-uniform on Fridays. No one ever challenged me about this. And y'know what, why would they? My trainers are sick – Mr Major wants me to wear my Hush Puppies, but he can bugger off. Anyway, my GCSEs are too crucial for me to go home and change. 'You want me to fail, sir? No, exactly. Now check this new jacket; it's got a Gore-Tex outer shell, Scafell Pike Storm Protection, and Dual-Altitude Wind-Blast Technology. Hiking? Nah, just looks sick, my brudda.'

---

1   'Concepts like inference and analysis can be powerful; they provide us with a new framework for thinking about our experiences. It's only when they become misconceived as skills which improve through practice that they lose their power': David Didau, *Making Kids Cleverer: A Manifesto for Closing the Advantage Gap* (Carmarthen: Crown House Publishing, 2019), p. 259.

During breaktime, my friend Connor ran up to me. 'Saw you on television,' he said.

'What?'

'You were on TV last night.'

'What the fuck? Don't lie.'

'I'm not. *Danny Dyer's Deadliest Men*. Check it out.'

That evening, I browsed the TV for *Danny Dyer's Deadliest Men*. Sounds awesome, I thought. About time I got some recognition. BBC One? No. ITV? Nah, keep going. I continued channel hopping until my thumb ached. Then, somewhere in the Nevada-like stretches of hinterland between Sky Movies and adult pay-per-view, I found it. According to the programme information, Danny Dyer was interviewing Barrington 'Baz' Patterson, a cage-fighter, bouncer, and former Birmingham football hooligan. To call the show 'low brow' would be an insult to Neanderthals everywhere. We need a new term – 'prognathous', perhaps, or 'Australopithecus'.

'I'm Danny Dyer,' said the intro. 'Playing hard men and acting tough has been my bread and butter. But now I've got a new role. I'm gonna be tracking down some of the most feared men in the country, on both sides of the law. I'm gonna find out what makes 'em tick. How they got their fearsome reputations. And why they're considered … some of Britain's deadliest men.'[2]

'YES THEN! How you like me now, Mr Major? I'm *deadly*.' I pictured him sitting on a futon at home with a ginger cat, sipping his Horlicks, a hot-water bottle tucked under his arm. Mr Major was about to witness the gritty reality. 'Serves him right for commuting from posh places like Daventry or wherever,' I thought. 'Won't be hassling me about Hush Puppies any more. Nor my target grades. Only TAG I'm gonna get will be the one that confines me to my house so I never have to bother with school again. My attendance record (76.7%) is about to become a Guinness one.' I cracked open a Diet Coke. 'Big man ting.'

---

2   *Danny Dyer's Deadliest Men*, series 1, episode 5: Barrington Patterson, Bravo (10 November 2008). Available at: https://www.dailymotion.com/video/x22jere.

The documentary started showing the Burges – the area where Coventry's urban planners had first decided to do away with ancillary concerns such as aesthetics and liveability – 'Yawn! I'm tired of those.' At the pub that afternoon, the architects must have spotted a beer garden ashtray with its flecked exterior and grimy, cavernous hollow. 'Eureka!' they said. In spite of various bottlenecks at the litter and broken glass factories, construction began and was completed the following day.

On screen, Danny and Barrington pulled up in a taxi. The camera pans to a McDonald's. Then, out I come with a few of my friends. Lacoste caps.[3] Black hoodies. Waterproof jackets. If David Cameron had walked by, he would've flung open his arms and hugged the lot of us right there on the spot.

You could tell we were 'deadly' because Danny couldn't hack it: 'I've only been down here five minutes,' he said, 'and already it's kicking off left, right, and centre. It's about 10 o'clock already – it's that mad mentality of the town. Nutty birds everywhere. And I feel a bit didgy,' the camera pans back to me and my mates. 'Even though I've got Barrington around me, I feel a little bit didgy. Let's jump back in the motor … lively.' All we did was walk out of a McDonald's.

I had to look up the definition of didgy. It means, 'when things become a little dodgy or dodge'.[4] Enlightening stuff, but there we go. I was out and about being a badman. Grades? Who cares? I'll probably pass. Doesn't everyone? I'm pretty sure everyone *has* to pass or the school goes bankrupt or something. Whatever. Did you watch *Danny Dyer's Deadliest Men*?

Back to the report. Here's the breakdown.

Business: I used to bring in a *Mario Kart* emulator on my memory stick and drive around Rainbow Road. 'Sorry, miss, but I don't really

---

3   Burberry caps were discontinued in 2004 due to their associations with hooliganism. Lacoste would do the same. What is today's answer to these sartorial identifiers? Unbelievably, it's the perm. See Paul Kelbie, Burberry Checks Out of Baseball Caps to Deter Hooligan Fans, *The Independent* (11 September 2004). Available at: https://www.independent.co.uk/news/uk/this-britain/burberry-checks-out-of-baseball-caps-to-deter-hooligan-fans-545812.html.

4   See https://www.urbandictionary.com/define.php?term=Didgy.

care what an invoice is – can't you see I'm firing turtle shells at Italian plumbers and talking mushrooms?'

Product design: for our final project, Mr Tudor had barked at us to pick the first thing that popped into our heads. 'The first idea is invariably the best,' he said. On no condition were we allowed to deviate. He pointed at me and I blurted out 'drinks dispenser'. Do you have any idea how difficult it is to fashion a drinks dispenser out of wood? Any predicted grade for design was unlikely to be water-tight so he prudently left it blank.

History: kicked off.

ICT: I was the academic equivalent of a minister without portfolio. Like Peter Mandelson, I'd be summarily dismissed numerous times before being let back on again because the teacher liked me. I had no chance of passing. A prince of darkness to keep the naughties on side? Perhaps.

Science: bottom set. My friends from that *Deadliest Men* episode were all in the same class, and since we'd taken on the East End hardman himself, no way did Mr Campbell-Bannerman stand a chance. 'Samuel should consider how his behaviour may be imped-ing his progress and disrupting the learning of others,' read the report. Strong words, but nothing a little talk with mother couldn't fix. 'Look mum, they just say this kind of thing because I don't have to revise. *I know things.* Sometimes, when I'm alone, I think about things like space or how we came from apes. Like Charles Dickens.' In the end, the school brought in a crack unit of teaching assistants to split up the class and teach us at opposite ends of the school. I sat in the science office while my teaching assistant told me what to do. 'Sir, what's an atom? It's not on the test … I'm just wondering.' 'An atom is an elementary particle consisting of protons, neutrons, and electrons,' he said. 'Wait, why are you writing? Stop that. *You said it wasn't on the test!'*

Finally, systems and control: nope, I've no idea what that is. Oh well, I'll take my G grades where I can get them (G means 'good', right?).

Up until this point, my secondary school career had consisted of bluff, bravado, and the most absurd level of blue-sky thinking. I'd run a pub … join a band … become a television thug. Unbeknownst to me, the thunderheads were gathering. An irrevocable storm that would send jolts through the financial market. Crackling booms that would rid me of my complacency. I would do better at A level than I ever would in my GCSEs – and all thanks to the carelessness of America's biggest banks.

TOO BIG TO FAIL? (KEY STAGE 5)

Jamie penned a memo to his two partners, in which he asked them if they were making a bet on the collapse of a society … 'If a broad range of CDO [collateralised debt obligation] spreads starts to widen,' he wrote, 'it means that a material global financial clusterfuck is likely occurring [...] The U.S. Fed is in a position to fix the problem by intervening … I guess the question is, How wide would the meltdown need to be in order to be "too big to fail"?'

MICHAEL LEWIS, THE BIG SHORT[5]

2008 was a year of changing fashions. Bankers on Wall Street had decided that solvency was rather passé and thought that plunging the global economy into recession was a neat way of introducing a little spontaneity. My family lost their pub. We had to go on the dole. Oh, and I wasn't allowed to open the front door in case it was a bailiff. Whenever my friends rocked up in black jackets they were in for a long wait, believe me. 'How do I know you're not a bailiff?' 'Sam, it's me, Ryan.' 'Hmm, that's exactly what a bailiff would want me to think.' 'Sam, open the door.' 'Sounding very aggressive today, aren't we, "Ryan"? I'm going to play some video games on my lovely flat screen. Hope that doesn't bother you too much.' I finished Year 11 with five C-grade GCSEs, including English and maths. 'Read it and weep,' I said to mum – she took it a little too literally. If I'd walked away from my education at Key Stage 4, I'd have been lucky to get a job at the Binley Mega Chippy.

Fortunately, there is a socio-economic Goldilocks Zone for misbehaviour; my family lost everything, so I was well out of it. Whereas

5   Michael Lewis, The Big Short: Inside the Doomsday Machine, Kindle edn (London: Penguin, 2011), loc. 2461.

before I had been so naughty that I was almost too big to fail, it now seemed like I was too poor to misbehave. I decided to get my head in a book so I wouldn't have to go to the Job Centre. It's why I don't have much faith in the sociological view of education, whereby 'schools and teachers [are encouraged] to use socio-economic background as an excuse for failure'.[6] The poorer my family were, the more of an incentive I had to achieve.

Ten years ago, Tesco Value had an aesthetic that, had it existed in the 1980s, could have reversed the decline of the Soviet Union. How? Just hold a tin of Value baked beans over Checkpoint Charlie and those fleeing the Berlin Wall would have gone running back to Gorbachev. 'Those poor capitalists,' Lech Wałęsa would have said. 'Sure, they have their Levi's, but have you seen Tesco Value?' Even the most overworked and under-provisioned labourer in Crimean Chocolate Bar Factory #4 would have given himself a hernia laughing at our Tesco Value and Sainsbury's Basics products.

It was at this time I stopped drinking. I didn't have much money and you didn't have to be a fortune teller to see what the plastic bottle and slogan of the Basics vodka portended: 'a little less refined, still mixes well at parties'. Keep going through that and I'll be living on a park bench in no time. Other products were no better. Basics porridge: 'not quite gruel – would still ask for more, sir'. Still table water: 'definitely not from the tap'. And as for birth control … well, make sure to pick up some Huggies on your way out of the store. No, I think if anything made me want to improve my grades, it was the disincentive of subsisting on economy-line toilet paper and Jaffa Cakes.

I decided to stay on at sixth form, but I'd only done this because my application to study interactive media at City College had been swiftly rejected. Never mind me telling them how I'd beaten *Mario Kart* on both 150cc and Mirror Mode; they were too hung up on the fact that I'd dropped business – 'Coursework? No, I didn't finish. I'm really *passionate* about beating Bowser, though.'

---

6   Robert Peal, *Progressively Worse: The Burden of Bad Ideas in British Schools* (London: Civitas, 2014), p. 83.

I used my education maintenance allowance (EMA) to buy all of the textbooks for the A levels I was sitting. I studied them, read them in the library, and read them before bed. We now know that reading and rereading information is not an effective revision strategy,[7] but I never learned anything in school. Looking through my Year 11 report, the emphasis is on 'exam-type questions', styles of writing – learning to 'discuss, argue, persuade, explain, describe, and inform' – or, hilariously, 'developing the key skill of understanding the questions'. Whoever penned the last entry must have had site services breathing down their neck to pack up already: 'Yes, yes, I'm just finishing. I won't be much longer.'

I still find it hard to accept that I struggled in any of my GCSEs. Don't you know that I have an ASDAN Key Skills in Problem Solving certificate (Level 2)? That's right. It's certified by Ofqual, the Welsh Assembly, and a professor of education from Oxford University. I don't know who else accredits it – George R. R. Martin, perhaps? Either way, these decontextualised skills weren't helping anybody. As Didau says, 'what does it mean to be skilled at making inferences? Nothing: it's indistinguishable from being knowledgeable.'[8] With the textbooks, I could grapple with concrete knowledge, and I used them in a brute and simplistic manner. Read, repeat, memorise. Eventually, I also created my own flashcards, quizzed myself, and wrote essays. Nothing fancy. And all on a little £10 desk from IKEA. 'Four legs. What more do you want?' Eventually, I secured A*, A*, A*, A, A in my A levels, and I attribute it entirely to the textbooks.

I was never a high-attaining pupil, and until recently, the only time I'd ever heard of a G&T was at Wetherspoons, but once I'd got hold of those textbooks … it didn't really matter. I could grind it out like nobody's business. I even bought an A level with my EMA (government and politics – not the grade, but the right to sit the exam since the school didn't offer it). I studied it for two months, sat the exam, and got my fifth A level. Those Edexcel textbooks really did the trick.

---

7 'Retrieval practice – recalling facts or concepts or events from memory – is a more effective learning strategy than review by rereading': Peter Brown, Mark A. McDaniel and Henry L. Roediger III, *Make It Stick: The Science of Successful Learning* (London: Belknap Press of Harvard University Press, 2014), p. 3.

8 David Didau, *Making Kids Cleverer*, p. 234.

At the end of sixth form, I went to the University of Nottingham, a Russell Group university. 'Not exactly Oxford, still red brick!' Three years after enrolment, I would graduate with a first and become a teacher. Whenever I tell people in the office how naughty I was, they just laugh and tell me how naughty they used to be: 'Well, this one time at St Dunstable's, we unhooked the velvet rope from the stanchions and jumped the queue for the smoked-salmon sandwiches!' Meanwhile, I'm having flashbacks of Danny Dyer and a Birmingham Zulu warrior fleeing in a taxi after an encounter with me and my mates. Go figure.

Chapter 2

WASTEMAN TEACHER

Ah, 'tis the story of the wasteman teacher. If you enjoyed burning small insects with a magnifying glass as a youngster, then this is the chapter for you. An inverted how-to manual for how to teach – or how not to teach. Play the audiobook version backwards and hear croaky, guttural messages, such as 'Discovery learning is the best' or 'Give your scholar no verbal lessons'.[1] But, there is a lot to learn here, as with the Book of Revelation or Shakespeare's *Titus Andronicus*, where everybody gets baked in a pie and lives happily ever after. The moral? God knows. I hear that mindfulness helps.

LITTLE ALFRED

I'm ready for my first term in a school. My application to Chelmsley Wood Academy has been accepted. The job title: graduate learning coach. Their ethos: to provide opportunities to children from a diverse range of challenging backgrounds. Their Ofsted rating was 'outstanding' last year, recently demoted to 'good'.

I'm buggered in terms of transport. I didn't take my driving test when I should have, so now I've got to bus and train it to Marston Green, walking the remaining three miles there and back every day. Oh well, should keep me fit.

It's my first day. I've got brogues, tweed trousers from Topman, and my shirt's so white that its albedo could lower my carbon footprint. I had my hair done yesterday too. 'Looking shaaarp, boss,' the guy at Istanbul said. The Turkish barbers are the best. They don't have the sham-Edwardian coat hooks or a PlayStation in the waiting bay, but at least they don't make dead conversations about the top ten boozers in Coventry.

---

1   Jean-Jacques Rousseau, *Emile, or Education*, tr. Barbara Foxley, Kindle edn (London & Toronto: J.M. Dent and Sons, 1921), loc. 1111. Available at: https:// oll.libertyfund.org/titles/2256.

The button flashes as the train pulls up at Marston Green. I get out and watch it leave. There's a crowd of kids in blazers waiting by the station. They're boarding a bus. One boy thwacks a girl with a fizzy strawberry cable. 'Oww, *bastard*,' she shoves him on his arse. The kids laugh as they file past the driver.

As for me, I'm still in morning mode, the scenes of the day filtering gradually through perception. Being tired is like cling film for the senses. You're there but not fully present. I look at my shoes and briefly forget what a shoe is, until some upwelling of consciousness reminds me that I'm a human, humans have feet, and that our feet are shod with shoes. Funny how we can glitch out like that; an impenetrable diamond viewfinder of reality dissolving into the insubstantial.

This meditation over, and I'm at the school. Yet another glassy private finance initiative (PFI) build, just like every other identikit school. Children breeze past on bicycles, chain-wheels clittering as they round the bend. Rain spatters and girls walk with their hands covering their faces. It's quite disconcerting. Like Magritte's painting of the man with the apple in front of his face – *The Son of Man*. Only the daughters of Chelmsley Wood are a little different because when they pull their hands from their faces, they're revealed as crumbling Egyptian monuments: more foundation than the Sphinx and Great Pyramid combined. What strange customs. Pupils from Kingsbridge, the twin of Chelmsley Wood Academy, straggle to school, shivering in their grey jumpers like a melancholy army.

Going through the gates feels daunting. There are kids there and I'm not sure where to look. I'm not scared. Not yet, anyway. But it is awkward as an adult when you first interact with children – where do you look? I look at them; they look away, then down at the floor. Fair play, I guess this is the pattern: adults make eye contact and kids break it. Later on, I'd understand more deeply that persistent eye contact is one of the most critical subroutines of an adult's authority.

I'd been at the school for INSET on the Monday and Tuesday but this was different. Teacher training was done. I was now scanning my emails and reading my timetable. Seven hours of literacy. Two Year 7s, a Year 8, and one Year 9 class. God knows what I'll do.

My boss, Mr Bentley, bounced about the office. My colleagues whispered something about him being 'so autistic' but 'a great guy', nevertheless. The bloke seemed alright to me. He had a knowing smile on his face. He offered us some chocolates but I said I was alright.

'Right, let's get started, shall we?' He installed himself at the desk, while we – the teaching assistants – sat dotted around the narrow special educational needs (SEN) classroom. 'Sam, you're on literacy. Kathy's got some resources for you in 3B08, OK? Good. David, you're taking Year 8 for literacy as well as Sam, so be sure to communicate where you get up to today. Right ...'

He proceeded in the manner of a friendly robot, tracking our names on a printed spreadsheet and issuing directives: 'Got it? Yes, OK.' His buoyancy imparted a confidence that felt strangely artificial. The kids have all been in registration so the school is quiet. Then, 9am. The electronic bell made a noise that on *Casualty* would signal a cardiac arrest. The day had begun.

I raced to Kathy, grabbed my folder, and returned to the SEN galley room to teach the Year 7s. The kids were so happy to see me. 'Wow, sir, are you our new teacher?' That's me. 'Were you on *Coronation Street*?' Erm. 'Sir, are you married? You look married.'

'Right, let's get settled!' I said, my teacher voice hitchingly diffident, like the roar of a lion cub. 'Sit where you like and we can go around and introduce ourselves.'

Little did I know that I'd already made about twenty mistakes that would leave this class out of my control for the remainder of the year.

'Wow. Yes, sir!' said Alfred. 'Three cheers for sir!'

'Yaaayyy,' the kids erupted.

My Bentley walked in, 'What on earth's going on in here?'

'Just introducing ourselves,' I said. 'Alfred's been cheering me on.'

His irritation subsided. 'Ah, well that's OK, isn't it? And how are we today, Little Alfred?'

'Good, sir! Mr Elliott says he's gonna put on a YouTube!'

'Is that so, sir?' he asked.

'What – erm, no. We're introducing ourselves.'

Mr Bentley nodded and smirked before bouncing back out of the room again.

The first 'lesson' went fairly well. The pupils introduced themselves, we talked about writing, and at the end I had them sketch a poster of what they wanted to achieve that year. One boy named Rahan asked how to spell 'literacy'. I went over to the whiteboard and began, 'L-I-T-E-R-A-C-Y. Like that.'

Rahan squinted, stuck his tongue out in concentration, and set to writing: 'Litrussy'.

'Don't worry,' I said. 'We'll get there.'

Towards the end of the lesson, the pupils affirmed once more that I was their greatest ever teacher, and asked to be given a homework. I'd heard a pupil mention *Minecraft*, so I had an idea. 'Right, guys – we've got a few minutes before the bell. The homework is this: in English today, your teacher's going to talk to you about a book called *Skellig*. It's about an angel in somebody's shed. I want you to recreate the scene on *Minecraft* – can you all do that?'

'YEEESSS, OMG, yes, sir's the best!' said Alfred, practically punching the air before stopping himself in a spasm, then kneeling on the ground and salaaming rapidly up and down like he was on the fritz. The others were cheering as well.

'Yep, that's what we're doing,' I affirmed, watching as two teachers walked by, one smiling, one frowning. Like theatre masks.

It's the end of the day and I'm out of the gates. The kids maelstrom across the car park. One teacher is inexplicably wearing flip-flops and a pair of shorts. A personal joke of some kind, since a gaggle of kids stand around bantering him. He nods, smiling as broadly as the autumn sun.

I'm up the road listening to my iPod when I sense something across the road and off to my left. It's Alfred and my Year 7 class standing outside a Nisa Local.

'MR ELLIOTT, OH MY GOD,' they shout, running across the dual-carriageway to greet me. Oh lord.

'Boys,' they'd just finished football practice and none of the girls were there. 'Calm down. You've just run across the road there.'

'Yeah, but we run fast, sir,' said Kian. 'Like Sonic the Hedgehog.'

'Only hedgehogs I ever see are roadkill, Kian,' I said. 'Besides, I gotta get home. I can't sit around talking to you guys – I've got to catch the train.'

'Sir,' said Alfred, his eyes smiling but his mouth too full of Doritos to participate. 'You got to have a Dorito. C'mon guys, Mr Elliott needs sustenance [Year 7 Word of the Week]. He's got a train to catch.'

'Nah, I'm OK. I'm on a diet.'

'C'mon, sir – please!' said Kian. 'Just one!'

I have no idea why they wanted me to have a Dorito, and then one of Kian's Starburst, and then a cheese curl from Rahan. I had a dim sense that this was the opposite of what parents imagine when they say, 'Don't take candy from a stranger.' Here's me, trying to get away, but I'm accosted by children force-feeding me sweets. After my last Wotsit I said, 'That's it now, I've got twenty minutes. I'll see you on Friday,' and walked off. The kids waved me away like I was boarding the *Titanic*. Little did I know, I could just as well have been.

The class soon became difficult. When you start off on such a high, and impose no authority, the pupils form inappropriate attachments to you. At first it was flattering. Some of these pupils, especially Alfred, had such a high regard for me. Even when they misbehaved and I'd begin to despair, they'd turn around and tell me, 'C'mon sir, you know you're our favourite.' Then I'm whipped into action again, going back to the PowerPoints, coming up with some new and engaging initiative. But I was killing myself doing it, and, in the end, merely dumbing things down. When you do this continually, you'll soon forfeit any respect you might have had.

I still miss those kids, and there will never be a phase like that in my career again. If I'd started off properly with clear rules, routines, and expectations, I could have made a difference to their lives. I'm sure they turned out fine without me, but it's still a shame when you know that you dropped the ball instead of gripping it with every fibre and ligament. I hope those kids turned out alright.

KNEE-JERK RESPONSES

The week after I began with Year 7, I took on my first Year 9 class. These kids look enormous. One of the girls is six foot two. Which makes it all the funnier that we're all cramped into 2U07, a room so small it could give a fruit fly claustrophobia. There are dyslexia-friendly board games on shelves that wrap around the perimeter of the room. The Young Amazon cracks her head on the metal shelf bracket, 'FUH – ow,' she corrects herself. 'Sir, do we 'ave to be in here?'

'Yeah, sir, this is dead,' said Damian. 'I feel like I'm in one of them clown cars.'

I looked around. Only five pupils had the luxury of a desk and chair. Another, Ibrahim, knelt on the floor beside his best friend, Ben. Kiera and Tamara leant across the cupboard counter-tops, resting awkwardly on their elbows. One boy, Macaulay, looked out of the window.

'Right, guys, shall we introduce ourselves,' I said. 'My name's Mr Elliott and I'll be teaching you literacy.'

'Can I start, sir?' asked Kiera, languidly raising her head. The absurdity of reclining on a cupboard seemed to escape them. Strangely, their Dickensian plight imparted a kind of camaraderie, as though they'd internally branded themselves 'The Cupboard Girls'.

'Nah, me,' said Owen. 'I'm starting.' I nodded. He proceeded. 'Right, so I'm Owen. My favourite subject is girl-pulling – luckily, got Mr Elliott here to teach me how. And when I grow up, I wanna pull girls like ma brudda Mr E. C'mon sir, my guy, my guy.' He raised his fist expecting a bump, not to be let down with one.

'Owen, that's not appropriate. If you make that kind of comment again, I'll be forced to give you a C1.'

'C1 – wah? C1 – waaah? Ay, you know that's a verbal warning, right?'

'Right?'

'So, you've just given me a C1.'

'I haven't yet, Owen, but if you continue to challenge me then I'll have to give you a C1.'

'Oh, my days! Are you dizzy? Man's giving C1s for C1s now. Look, just give me the C1, I don't mind.'

'No, you've not earned it.'

'For *fuck's* sake,' said Owen. 'What about now?'

'Outside,' I said. When you're first on the job and you hear a kid swear you almost always send them out. It's a knee-jerk response but you don't know what else to do.

Owen was rather pleased to be sent out and stood patiently by the door.

'Don't mind him,' said Tamara. 'You should see him with other teachers. He's fucking mad.' Tamara jumped like she'd knocked a Ming vase off a pedestal and clasped her mouth. 'Sorry!' Yet I sensed a vague glimmer in her eye.

So, this was the first lesson. One month later and times had changed. Marius sat in the middle of the room flipping a two-litre bottle of Pepsi. Owen was kneeling on the floor on the opposite side, pounding the table.

'C'mon, Marius – you nearly got it. Oh, shit, you almost got it den! C'mooon,' he roared.

'Look, boys,' I said. 'We've got to get this literacy pack done by the bell.'

'Yeah, sir, chill. We got this. Just a few more flips,' Owen said, his grin wide enough for a canine extraction. 'You don't understand *this* bottle, sir. We been trying to flip it all week but it *never* lands. But Marius almost has it.'

Kiera and Tamara were drawing pictures in felt-tips. Damian was hopping around the room. And Macaulay came over to start mocking Marius.

'Marius, when's your dad gonna get a fucking job?' he said, before wheezing into laughter, beads of water squirting out of his eyes and running down his rosy hamster cheeks. 'Sir, you know Marius is a dirty little benefit scrounger?'

'Macaulay, enough!' I said. 'You say that again and you'll be staying behind after school for an *hour*.' I enunciated it loudly.

Macaulay waved his hand as though dismissing a waiter who'd told him his card was declined, as if to say, 'I couldn't possibly enter into *this* discussion, right now. Can't you see I'm having a good time?'

'Marius,' said Macaulay. 'His dad,' pointing squarely in Marius' face, 'is on benefits. And guess what? He says his back's all better now. But he's gonna *stay* on benefits because there's no jobs that pay as well.'

Marius shifted uncomfortably. He's stopped flipping the bottle now. 'Look, he'd only be back in construction, and he might put his back out again so ...'

'So fucking what?' said Macaulay, becoming hysterical. 'He's a scummy, grimy, scabby little dosser. I bet he's never even clipped his toenails and they're all about an inch long – and yellow. Needs to get some fuckin' Curanail. Dirty little dosser. I ...'

'MACAULAY, OUT!' I said. 'RIGHT NOW!'

'Ooh, watch out, Mr Elliott's about! Sorry,' he started mocking me. 'Ooh, sowwee.'

'What's Curanail?' asked Marius.

'Marius, no,' I said.

'Basically,' said Macaulay. 'Your dad has a fungal infection on his big toe. It's bright yellow like a fuckin' lemon. Serious. Like a radioactive banana, my brudda. Dutty man.'

'Well, how do you know what Curanail is?' I asked. 'That's a pretty specific thing to know, don't you think?'

'Er – adverts. I seen adverts,' said Macaulay. 'Look, sir, you're not gonna ring my mum, are you?'

'Of course I am,' I said. Marius was nodding.

'Oi, nah, c'mon sir. Low it,[2] fam – I thought we was bruddas.' Macaulay had tears in his eyes again, but not from laughter.

'Nah, no way you getting away widdat shit,' said Owen. 'Talking about benefits 'n that.' Owen, by now, had finished laughing at Macaulay's little diatribe and wore an expression of mock severity.

Macaulay tried to barge past me but knocked himself back a little. Owen snorted with laughter. Macaulay, wiping away tears with his blazer sleeve, ran out of the room.

'Don't worry, sir,' said Kiera. 'He's always like that. You should see him with Mr Craven. He's *much* worse for him.'

'Yeah, sir, you're doing alright, y'know,' said Owen. 'And, look on the bright side, at least he didn't crop-dust us this time.' Owen was referring to the time I'd sent Macaulay out and he'd farted. 2U07 had been left with the smouldering stench of sulphur and rotten eggs. We evacuated into the gathering area known as the Heart

---

2   'Bastardisation of "allow it", often used by youths who have been rude/ outrageous and then wish to compound the effrontery by telling you to metaphorically "chill out".' See https://www.urbandictionary.com/define. php?term=low%20it.

Space, and I spent forty-five minutes trying to salvage the lesson – to no avail.

For the remainder of the year, the lessons were much the same. They oscillated between extremes of jaded apathy and energetic slagging matches. The Cupboard Girls were great and often opined that things would have been much worse for Mr Namby, Mr Pamby, and *especially* Mr Stockholm. The sheer thought of his lessons made me want to breathe into a brown paper bag.

Year 9 is a time of transition, and my life was made easier by the waning fortunes of Macaulay. He'd started off the year as a popular lad. He had his own YouTube channel where he swore at 8-year-old children on *Minecraft*. He had a dog, which he occasionally walked up to the school gates. And he had a pair of Hugo Boss glasses, which he always boasted of in class and which seemed to impress some of his peers. He'd elbow Damian and Owen aside and take his glasses off, sweeping all exercise books and stationery onto the floor, before installing the glasses on an imaginary plinth. 'Soz, sir, gotta flex on dese youts,' he said, which, translated literally, means, 'Sorry sir, I am impelled to boast of my material wealth for the edification of these young children.'

As with Bertrand Russell's chicken, however, which is fed every day of its life until at last the farmer wrings its neck, Macaulay was fattened seemingly for the purpose of his own social slaughter. One day, after school, Marius' cousin came down and punched him so hard in the face that his incisors came through his upper lip. Talk about teething problems. Macaulay was never the same. He sat in my lesson flinching from anything even approximating a gaze from the direction of Marius. Even his dog died – it got crushed by an Eddie Stobart, apparently. Perhaps another angry cousin. Soon after, Macaulay changed sides of the year.

Did my Year 9s learn anything from me? I doubt it. As with Year 7, I went back to the drawing board again and again, devising new ways of imparting knowledge through minimal effort. Sadly, this idea is the learning equivalent of perpetual motion: you cannot learn without effort; effortless learning is an oxymoron. Since I'd forfeited the respect of my class, they would never work for me, and although we liked one another, it sadly wasn't enough.

I felt bad for these kids. I had three hours a week with them. Damian, Marius, the Cupboard Girls, Young Amazon, and even Owen – they all had aspirations. Sure, they were naughty, but I should have been stronger. I only ever wasted their time.

TEACHER TRAINING IN LEAMINGTON

For example, a recent topic around caves started with a darkened classroom devoid of all adornments. This was closely followed by a trip to a cave.

AN EXAMPLE OF 'OUTSTANDING' TEACHING FROM AN OFSTED REPORT

'So,' she said, 'how did you think that went?'

Images of children reading off an emoji sheet sprang to mind. 'Given what you know about Nazi propaganda, why am I showing you these images?' Pupils had to infer from a speaker emoji, for instance, that Hitler had installed speakers on telephone poles to broadcast virulent rhetoric. Meanwhile, several children were deputised as 'Gestapo agents' to police the work rate of the class and censor anything vaguely subversive. I'd outdone myself this time.

'I'd swear, but I don't want to fail Part 2: Professionalism along with everything else. I personally thought the lesson was a load of junk.'

'Yes?' said Marian.

'These are the kinds of lessons we see highlighted as good practice, so I sought to emulate them, and because my usual style is fairly teacher led, I wasn't sure how to police it all …'

'And that's where the Gestapo came in?' said Marian, inserting dashes and dots beside each of the Standards.

'That's where the Gestapo came in,' I affirmed.

'I've spoken to your mentor and she says your behaviour management is usually excellent. Could you not have fed that level of control into your group tasks?'

'No, because when I do group work everything spirals out of control. If my lesson doesn't have an impeccable structure, the kids don't wanna know.'

'Hmm,' said Marian. Evidently my condition – collatiophobia or fear of group work – was quite advanced. Metastasised almost. She'd need drastic measures. 'I'm not going to sugar the pill, Sam. The lesson was – well, I don't want to violate Part 2, either, so I'll leave it there.'

'Are you going to give me QTS?[3] I got QTS last time.'

'No,' she said. 'Having looked through all the sub-standards, it's mostly "working towards". Through much of the lesson, learners were either passive or overly engaged, and engaged by extraneous material at that, such as one of your Gestapo asking whether one of the boys could be tied up for writing, "HITLER'S A FUCKIN MONGOLOID".'

'Archie,' I said.

'Archie,' said Marian. 'I spoke to him outside and he's a charming boy. Lives over in Lillington, so things are tough. You didn't make the boundaries clear enough for him.'

That's because it was a group task, I thought. You might as well sack all the air-traffic controllers and complain about the high incidence of Boeing 737s landing on the M25.

'And then there was the matter of the word search at the start,' she said.

'Word search?' I asked. 'Oh, you mean the crossword. What's wrong with that?'

'Word searches are not a skill,' she said. 'They're also passive. You could have started the lesson with a hook of some kind. I wrote one during the observation: "If the senior Nazis were Mr Men characters, which would they be, and why?" This requires a lot of skill, since they'll be able to work out that Joseph Goebbels is undeniably Mr

---

3   QTS stands for qualified teacher status. In ITT, it's the name for a passing grade.

Bump, as it says in the textbook that he had a club foot, and Heinrich Himmler could be Mr Clever, because they both wear glasses. But it doesn't have to be fancy. You could have easily started with a quiz.'

'It was a crossword,' I said. 'A crossword is a quiz.'

'Maybe, but it involves drawing lines between letters, so while it's good for spellings, it doesn't relate to subject knowledge. It's also quite passive.'

'Look,' I said, about to explain the difference between a crossword and a word search, but what's the point? This poor woman doesn't even know what passive means and I'm going to try to haggle for a better grade? She's made her decision already and whatever the Teachers' Standards do or don't say, I'm going to be graded 'working towards'. 'OK,' I said, as I chose to sit back and disengage from her entirely as she set about the superfluous task of euthanising my stillborn career.

'FUCK MR ELLYOT'

I soon moved from Leamington to a school in Coventry known as Wormwood. It was apparently both Outstanding and World Class – always capitalised and don't you forget it. Quite an enterprising academy, they seemed to have garnered every available accolade. This was because the head teacher was the sort of person who'd have run a soup kitchen in the playground if there had been the slightest chance of the school earning Michelin-star status. The school itself was actually Terrible and below par even for Coventry. Nevertheless, the awards reminded me of one time when I threw a pen against my bedroom wall and then covered the ink splatters with Panini World Cup stickers. 'Look, mum! Look how World Class my room is.'

'Honestly, you're going to love this class,' said my mentor. 'They're amazing.'

'Oh yeah?' I said.

'Yeah. You won't have to lift a finger.'

Three months down the line, and I've resorted to the unorthodox tactic of telling the class that it's my birthday, in the hope that they'll stop flipping bottles and at least look at the starter task.

'Yes then, sir!' said Sameer. 'It's sir's birthday. Let's sing "Happy Birthday", c'mon.'

Three renditions later, the final one finishing with a piercing falsetto, and the bell rings. Class dismissed. As is often the case with birthdays, I have wrappings to pick up and throw away. Daim bars, M&Ms, and Fruitella. Could have saved one for me.

I guess it was my own fault. I took my mentor literally, assuming that this would be the class I could finally trust with group work. For my first observation, I introduced a carousel activity – pupils had to take down information from A3 posters I'd dotted around the room and write it up on a sheet. There was then a class debate where the pupils would green-pen what they had missed. The feedback, as usual, was entirely vacuous. Carol, the ITT woman, told me to set up a video camera to film a disengaged autistic pupil who'd opted out of my lesson by reading *2001: A Space Odyssey* at the back of the class. After Carol had left, my mentor said, 'Please *don't* do that, since it's against the law.' Anyway, I doubted that the pupil liked HAL 9000 so much that he'd opt to test-run Wormwood School's very own beta version.

Nevertheless – feedback aside, I was given 'good' this time – this lesson marked the biggest decline of my teaching career. From here on out, I would triumph with every other class except this one because I'd forfeited their respect from the get-go. This put me in a remarkable position, since not only did I soon become one of the strictest and most fearsome teachers at Wormwood, but I was also remorselessly terrorised for three hours a week. First, when they were in Year 9 and then into Year 10.

The litanies of disruption appeared never-ending. Rahan would be reading Arthur C. Clarke, yet again, and the pupils would be screaming at him, 'Put it away! Sir's trying to teach!' One lad, Ezekiel, would get out of his seat to put his chewing gum in the bin. He did this while giving me a determined look – call it conspicuous consumption. He and his friend, Luka, were high-attainers who'd taken against me from the very beginning. Their disruptions were subtle but effective. They'd mumble over me while I was speaking or incite others to holler or jump out of their skin. One boy – everybody called him Chihuahua – was practically feral. Ezekiel and Luka had trained this boy. They would whisper that I wanted to speak to him, so that he'd randomly wander over to me in the course of my instruction, or tell him, 'Put the textbooks back in the cupboard like Mr Elliott asked. At the back, under the display.' Next thing you know, I'm spending forty-five minutes griping about not having any resources, fist-shaking at whatever Greco-Norse deities had deigned to punish me in such a manner.

I tried to teach the lesson with a board pen but it went something like this:

'OK, we all know that Hitler was very *evil*,' I said, dragging the word out as I stalled for time. I drew a picture of a Swastika on the board.

'Oi, Chihuahua, what the fuck?' said Luka.

'Language!'

'But, sir, your pen!'

Sure enough, Chihuahua, snarling, had gnashed and shattered the biro I'd lent him between his teeth. He was attempting to rub ink from his lips with a sheet crumpled and torn from his exercise book.

'Urghhh, Chihuahua,' said Millie and Shayna. 'Grrrrooosss!'

'He's got a fucking bogey as well,' Sameer shouted. 'URGHHH!'

The class was in uproar. Chihuahua had gone too far this time. Meanwhile, I'm saying '3 … 2 … 1 …' more times than an un-unionised race starter and, similarly, all I'm doing is firing off blanks. This class stopped listening to me long ago. It's funny because I'm named after Patrick Swayze in the movie *Ghost*. He plays the protagonist, Sam, who is shot by a mugger to return as a disembodied spirit. Only after taking this class could I fully empathise with my namesake.

This continued throughout the whole of Year 9. Chihuahua became increasingly aggressive. Near the end, he was practically rabid, and took to 'mad-dogging' me – staring aggressively as I sat in the office. He'd knock on the door and ask to speak to me.

'Where's ma Ellyot?' he'd demand of a senior teacher.

'Hold on, Chihuahua,' said Miss Blunderbuss. 'Mr Elliott, you have a visitor.'

Christ on a tractor-driven chariot, I'd think.

'Sir, you're not gonna give me a detention for yesterday, are you?' he said. 'Look, my mum said I've got to up my medication because I get a bit ...' he pulled an expression like a mime dropping LSD. 'You know, so is that OK?'

'Look, Chihuahua, I have to hold you to account for what you did. You disrupted my lesson. And, hey, people are trying to learn. Your antics are holding everybody back. And you know what? You're really letting yourself down.'[4]

This inane conversation continued for the rest of lunch. Chihuahua's eyes were darting around the room as though several tennis matches were occurring simultaneously in the ether. He'd tell me variously that (a) he wasn't coming to my detention, (b) I was his favourite teacher, (c) actually he'd like to be in detention, (d) it was out of order to give him a detention when I hadn't noticed Luka prod him with a shatterproof ruler shank, and (e) he needed more meds, or wasn't getting enough meds, or that 'I'm a lil bit loOoOopy, sir.' I was starting to feel like I could do with a visit to Dr Feelgood myself.

Chihuahua got progressively worse. Soon, he was telling me he did taekwondo and pratting about around the tables doing karate chops. Then, he'd be outside the office every lunchtime asking,

---

4   This was my BTEC attempt at a restorative conversation. There is mixed evidence for these, even when done well. In some cases they can reduce bullying. In others, they can lead to increased levels of antisocial behaviour. They have yet to be shown to work in the absence of 'parent meetings, firm disciplinary methods, and improved playground supervision': Didau and Rose, *What Every Teacher Needs to Know About Psychology*, pp. 185–188.

'Where's ma lil Ellyot!' During lessons, he made a number of inappropriate comments, including telling me that he was in a gang and that, 'Ma mandems shank up all kindsa bruddas, get me?' Translated literally, it meant that he and his gang stabbed people; it sounded absurd coming from him. The only 'gang' I could imagine him being in was the Hair Bear Bunch. I had to spend half an hour reporting the incident. Can this kid give me a break? He takes up around 35% of my workload as it is.

Later in the year, things with Chihuahua got dark. I'd had a haircut and he told me I was looking 'spicy', and offered to ask out the woman on reception for me. I explained that this was improper behaviour. He started saying, 'Whaaat? What, sir?' I said, 'Chihuahua, be quiet!' His head lolled back with his mouth open and he was screaming. I couldn't let it continue, so I shouted. 'CHIHUAHUA!'

'Ayeee, SORRY DADDY!' Chihuahua shouted.

I've never seen a class react like this. It was like a Champions League final. Luka and Ezekiel were up in arms telling me that Chihuahua was gay and that I had to report it. Millie and Shayna were palpably disgusted. As for me, I just stood there confused. All he said was 'Daddy'. Do I really have to report this?

Finally, things came to a head with Chihuahua. I'd long been abandoned by the head of year for this class. He'd chalked me up as useless, I guess. Anyway, as I left the lesson, I turned back briefly and watched in awe as Chihuahua took a board pen and scrawled in a textbook. I was metres away but I could see what it said: 'FUCK MR ELLYOT.'

'Right,' I shouted. 'Chihuahua. Here. Now!'

'What,' he said, hackles rising.

'I saw what you did – go to the office, now!'[5]

'What?' he said.

---

5 Sending a pupil 'to the office' usually means either pastoral (the head of year) or the subject department (in this case, humanities).

'What?'

'What?'

'Yeah – WHAT – in the office.'

'Nah, fam,' said Chihuahua. 'Can't be speaking to man like that. Oi, watch now, yeah. Mr Ellyot tryna start on me. Watch what happens now, yeah.'

Next thing you know, an incident has been filed with the Year 10 team (I'd had the class for a year now). The head of year was so helpful. He decided that I was the problem, in spite of my impeccable record with my seven other classes, and did nothing to help. He took Chihuahua seriously, observing that he needed to 'Get it right with Mr Elliott.' He even gave him a fifteen-minute detention once for shouting, 'BIG MAN, WHAT THE FUCK ARE YOU GONNA DO!?' in the middle of a geography lesson he wasn't even supposed to be in. Is it right for teachers to be physically threatened in this manner? No, but it happens routinely, and a soppy head of year who allows this does more to lower the collective IQ of society than lead-based petrol and reality television combined.

The worst thing about incidents like this is the chronic stress they induce in a teacher. Although I was now an NQT, my workload was staggering, in spite of the fact that I arrived at 7am and left at 4.30pm every day. Now, I had the additional stress of parental meetings and having to justify myself. All because the head of year was more worried about careerism than his own colleagues.

In a way, I owed him one, since this was the moment I resolved to become a one-man behaviour unit. This was the moment I decided to turn my Year 10 group around. I arranged to meet Chihuahua's mum next Wednesday. Go time.

TURNING AROUND YEAR 10

If you ever have to meet with a parent about a pupil's behaviour, do the following: email every other teacher responsible for that pupil to request a behaviour summary. Next, go on to the behaviour management system and copy and paste every incident into a Word document. When teachers reply to your email, print them out. When you've printed both documents, you're ready to go.

Luckily for me, Chihuahua's were no regular goldmine but a once-in-a-generation platinum-laced meteorite. The depredations of this kid would've made the Ostrogoths blush. Teacher assaults, stabbings with pencils, even jumping down from a first-floor parapet. The juiciest entry was marked 'Theft', and recounted him stealing a vase and handbag from art, before barrelling into a pregnant Year 7 teacher. He'd run away, not even bothering to help Miss Blanche off the floor.

The meeting was quick and surgical, though far from painless. I presented each behaviour point to his mother like a barrister in a murder trial. 'There is the blood-stained knife, Your Honour, along with the CCTV footage, and, oh look, a signed confession to boot.' Chihuahua couldn't believe what he was seeing.

Needless to say, we never had another incident. His mum wanted me to be his mentor and look after him. She'd ring the school constantly asking to speak to 'Mr Ellyot'. Long after I'd left Wormwood, she'd still ring, asking for the nice Mr Ellyot to help her son who'd gone off the rails again. I see where Chihuahua gets it now.

But I was still firefighting. This had all been fun and games in Year 9, but now the children were bigger, naughtier, and embarking upon their GCSEs. I had to turn it around. The Year 10 department were bugger-all help, since all the head of Year 10 did was complain to my boss that I'd had a parental meeting without his approval. Maybe he should answer his emails, the useless … individual. Bloody contactless – leaves me no money for the swear jar.

My plan was straightforward: I'd try to go fully teacher led. Anyone who spoke over me would be given a detention, and if need be I'd phone home. Trainees and NQTs are reluctant to use phone calls home but they're very important. Parents often have no idea how their children behave at school, and it's not fair to blame them when you haven't initiated a dialogue. Nine times out of ten, they're more help than hindrance.

Lesson time. I arrive in class. The Year 10s are baiting me at the door while Ezekiel and Luka refuse to sit down. It's shambolic from the start.

'Alright, let's get going,' I said, slamming the door. 'Title, date. Get it down. Slide's changing, you've got a minute to get sorted.'

'Yes, Luka!' said Ezekiel.

'Wagwarn, Ez,' said Luka. 'You good, brudda?'

'Yeah, yeah, you know – oi, you know Idris shit himself?'

'Dooon't lie,' said Luka, bouncing out of his seat and shaking his fists like an ecstatic toddler. 'Why?'

'OK, you two,' I said. 'Warning.' I wrote their names in my Little Red Book.[6]

'Yeah, yeah,' said Ez. 'Moist geezer.' Dismissing me with a hand wave.

They carried on their conversation, I continued adding sanctions, and the lesson was less a train wreck than two cargo vessels in head-on collision. The difference was that I had plotted a future course, while their hull was breached and the stars were snuffed. My behaviour management, like an iceberg, hung ponderously beneath the waves.

That day, I stayed back and made some calls. 'Hi there, this is Mr Elliott from Wormwood School here – Ezekiel's history teacher.'

'Allo,' said his dad. 'How's he doing?'

---

6   For more on the significance of the Little Red Book, see 'The Little Red Book: Salvaging Power from Impotence'.

This is when you let rip. But it has to come from logic, not emotion. Ezekiel was four grades below target on his most recent mock. I said so. Ezekiel hadn't set pen to paper in weeks. I said so. This is the patter. You cannot become emotional since then parents will become defensive, and rightly so. Who wants to hear a fully grown man bitching about their child?

'Ahh,' he said. 'Can you give him a detention?'

'Sure, Mr Smith, I'll set an hour for tomorrow.'

'One hour?' he was incredulous. I grew anxious. 'Make it two, for God's sake. And can we do Thursday as well?'

Stunned by the level of support, I said, 'Sure, but make sure he has some extra lunch.'

'Will do, Mr Elliott, and thank you for your call. Please, if there are any problems, let me know right away.'

I said goodbye, hung up, and my eyes were glassy. I'd been struggling with this class for over a year now. The disruption: relentless. Respect levels: absolute zero. As for support … think pipe-cleaner splint for a broken spine. To have this level of assistance from a parent was truly gratifying.

The next lesson, I arrived early. Year 10s at the door again. Baiting me.

'Yes, Mr Elliott,' said George. 'My guy,' he held his fist out for respect. When a kid does this, ignore it: they're mocking you or detecting weakness.

'Get to lesson, George, or I'll ring Brian,' I'd anticipated George arriving and looked up his dad on SIMS. Suitably shook, George scuttled off to Miss Burley.

Ezekiel stayed quiet, his head hanging from his shoulders, suspended above the textbook. He wasn't happy but he wasn't disrupting – I took this for progress. Meanwhile, the real issue, Luka, is disrupting with his latest ally, Sameer. They'd hated each other before but since Ezekiel had been knocked out of the war, I guess they'd signed a non-aggression pact.

'Sir, what barbers you go?' asked Sameer.

'First task, Sameer,' I said.

'Look, if you wanna go barbers, try Manix in Foleshill. It's fully sick.'

'Nice, will bear that in mind.'

'Actually, no … you might get raped.'

'Pardon me?' I said. I wrote this down in the Little Red Book.

'Nooo, sir, not that book, c'mon. What you writing – I said *raked*. Like leaves. C'mon, sir, low it.'

'Just get on with it, Sameer. Don't make this any worse.'

Luka was meanwhile drawling away in his inimitable monotone. I could never really tell what he was talking about. It seemed to be gossip. This time it was about the new supply teacher in modern foreign languages, Mr Sangah.

'Sir, you hear about this new geezer. Mr Sangah. Oi, he's a pop star. Makes these cringey videos on YouTube singing bhangra 'n that. And he was in this Croatian soap opera as well.'

I'm not really sure what to do with this information. I'd been hearing about Mr Sangah all day – Wormwood's latest 'celebrity teacher', seemingly for all the wrong reasons.

'Look, this is his Insta,' said Luka, holding up his iPhone with a still image of Mr Sangah and an undulating, plaintive melody issuing from the speaker. I can barely believe what I'm seeing. Sameer's up behind his chair, gyrating inappropriately, and biting his lower lip like he's really into it.

'Jeez, what a banger,' he said. The girls are giggling away. 'Mr Sangah's on some next level.'

I sent Luka out and brandished the Little Red Book at Sameer again. He sat down, cowed for a change. Meanwhile, Luka's at the door, winding me up again.

'Sir, why do you hate me?' he asked.

'I don't hate you, Luka, I just want you to do your work. Away from the door, please. Look,' I said, stepping out of the room. 'I want you to stand by *this* plug socket. Don't stick your finger in it, either. If you move from this plug socket, I will give you an additional hour.'

'I've got an hour?' Luka asked. 'Sir, look, I know you want me to work. Hey, I want loads of things. I wanna get big muscles like you, to be honest.'

It should be stated here that Luka is very clever. He's one of the few naughties sociopathic enough to unabashedly admit that he's out to get teachers. It's always dismissed as a 'school-wide problem' but nobody ever does anything. As for me, what I see is barely a snippet compared to what he does to other teachers, some of whom he's apparently 'bullied'.

Often, the worst naughties are put through a managed move where they're passed between schools like a ticking time bomb lodged in an oven-baked potato, all because head teachers don't have the integrity to expel kids polluting the school ethos. Alternatively, naughties are dumped in the SEN department. Luka is clever enough that he doesn't leave a trace, so he's barely ever detained, let alone manage moved or isolated. Meanwhile, what you're reading here is him on a good day.

'Yeah,' he said, renewing his attempts to manipulate me. 'You got the guns, sir. Click, click, pow,' he cocks an imaginary pistol. 'Look, I know we don't always get on, but you're my favourite teacher. The best, in fact. Sure, we mess around, but we get it done, right? Sir, don't ignore me now, c'mon. I thought you were better than that.' He's soon bored of impersonating Uriah Heep and decides to tour the school. Nothing but crisp static from the Year 10 department.

In the end, the class were brought on side temporarily, although reversing the behavioural inertia felt like lifting an Atlas Stone. When you've lost all respect, you have to take drastic measures to recover the class. In order to stamp out the disruption, I rang about 60% of the parents, because although I've mentioned certain pupils by name, what you're reading in this narrative should be viewed like a silverfish on a skirting board. The book only supports so many names, and unless you're writing *Game of Thrones*, it's best to keep the cast to a minimum. So, take my word for it: the disruption was so extreme that it was almost unanimous.

When I'd rung all of these parents, the pupils were better behaved, but there was still the sense that this wasn't the real me.

'Sir,' said Jacob. 'You know you can't be strict. We liked your lessons when they were interactive.'

'Interactive,' I laughed, chewing my board pen like a cigar, 'that's one word for it. Nobody did anything.'

'I did, sir. So did Raihana.'

'Yeah, but you're different. You can block out the distraction and focus. That's very unusual. There are pupils in this class who struggle in terms of their reading, writing, and comprehension. They need silence in order to work. It's not fair if we have a noisy class just because you want one, is it, Jacob?'[7]

'I guess not, sir, I just think it's … different. You've changed so much.'

'How so?' I asked.

'I see you at the start of lesson with your Year 9s when I collect the books for Mrs de Milo. That's not teaching, sir, that's fear.'

'Excuse me?'

'The Year 9s. They don't say a word. They're like robots.'

---

7   In the famous 'marshmallow test' pupils could either receive one marshmallow now or receive two later. Many don't pass this test. The ability to self-regulate is associated with social competence, academic success, and verbal fluency. My advice? To reduce the attainment gap, save pupils from themselves and remove the distraction: see Bradley Busch and Edward Watson, *The Science of Learning: 77 Studies That Every Teacher Needs to Know* (Abingdon and New York: Routledge, 2019), p. 13.

'Listen, Jacob, you misunderstand teaching. We're here to work. Some of these kids don't have as many opportunities as you do. They aren't interested in learning. Has it ever occurred to you that in every group task, you and Raihana are the ones doing all of the heavy lifting? What does that leave for the others? You're implying that I'm selfish, but it's quite the opposite. I want every pupil to work, free of distraction, and to be given feedback on what they produce individually. Think analytically instead of emotionally and you'll see that I'm correct.'

Jacob didn't have an answer for me, but neither did he question my methods. I wrapped up the lesson and went back to the office. Thank God that's over.

TERROR TIME

Halfway through the spring term and Year 10 are almost manageable. They do their work. I'm criticised for not doing group work but you may as well yell at Pandora for keeping the box shut. I'm not dining out on the slender rations of hope ever again. I'll control everything that happens; if the Year 10 team don't like it, I'll simply ignore them.

But we had to make changes. One of my colleagues, the traditional, no-nonsense head of Year 8, Miss Champion, was having trouble with a pupil named Barry. I asked her if she fancied swapping Luka for Barry and she leapt at the prospect.

As King Duncan said in *Macbeth*, 'There's no art to find the mind's construction in the face.'[8] Perhaps not, but there is a science. According to psychologist Daniel Kahneman, the shape of a face allows us to assess dominance, with a strong, square chin being one sign. Check! Similarly, facial expressions, such as frowning, allow us to assess intentions. Double check![9] To put it bluntly, I had serious doubts that Barry was going to 'activate himself as a learning

---

8 William Shakespeare, *Macbeth*, Act I, sc. iv, ll. 11–12.
9 Daniel Kahneman, *Thinking, Fast and Slow* (London: Penguin, 2012), p. 90.

resource' for me anytime soon.[10] But all Luka ever did was get sent out and wander the school, thereby getting me into trouble for sending him out. Incredible, isn't it? I needed a kid who would just sit there, and since Barry was quite lazy, he was unlikely to spend the hour meeting his Fitbit quota.

I spoke to Barry for the first time on a rainy Thursday morning.

'Oh, looky here, my new history teacher,' he said, rubbing his hands together. 'Mr Elliott, how you doing!'

'You good, Baz?'

'Yeah, can't wait to change lesson. Miss Champion's such a bitch. You know she rang my mum for no reason?'

'You'd stamped on Caleb's head,' I said. 'Anyway, Baz, don't go thinking I'm a light touch.'

'Yeah, I hear you got steee-RICT,' he said, laughing. 'Don't matter cuz you're still getting terrored. Oi, Sameer,' Sameer padded over to us. 'Terror Time soon,' Barry smiled.

Sameer was afraid of me now and had the good sense to keep his mouth shut. He smirked nevertheless.

'Yeah, watch,' said Barry. 'Nooo long ting. Terror Time soon, my brudda.'

'Look, lil Baz, you're not a scratch on Luka so stop acting it. My Year 10 – they're sorted. I'm not letting anyone mess it up. I'll ring your mum, I'll ring your dad, even your Great Auntie Gertrude if I have to. Whatever it takes.'

'Sameer, you know Sammy Elliott here went to school with my cousin?' he was grinning so widely I thought his head would drop off at the cheeks. 'He used to be in a gang. CV2 lads.'

---

10 Kathy Dyer, 5 Formative Strategies to Improve Student Learning from Dylan Wiliam and NWEA, *NWEA* (14 February 2019). Available at: https://www.nwea. org/blog/2019/5-formative-strategies-to-improve-student-learning-from-dylan-wiliam-and-nwea.

I took my cue to end the discussion. I did know Barry's cousin. He'd tried to swig some of my neon-green alcohol once without paying, so we'd got into a fight outside Tesco. He bit me on the stomach, one of his friends hit me across the legs with a wooden beam, and I slammed his head against a metal fence. It ended outside the Cadbury Shop when a friend pulled up in a Range Rover to referee a rematch. We fought, he bit me again, and we ended the fight more through inconvenience than exhaustion. We became mates and went to the gym instead, after I'd had a tetanus shot at Walsgrave Hospital.

Next week, and I was ready. Year 10, period 4 – Terror Time. It's on. The room was silent. Daniel handed the books out and they wrote down the title and date. Barry arrived five minutes after the bell.

'Yo, wagwarn, sir?' he said. 'My guy,' he tries to fist-bump me while bending the knee slightly. Absurd. Same routine, same patter. He's trying to mug me off.

'Siddown, Baz,' I said. He lopes to the back of the room to Sameer.

All's quiet on the Western Front. No shelling, no sniping, and not even the dull rumour of warfare. My phone calls did the trick.

This proceeds for a week or so. Barry has been remarkably quiet. The pupils are punctual and engaged. Sure, Barry turns up late, but at least he does me the courtesy of handing in a forged note. We entered into a Golden Age. Sameer said he liked history. We scrutinised the exam paper together and the pupils put effort into their recall tests. Finally, I'm able to teach.

That weekend, I decided to go to the gym, and who should I see but Luka and Barry. 'Yes then, Mr Elliott, wagwarn?'

I still hated them, but since things were going well with Year 10, I nodded. I pointed out that they were doing squats on a shoulder press and suggested moving to the leg extension machine.

'Sound, bredda,' said Luka. 'My guy Mr Elliott got the guns – pump action!' he reloaded an imaginary shotgun. 'Come, fatty,' he said to Baz.

The next week, things improved further. My mentor observed me and congratulated my exemplary practice. Clearly, she said, mixed-ability seating plans were the way forward. 'Haha, yeah,' I thought. 'Mixed ability – those *able* to disrupt and those *not able* to disrupt, because they're either facing a window or sitting by my desk.'

Nevertheless, I had a sense that it couldn't last forever. When you forfeit respect, it's a permanent loss. You can buy yourself respite. A week, or maybe a fortnight, if you're lucky. But a teacher will always bear 'the indelible stamp of his lowly origin'.[11] I'd explained this to countless mentors and managers. They would always say no, raising a sententious finger like Hermione Granger performing a wand flick, and explain that it was my AfL, my differentiation, or my teaching and learning. This worked out nicely for them since they could observe me and tick the relevant box, sidestepping discomfiting notions of pupil disruption.

The following week, another lesson. This time, a gaggle of Year 10s erupted into my classroom during the starter activity. 'Is this the guy?' they asked. A girl nodded.

'Oi, Mr Elliott,' said a boy with acne I can only describe as acupunc-tural. 'Shayna fancies you.' I'm not sure how to respond. 'Some of these Year 10 girls, sir, they think you're summat special.'

'Right,' I said. 'Lesson time, off you go.' I turned to the class. 'For the starter today, can you …'

'Some of these Year 10 girls, sir,' said the boy, opening the door I'd closed. 'They've been saying all sorts. Trust me – you could pull bare girls, sir.'[12]

Another girl stumbles into him. 'It's him!' she jabs a finger in my direction. 'Shayna loves you!'

---

11 Charles Darwin, *The Descent of Man, and Selection in Relation to Sex*, Kindle edn (New York: Createspace, 2017 [1871]), p. 354.
12 Bare means 'a lot', as in 'This Uber driver's on a big man ting! Bare tunes. Five stars coming your way, my brudda.'

I continued: 'Can you list the biggest advances you can remember from the Medical Renaissance? For example, remember Leeuwenhoek?'

'The guy who sounds like coughing up phlegm?' said Sameer.

'That's the one. What did he …'

The finger-jabber strutted past me and sat in my chair. Is this for real? Do I shout?

'Hello,' I wave to the girl. 'Lost?'

'Don't talk to me like that, Mr Elliott,' she said. 'Shayna loves you and she spent seven hours making you that poster of the Yalta Conference – I helped her. And where is it? You haven't even put it on display.'

'Look,' I lowered my voice. 'I can't do any displays in this school, OK? It's some marketing thing. I explained that to Shayna – who are you, anyway?'

'Kelsey,' she said. 'And you do realise that Shayna's off today because she's so upset? She's been working so hard for you and all you ever say is "good" or "well done".'

I think to myself, what the flip does she want, expiation?

The lad butts in, 'Sir, do you ever, like, flex on guys. Y'know, take their girls 'n that?'

'If you don't go, I'm going to escalate this,' I said.

'Give her a detention, sir,' shouted Sameer. 'It's what she wants.'

'Shut up, Sameer,' said Kelsey.

'Right, you're in a lot of trouble now,' I said, lamely.

This was the point where I lost control of Year 10 for the final time. Kelsey came into every single history lesson of mine, even though she was meant to be in geography with Miss Burley. I informed the Year 10 team. Speaking to myself again, obviously; stress levels amplifying my interior monologue to a sonorous squeal – what had formerly been static was promoted to audio feedback so loud it could desolate Glastonbury. It happened seventeen more times, the drama ratcheting up with each instalment: 'Shayna's written a poem about you, sir! How can you be so heartless? I'm gonna stay here until you apologise.' I could hardly believe that my downfall would be this much of a farce.

Eventually, the Year 10 team rang home and gave her a detention. It didn't work the first time, or even the second, but after the third, all I ever saw of Kelsey was an accusatory glance from the doorway as she hustled to geography. The lad would still stop by to tell me how many girls I could pull, phrasing it speculatively, like a word problem: 'So, sir, if you were in a pub, and there were seventeen girls, but you could only pull three, and you only had enough money for two drinks …' Then he petered out as well.

But these disruptions were merely the prelude because the sleeping giant, Barry, had been studiously taking note, but not on the Medical Renaissance. Then Shayna returned. Apparently, she was better, but so far as I could tell she had four humours and they were all bile. She, Barry, and even Luka, who was so regularly kicked out of his lesson that he took any chance to visit his old sparring partner, began a terror campaign so remorseless it made the French Revolution seem like a bit of argy-bargy.

I couldn't speak: they talked over me constantly. I couldn't mark: Shayna would kick off because I'd said Raihana's work was 'great' and 'excellent', whereas hers was merely 'excellent' and 'very good'. Worst of all, I was being observed and blamed for this, due to the erroneous idea that my teaching and learning was at fault.

Sadly, I lost the battle with this class, in both Year 9 and Year 10. A double rout. Two years of education lost. And all because my mentors never trusted that once a trainee/NQT loses the respect of a class – an inevitability when you're encouraged to 'try new things' with a frequency bordering on the neurotic – they can never recover. At least not until they're fully conversant with the principles of behaviour management. But hey ho, I was changing schools.

In the final lesson, I showed Year 10 my reflection log, where I'd compiled signatures from all of my favourite pupils in my other classes. I turned to a blank page and asked them if they'd like to sign it. They all cheered (strangely, despite terrorising me, I was one of their favourites; they were genuinely eager for closure).

'Oh, good,' I said. 'Well, I'm going to sign it for you,' I took my board pen out of my blazer, bit off the cap, and began scrawling black ink methodically from the top to the bottom of the page.

'Nooooo!' shouted Shayna. Sameer was distraught. Even Luka, slouched in the door frame, looked rather glum.

As I filled in the page with cross-hatchings and jagged spirals, Ezekiel, who had recently met his target grade and who hadn't spoken since I'd rung his dad, smiled. 'Look, sir,' he said, standing up. 'You think it's all been for nothing, but just think how much *stronger* you'll be.'

How right he was.

Chapter 3

THE PRINCIPLES OF BEHAVIOUR MANAGEMENT

In this chapter, you will find all you need to know about behaviour management. It is replete with institutional overviews, psychological principles, and certain heuristics that I've distilled from my own practice. Abide by the principles and kids like Barry, Luka, and Chihuahua will fall into line.

We start with mindsets – don't beg it! – before moving into the psychology of the behaviour system. Teaching isn't a video game where you can button bash or spam X. Only a varied approach will work. But occasionally the inadequacies of the school system serve as obstacles. Complaining is all very well and good, but you need strategies. By the end, you'll know how to (a) get help from year heads, (b) collect detentions in the absence of a school-wide policy, and (c) manipulate pupil culture to secure your own following. Remember, behaviour management isn't easy but it is essential.

STOP BEGGING IT: WHY THE RELATIONSHIP COMES THROUGH THE LEARNING

Any teacher who tries to befriend his or her pupils will immediately be known as a 'beg' – the worst insult a pupil can ever level against a teacher. The teacher accused of 'begging it' will be that same teacher you might already have seen in the staffroom. They invite children into the office, talk to them about their personal lives, and laugh after every sentence like it's cocktails at Cosy Club. When you are told that good teaching is 'all about relationships', this is exactly the opposite of what is meant.

I'm a believer in what I call 'educational materialism'. The social superstructure of the pupil–teacher relationship should emanate naturally from classroom practices. In other words, by trying to foster good relationships with pupils before teaching competently, you are putting the chariot before the horse. Without exceptional teaching, the relationship is unbalanced, stationary, and liable to tip over.

The relationship really does come through the learning, and this is partially due to the Benjamin Franklin effect, discovered when Franklin managed to turn an enemy into his friend, not by doing favours for him but by having his enemy lend him a book. The enemy rationalised it as follows: 'I am doing a favour for Benjamin Franklin; therefore, he must be a friend of mine.' As Franklin put it, 'He that has once done you a kindness will be more ready to do you another, than he whom you yourself have obliged.'[1] If all books on classroom management were lost tomorrow in simultaneous raging fires, along with a DDoS attack that wiped out every Kindle edition,[2] I would happily substitute this single quotation.

When you teach a lesson, you need to delegate difficult tasks routinely, and through this the pupils will develop a strange kind of regard for you. Moreover, this relationship is an appropriate one. By contrast, if you have an emotional relationship with a pupil, this is a problem, since the banter they have with you can serve as a contending source of social reward. Instead of performing well on a knowledge test for you, they may decide to impress you by telling you your tie looks nice, or that they saw you in Lidl last Saturday and you were in the alcohol section. Remember, you are there to foster relationships, not the pupils themselves.

The worst part about having emotional relationships with pupils is that it makes life harder for every other teacher. I hate to admit this, but at Chelmsley Wood Academy I was a 'celebrity teacher'. I talked to the kids like I was their drunken uncle, and my banter was like something the Greek gods would chain you to a rock for. I would always stop to laugh and joke with pupils. And then, whenever I had to collect a pupil for intervention, I think even Jesus of Nazareth

---

1   Walter Isaacson, *Benjamin Franklin: An American Life*, Kindle edn (New York: Simon & Schuster, 2004), loc. 1970.

2   DDoS (distributed denial-of-service attack) is an acronym rather like DNA. Many know what it is but few know what it stands for.

would have drawn a lacklustre reception by contrast with the 'absolute legend' that was Mr Elliott.

And y'know what, becoming a 'celebrity teacher' doesn't even work.[3] Pupils do not regard their teachers as peers. The odd one might be considered 'alright', but this doesn't increase their capability as a teacher whatsoever. Wherever teachers cultivate these personal ties, they leach from more nourishing crops, such as knowledge and literacy, which serves to blight the harvests of those responsible for GCSE results.

I almost believe that the best way to conduct oneself in teaching is to be 'too strict to fail'. This is quite an absurd way of putting it, but what I mean is that you cannot fail because your lessons are so on point they would make a porcupine blush. In fact, one of the funniest things I've found is that if I deliberately show pupils that I couldn't care less what they think, they seem to respect me even more.

Since leaving Chelmsley Wood, I have had various cult followings where pupils actually find the consistency of my strictness to be comforting. The pupils you push hardest will like you the most.

SALIENCE: HOW TO TELL OFF A CHILD THE SCIENTIFIC WAY

Willenhall in Coventry is one of the most unemployed areas in the United Kingdom.[4] It's where I live. One Sunday, I took a walk past the Precinct, within the Beer-muda Triangle of Ladbrokes, Heron Foods, and Willenhall Social Club. Two women were walking along with a small boy on a tricycle trundling ahead of them. 'Get the fuck off the bike, ya little wanker,' one said, turning to her friend. 'Yeah, listen to ya fookin mam. Kids, what the *fuck* is wrong wivvum?' My

---

3 'There was no correlation between how much students rated the effectiveness of their teacher and how much they actually learned': Busch and Watson, *The Science of Learning*, p. 21.

4 It is ranked twenty-sixth for unemployment out of the 35,000 or so 'neighbourhoods' (lower layer super output areas) in England – see: http://dclgapps.communities.gov.uk/imd/iod_index.html#.

jaw hung open like a wardrobe in a removal van that brakes too suddenly. I watched them as they passed me, nodding to each other in amiable consensus: what a little twat the boy on the tricycle was.

These are the children that teachers are going to have to deal with in secondary schools. They've been called every name going. Their parents have yelled them into the ground more times than they can remember. Once, I even saw a mother squaring up to her 9-year-old son at a bus stop, like a weigh-in for the newly combined feather-weight/cruiserweight title. How am I to discipline a child when this is what they're used to?

Where did it all go wrong for these terrible parents? Quite simply, it has to do with the psychological principle of social salience – salience meaning 'to stick out'. When something is rare or infrequently encountered, it is salient in our minds. For instance, if you saw a purple cat with green spots, fluorescent eyes, and a small lion's mane, you would probably pay attention to it as you googled 'psychiatrist near me'. By contrast, we pay less attention to things we have encountered many times before.

What the parents have done is sworn and shouted at their children so much that the kids now have a higher tolerance for it. The first time you tell little Timmy to 'fuck off', you have called your own bluff. If I were little Timmy and my mum shouted at me like that, I wouldn't care, because this is her max setting. If I can do what I like and only have to be sworn at – which she's done before anyway – well, that's a price worth paying.

How do we discipline according to the principle of salience? Authority depends not on what you say, but on what you don't have to say. And if authority is the mortar holding the walls of our educational establishment together, then the bricks are the inconveniences we can cause pupils. To tell off a child properly, think: 'How can I inconvenience this child?' There are many ways of doing this – for instance, isolating pupils is an oldie but a goodie.[5] This means taking the pupil out of circulation to sit with you all day. You can ring the parents if you have a professional telephone manner. One of my favourite methods is what I call the 'uncertainty principle'.

---

5   I discuss isolation in more detail in 'How to Use the Behaviour System'.

Mike Tyson once spoke about fear and said that the craziest thing is that our greatest fear never actually happens.[6] To make the uncertainty principle work, calmly explain to a pupil that they are in a lot of trouble for what they have done and that you will get back to them with the punishment at the end of the day. If it is already the end of the day, explain you will have to think about speaking to their parents and you will get back to them tomorrow.

Human beings cannot abide uncertainty. It is our instinct. Maybe it evolved to allow for a secure food supply in hunter-gatherer times. Whatever the origins, it's there. In the interval between you telling the child and deciding on the punishment, their own anxieties will do most of the disciplinary work for you. They will envisage various worst-case scenarios where their phones are refunded for book tokens, or mum and dad are hauled in front of the head, perhaps with some random Ofsted inspectors with clipboards standing by.

HOW TO USE THE BEHAVIOUR SYSTEM

Ironically, the teachers most feared for giving out detentions are also those who give out the least. Why is this? Because of deterrence. In life, the biggest, strongest, and tallest – the ones who look like the best fighters – wind up fighting the least. They are so intimidating that nobody would ever take a swing at them. Similarly, a country with a stockpile of nuclear weapons will only rarely have to fight a conventional war, unless they find oil in Iraq or something. In many ways, teaching is similar.

However, deterrence is not just about being the strongest. In teaching, it has more to do with mental acuity than physical prowess. If you overuse the behaviour system, it doesn't work. There should be a scarcity value to it. One of the reasons why nuclear weapons are so scary is because they are never used. If there had been more conflicts where nuclear bombs had been dropped, we might be less

---

6   Tony Gonzalez, Heavyweight Mike Tyson on Why He Loves Fear [video] (21 February 2020) at 1.33. Available at: https://www.youtube.com/watch?v=zeRlmGTMZM8&t=2s.

scared of them today, since we'd have become sadly inured to the impacts of nuclear shockwaves, heat blasts, and radioactive fallout.

Please don't misunderstand me: when I say use the behaviour system sparingly, I'm not saying never use it at all. This is ASBO Teacher, for Christ's sake. If you're looking for Hippie Teacher, there's a book called *Summerhill School* you might like.[7] Neither am I advising you to ask your barber for a tonsure, don a hair-shirt or waft incense sticks at misbehaving pupils. But you must use salience to your advantage. Think about guns. In the United States guns are ubiquitous. You can buy ammunition at Walmart. Some people take their guns to church with them. In many states, child-friendly shooting ranges are available for thirteenth birthday parties.[8] Yet, when I go to the train station and see an armed police officer, I feel like a man who has swallowed a fridge magnet undergoing an MRI scan. When I see a weapon like that, having never seen one before, I am intuitively more afraid of it than I would be if I'd shot an apple off of a crash-test dummy to celebrate my high-school graduation.

You have to avoid becoming 'that teacher' – the one on the behaviour logs giving out C2s for everything from 'shit haircut' to 'shoelaces untied'. As a form tutor, I take one look at the fifty-seven behaviour points given by Mrs Winfrey to Year 9 in the space of a single day and I ask myself two questions: firstly, did she really stand there at the front, pointing and proclaiming, '*You* get a point, *you* get a point … *everybody* gets a point'? Secondly, how useless can this staff member be? If you can punish a single, salient instance of misbehaviour, however, the class is yours.

Praise in public (PIP) and reprimand in private (RIP) were the two best takeaways from my ITT year, the Nando's I had at the end of it being the third. You must reprimand in private as often as possible. For instance, pupil A has just said to pupil B, 'Shut the ____ up, you little ____.' You can fill in the blanks on that one. If I were to shout and challenge this behaviour in front of the entire class, well, pupil A is already in a lot of trouble and has nothing to lose but the chains of being in the restrictive classroom environment, so he will mouth

---

7 Alexander S. Neill, *Summerhill School: A New View of Childhood* (New York: St Martin's Press, 1998).
8 See https://gunforhire.com/shooting-range-kids-parties.

off at me. For certain peer groups, this behaviour is impressive and will secure for him the status of a desk-bound William Wallace.

How should I handle this situation? When the rest of the class is busy, distracted, or productively engaged, I would go over to pupil A, crouch beside him, facing in the same direction, and quietly tell him to go outside or to the office. In reprimanding him, I would impress upon him how serious the offence was, and I would act like the offence was so serious that I really do not know what my next steps will be.

It is important to amplify the severity of what pupil A has done. Even if he had only said, 'Shut the hell up, you little nincompoop,' I would still have to make a mountain out of a molehill in order to induce contrition. If pupil A had said what you likely imagined he did when you filled in the blanks earlier, I would isolate him, ring his parents, and arrange an hour's detention.

Isolation has had a bad press recently, what with pictures of isolation booths being shared on the internet and the launch of the Ban the Booths campaign.[9] Oddly enough, the image on BBC News which inspired so much outrage was a screenshot from Corporate Office Furniture Limited and is unrepresentative of the school isolation system.[10] I'm not sure what else outsiders think about isolation – maybe that it entails handing in homework via fax machine, fetching drinks from the water cooler, or filling in VAT returns for the number of biros that exploded in the last quarter. If we have a problem with people sitting in booths, maybe we should look at libraries, offices, and call centres while we're at it. For most teachers, isolation simply means separating a pupil from peers in their regular classes or taking them out of circulation.

And if you think isolation booths are bad, trust me, a Year 8 pupil would rather release his pet hamster into the wild than spend Friday period 5 in a rowdy Year 10 class – what isolation usually means. Meanwhile, one pupil managed to rack up an astonishing 240

9   The Ban the Booths campaign lists all of its recent press here: https://banthebooths.co.uk/press.

10 For more on this see Andrew Old, Isolation Booths, *Teaching Battleground* (2 January 2020). Available at: https://teachingbattleground.wordpress.com/2020/01/02/isolation-booths.

isolations in one of these booths.[11] Pardon me, but they can't be that 'draconian' and 'hurtful' if you repeat the experience another 239 times.[12] In any case, unless the school was going for the Guinness World Record, they should have realised that it wasn't working and arranged for alternative provision.

Back to pupil A. Could I have reasoned with him? No. The psychology of appeasement is very real and not merely a bedtime story that history teachers tell their pupils to put them to sleep. If I had not given a proportionate sanction, pupil A would have chalked it up as his own personal annexation of the Sudetenland, and he would have then scouted the classroom horizons asking himself, 'Now, who's Poland?' In this very simple scenario, my sanction dealt with pupil A effectively.

Obviously, for smaller transgressions, a frank, honest, and threat-laden conversation, perhaps seasoned with granular observations that pupil A is 'better than that', would suffice.

'WARLORDS IN A FAILED STATE'

I first saw this phrase on David Didau's blog and was struck by it immediately.[13] It seemed to encapsulate the essential difference between teachers at St Cumberbatch School and those at Grimshaw Academy.

Schools in thatched villages or downwind of Victorian townhouses are fundamentally different from those huddled beneath glowering tower blocks. Some of the most dispiriting areas imaginable are the Radburn estates of the modern cityscape. If you've never seen them, they look like holiday homes slathered in concrete. As if an architect got stoned one day and asked himself, 'What if a house could look like a giant's lunchbox?' They bring to mind the words of

---

11 Charlie Haynes, 'I Was Put in a School Isolation Booth More Than 240 Times', *BBC News* (15 April 2015). Available at: https://www.bbc.co.uk/news/education-47898657.

12 Ban the Booths, Moral Rights and Wrongs (16 December 2018). Available at: https://banthebooths.co.uk/blog/rightsandwrongs.

13 David Didau, An Argument for Order, *The Learning Spy* (24 October 2014). Available at: https://learningspy.co.uk/behaviour/an-argument-for-order.

Bill Bryson, who, trying to capture what was going on in the minds of architects in the 1960s and 1970s, claimed that maybe there had been 'an ugly building competition. For the better part of a decade, architects had been arriving in the area and saying, "You think *that's* bad? Wait'll you see what *I* can do." '[14] However we explain the 'mad seizure' that gripped the town planners of that era, we can at least infer the social consequences for today.

During my training, I had worked briefly in a school near Leamington. The children there were courteous, polite, and utterly incomprehensible. They had strange rituals like working silently in class and putting the chairs away after lesson. The only naughties came from a tower block over in Lillington. It was very different from Chelmsley Wood.

The Leamington kids were well behaved. Did the leadership team deserve the credit? No more than the self-service woman at Tesco deserves a raise for shouting 'Next!' seventeen times in a row. Why were the pupils so nice? Maybe take a walk around Leamington and you'll see for yourself. Tree-lined boulevards, parks lit by Victorian lampposts, terraces seemingly plagiarised from a Virginia Woolf novel. The area inspires pride.

This tale of ~~two cities~~ one spa town and a tract of urban sprawl brings to mind the phrase, 'the personal is political'. The school environment is shaped by what happens outside of the school, between pupils and their peer groups within the fringes of their built environment. When you work in tough schools, the atmosphere is thick and there is the dim sense that you'll be felled and trampled on if you're not 'on it'. Classes in Leamington could self-regulate, whereas the motive in tougher schools is to test the teachers. The only way to teach effectively is to take stock of the prevailing honour culture and exude an authority that is calm, fierce, and utterly unyielding.

Because I had trained in Chelmsley Wood – an area so deprived it makes Coventry look like the Emerald City of Oz – it meant that Leamington simply wasn't my skillset. Teachers in the staffroom loaded up on camomile tea and debated the goings on in 'Orkney

14 Bill Bryson, *Notes from a Small Island* (London: Transworld, 1993), p. 40.

Death Mysteries' or 'Formaldehyde on a Gurney' or whatever. Like many of the extras, I needed resuscitation. Going from a deprived area to teach in a more privileged one is like quitting Formula 1 to take up competitive go-karting. Perhaps this is unfair: these teaching experiences are just different kinds of games, like Monopoly and Scrabble. Kids with money and kids who jumble their spellings.

Strangely, I missed the adrenaline surge of tackling naughties, so I left and took a job in my hometown. Sent to Coventry, so to speak, because I never spoke to my Leamington colleagues again.

AN INSTITUTIONAL PERSPECTIVE

Inner-city comps: they're exciting but challenging. All the more so when management isn't supportive.

At Wormwood School, there was no isolation unit. If there is no isolation unit, how do you remove bad children from circulation? Firstly, you pathologise bad behaviour. Secondly, you foist naughty children on to the SEN department to be supervised by unqualified teachers.[15] This is unconscionable. I don't know the precise reasoning behind it. It may have something to do with the fact that 'more than one in five English children is identified as having Special Educational Needs (SEN), five times the EU average'.[16]

This practice deserves a dressing down. Whenever I speak to parents about behaviour, they often ask me what's going wrong. I'm always honest. If Jaskaran pulled another pupil's trousers down, I don't think you'll find that condition in the American Psychiatric Association's *Diagnostic and Statistical Manual of Mental Disorders* (DSM-5). Maybe I'm wrong and adversarial dysrobic syndrome is both real and tragic. But something tells me it's more devastating for

---

15 Guidance states that 'Schools can adopt a policy which allows disruptive pupils to be placed in an area away from other pupils for a limited period, in what are often referred to as seclusion or isolation rooms': Department for Education, *Behaviour and Discipline in Schools* (January 2016). Available at: https://www.gov.uk/government/publications/behaviour-and-discipline-in-schools.

16 Peal, *Progressively Worse*, p. 2.

the child on the receiving end, the one with the *PAW Patrol* underpants.

This is not to say that the imperial SENCo is entirely without clothes. There are many pupils with genuine conditions who need support, understanding, and additional provision. It only becomes a problem when these are swamped by characters who abuse their privileges or those who are just straight-up ASBOs in training. In *On the Edge*, Carroll describes the 'nervous "fuck off" of the young school bully uncertainly flexing his muscles'.[17] If, at this point, a staff member swoops in and notes that the pupil is SEN, they have done unimaginable harm, since naughty pupils will now have the right to sit among the most vulnerable pupils in the school. SEN departments, pull your socks up; *Lord of the Flies* is a novel, not a blueprint.

Detention policy is also important. When you're expected to deal with detentions yourself – known as 'taking responsibility' – SLT have abnegated their responsibility to secure the 'safe and stimulating environment' demanded by the Teachers' Standards.[18] You have to consider that it simply isn't possible for a teacher to be in the five places at once necessary to (a) teach a fifth-period lesson, (b) collect detainees from science, (c) collect detainees from English, and so on … Have SLT been sniffing their board pens? Clearly, visual and auditory hallucinations are playing some kind of role here.

There will be times when year heads don't back you. In this scenario, do as Tom Bennett recommends and 'manage upwards: know the school behaviour system backwards, then if support from the school isn't forthcoming, they can be "reminded" of procedures that have been publicly agreed'.[19] A tactful way of doing this is to hurl yourself on the floor and make a guttural squealing noise. Be sure to thrash about a bit and pinwheel your arms and legs. If you're going to spit your dummy out, do it with flair. Am I joking? Only slightly. The point is that if the school is not supporting you, they are putting you in danger. Is that illegal? Probably. But we're teachers and we don't have the money to sue anybody, so my advice is that if things are

---

17 Carroll, *On the Edge*, loc. 1477.
18 Department for Education, *Teachers' Standards: Guidance for School Leaders, School Staff and Governing Bodies* (July 2011), p. 10. Available at: https://www.gov.uk/government/publications/teachers-standards.
19 Bennett and Berry, Behaviour, loc. 922.

going wrong, say either 'I have rights,' 'I'm speaking to my union,' or 'I should have become a lawyer *like every other person in my family.*'

Although Chelmsley Wood was tough, they had what I call a 'point-and-click' detention system. This should be the model for all schools and no bright spark should ever change it. If a child misbehaved, you logged the detention and they were brought to you at the end of the day.

Naughty children are not to be swept under the welcome rug while school leaders sit at the porch, mocktail in hand, whistling as they nod to the postman. Not unless you're prepared to ask yourself, 'Who is the doormat in this analogy?'

In terms of myself, taking responsibility for bad behaviour meant becoming a one-man behaviour unit. And this is an absurd thing for any teacher to have to do. I have friends who are teachers in Spain and Italy who rip me about British schools being an experiment in crowd control. Read Lucy Crehan's *Cleverlands* if you want something weightier than anecdote.[20] But I think that is underselling it a little. There are journalists who would dream wistfully of being kidnapped by Somalian pirates again after spending twelve minutes in some British classrooms.

Since this is what we're dealing with, in this chapter I'm going to tell you how to become a one-person behaviour unit. Before doing this, however, I need to go over the kind of advice that is peddled in ITT. I remember a session which opened with a PowerPoint that showed a Tex-Mex dip selection. 'Which is your favourite?' the presenter asked. The implication was that some would go for the guacamole while others would prefer spicy salsa. Accordingly, you wouldn't force a friend who had expressed a preference for Thousand Island dressing to settle for sour cream and chive, would you? Behaviour management isn't one-size-fits-all, dummy. Some pupils will want

---

20 Lucy Crehan, *Cleverlands* (London: Unbound, 2016): specifically chapter 11, along with: 'This is due to the cultural importance given to *gaman* in Japan, [which means] "enduring the seemingly unbearable with patience and dignity"' (p. 65) and 'Teachers don't often pick out individual children that are being naughty; if one child is misbehaving, it is the whole class's responsibility to make sure they fall into line' (p. 72).

the full-bodied and wholesome Mr Elliott; meanwhile, other classes will want you to resemble a cucumber and mint yoghurt dip, which is invariably preferable to peri-peri sauce. 'What about people who *like* spicy food?' asked one trainee. 'The point', said the presenter, 'is that everybody can tolerate a little tzatziki, can't they? Whereas if we stick in a habanero chili pepper, we've likely driven everyone away.' And there we are ... strict = spicy; therefore, never be strict. Welcome to the learning buffet, ladies and gentlemen, a Nando's inspired concept even less useful than takeaway homework.

But behaviour management isn't a buffet, a diner, or a sushi restaurant. It is much simpler than that. Behaviour management is a line. On no account is anybody to cross it. This line is made harder to police when you're told to experiment with seemingly random and untested activities: 'Ensure that you smile, nod, and tell all the children how excited you are for the lesson ahead.' I understand the psychology but I don't think it's very helpful. Any attempt to Disney-fy learning leaves pupils underprepared for hard graft.[21] You'll be terrorised, exhausted, and your results will suffer.

As adults, we have a tendency to oversimplify what it is that pupils like. 'Win them over', you're told, or, 'Building relationships is so crucial'. I disagree. If pupils are embarked on a learning journey, what they want is a bus driver – a cool and formal operator who will flip down the ramp for those struggling to board. That's about it. They don't want any nurturing. I went to Disneyland as a child and got into an argument with my mum because I wouldn't hug Goofy. 'I've paid good money for this,' she said. 'You could show at least some appreciation.' But that's because I sensed that 'Goofy' was just a creepy man in a suit. You would not believe how attuned pupils are to insincerity. When we grow up, we seem to lose this ancillary sense. Kids, however, will taunt you mercilessly for your false enthusiasm. So, just be yourself. Coordinators telling you to 'get excited' are like a travel guide recommending wearing a Clifford the Big Red Dog T-shirt to the running of the bulls.

---

21 'Learning happens when people have to think hard': Robert Coe, *Improving Education: A Triumph of Hope Over Experience*. Inaugural lecture of Professor Robert Coe, Durham University, 18 June 2013 (Gateshead: Centre for Evaluation and Monitoring), p. xiii. Available at: http://www.cem.org/attachments/publications/ImprovingEducation2013.pdf.

Could remorseless enthusiasm work with some classes and teachers? Sure. But is it going to work in *every single circumstance*? No. And if it's a tough school, it won't work at all. Trust me. Don't smile until Christmas, and if you're worried about coal in your stocking, so be it. More fuel for the furnace.

I will never understand why trying experimental activities is seen as such an unconditional good. Primarily, teaching should never be *about* the activities in the first place. It is about subject knowledge and instruction, and you should only deploy an activity when it assists your teaching. An activity has to meet two conditions before you consider using it. Firstly, will it cause the permanent change in long-term memory that constitutes learning? Secondly, is it better than anything you could achieve through a simpler method, like a quiz, essay, or questioning? If it's not simple, it's likely junk.

Telling teachers to try experimental activities for no clear reason will mean that they successively lose their hold on the class. The story of 'Wasteman Teacher' is the story of what can go wrong when you deploy cumbersome educational gimmickry. If an activity fails, the pupils will begin to disrupt, and nothing will diminish your status faster than whole-class disruption. It is so unfortunate that we are telling trainees to experiment. Watch as coordinators come over all glassy-eyed: 'I miss my training year. There was so much room to experiment.' No, if anybody should be experimenting, it's the established teachers – those who have mastered the basics such as discipline, firm questioning, and subject knowledge. The ones who can adapt in the face of a mishap.

You don't see drivers with L-plates pulling donuts and skidding round corners, before hurtling off a ramp and flying through a flaming hoop installed above the Coventry Canal.[22] Teaching is much harder than driving, so why should it be any different?

---

22 For this level of danger, try the Coventry ring road.

DEINDIVIDUATION: WHAT YOU'RE UP AGAINST

The Holocaust and Black Friday have more in common than you'd think. And there's a reason that peaceful protests often erupt into orgies of violence. You might not have heard of the word 'deindividuation' before, but you'll have experienced it in one form or another. Football games, university chants, and even at the pantomime: 'Look out, he's behind you!'

But what is this word and why do we need to know it? Deindividuation is defined as any 'situation in which individuals act in groups and do not see themselves as individuals, thereby facilitating antinormative behaviour'.[23] To put it more bluntly: it means that people act like yobbos in crowds.

Before we proceed, it is important to understand that there is a darker side to human nature. In *The Blank Slate*, psychologist Steven Pinker disproves the myth of the noble savage, and in *The Better Angels of Our Nature* he cites evidence that death rates among tribal societies are far higher than in modern societies.[24] What this means is that our default setting is to engage in group violence; there's a reason the people of the Yanomamö tribe of Venezuela perform every kind of atrocity imaginable short of playing ten-pin bowling with severed heads. And it's because there isn't an officer in a high-vis jacket popping out of the shrubs to cuff the little yobbos.[25]

Where there are strong institutions that disseminate and enforce laws, we have what Thomas Hobbes called a leviathan – a strong

---

23 Felipe Vilanova, Francielle M. Beria, Ângelo B. Costa, and Silvia H. Koller, Deindividuation: From Le Bon to the Social Identity Model of Deindividuation Effects, *Cogent Psychology*, 4(1) (2017). Article: 130810. Available at: https://doi.org/10.1080/23311908.2017.1308104.

24 Steven Pinker, *The Blank Slate: The Modern Denial of Human Nature* (London: Penguin, 2003), p. 118; and Steven Pinker, *The Better Angels of Our Nature: A History of Violence and Humanity* (London: Penguin, 2011).

25 You might think it's unfair to call the Yanomamö tribespeople 'yobbos', but consider the following from Pinker's *The Better Angels*: 'The Yanomamö are one of many foraging peoples that kill more newborn daughters than sons' (p. 498), they 'go to war to abduct women or avenge past abductions' (p. 686), and the percentage of those who die in warfare is more than five times higher than war deaths for twentieth century Europe (p. 48).

state that creates order – to stop people beating and burgling one another. In the absence of this, there will be 'continual fear of danger and violent death; and the life of man, solitary, poor, nasty, brutish, and short'.[26] Then again, Hobbes was born a long time before the advent of mood-boosters like Centrum MultiGummies vitamins, so maybe we should take his dour verdict with a pinch of bath salts. Life is obviously much better than in the seventeenth century.

The problem is that society is only better today because of the laws and rules that we take for granted. The solitary poverty derided by Hobbes steals back over society in those pockets of anarchy that still exist in disadvantaged urban areas, like patches of damp in an otherwise refurbished home.

Once we accept that primitive man was not some kind of cartoon character who lived among talking animals, and appreciate our default setting of group violence, we can get a sense of how deindividuation might look in a school setting. The *pupils and their peer group* are opposed to the *teachers and their peer group*. That's how it is. Like when Coventrians observe that people from Nuneaton have six fingers, or when people from Nuneaton disparage Lady Godiva for her infamous third nipple. Do either of these have any basis in reality? No, it's simply a tribal mentality that we're all guilty of – especially those Brummies with their God-awful accents: 'G'day mate, 'ow's abaht a pint a' rippa?' Whoops, I'm thinking of Aussies.

I remember one lesson vividly from when I was a pupil. I was in Year 8 and our French teacher, Mr Port-Manteau, was shouting at us. He was furious. My friends and I were putting our hands up to ask stupid questions, and I think he thought we were *les incompétents*. I remember him gesticulating fiercely at us, jabbing his fingers into his forehead, before sighing and strutting prima-donna-like out of the class. Then a member of SLT would remonstrate with him, and he'd be frogmarched right back into *la zone de guerre*.

Thinking back to that French lesson, I understand how I was able to become deindividuated. There were pupils who were just as disruptive as me all spouting off, so that allowed for a diffusion of

---

26 Thomas Hobbes, *Leviathan* (London: Pelican Classics, 1979 [1651]), pp. 62–63.

responsibility, which researchers like Philip Zimbardo have shown to be linked with 'aggressive behaviour'.[27] Furthermore, deindividuation theory originally posited the need for 'a conductor' – someone who 'plays a decisive role' by swaying the opinion of the crowd.[28] In this case, a boy named Joel was the Henry V for us little disruptors – we happy few. He told us to storm the breach, and you better believe those Frenchies got routed. *Sacré bleu*, indeed.

Another factor was a lack of accountability.[29] Deindividuation means that no single person was responsible for the disruption. As Benjamin Franklin put it, 'we must, indeed, all hang together, or most assuredly we shall all hang separately'.[30] But lack of accountability on its own is not enough. On a test administered at Harvard, participants tended to cheat on a test when they were allowed to mark the test and shred it at the end, telling the experimenter their results verbally rather than handing in the test sheet.[31] Although they cheated when they could get away with it, they only cheated slightly more than the control group, who physically returned their tests and were therefore accountable for their behaviour.

This suggests that although anonymity alone can encourage you to behave immorally, it is only the precondition for the kind of deindividuation that leads to French teachers losing their visas. Anonymity removes the accountability for the behaviour, but someone then has to step into the moral vacuum and become the conductor. Sadly for our French teacher, he wasn't up to snuff, but little Joel was.

---

27 Vilanova et al., Deindividuation, p. 7.
28 Vilanova et al., Deindividuation, p. 2.
29 Vilanova et al., Deindividuation, p. 11.
30 Isaacson, *Benjamin Franklin*, p. 313.
31 Dan Ariely, *Predictably Irrational: The Hidden Forces That Shape Our Decisions* (London: HarperCollins, 2009), pp. 200–201.

BECOMING A ONE-PERSON
BEHAVIOUR UNIT

Now we have the fundamental knowledge in place, we can look at what it takes to become a one-man (or woman) behaviour unit – or a warlord in a failed state.[32] Remember: the whole idea of being a warlord is meant strictly as a metaphor. Many CEOs of Fortune 500 companies have read Sun Tzu's *The Art of War*. It doesn't mean Burger King is going to launch a Tomahawk missile into McDonald's HQ and blow the Hamburglar to the dark side of the moon. Besides, Sun Tzu says that 'the skillful leader subdues the enemy's troops without any fighting'.[33] So please, if you're quite literal-minded, maybe go over this paragraph again so that you don't end up like poor old Mr Port-Manteau.

To start, rid yourself of any ideas that will cloud your judgement. If a child has attention deficit hyperactivity disorder (ADHD), you should hold them as accountable as everybody else. If they tell you they're autistic, respect it and work with them. But you would have to have pretty low expectations of these children to see them misbehaving and to say, 'Oh well, they have a *condition*.' Accommodate their needs, but remember that nobody is exempt from good behaviour.

Quick aside: I have a few 'pupil profiles' in front of me now. They're usually drafted by teaching assistants and members of the SEN department. I actually made about thirty of these one afternoon at Chelmsley Wood, when my boss emailed me a PowerPoint with 'the kinds of things you should put in them' and asked me to have it done by 4.30pm. The PowerPoint contained stock comments in word bubbles such as 'eye contact makes me uncomfortable', 'I like sitting next to my friends', and comments corresponding to autism suggesting that these pupils find the world scarcely more comprehensible than William James' 'blooming, buzzing

---

32 I know that whoever coined this phrase didn't intend it as an aspiration. In the absence of a Hobbesian leviathan in schools, though, it seems a more legitimate goal than 'continual fear and danger' of getting terrorised.

33 Sun Tzu, *The Art of War*, tr. Lionel Giles (London: Luzac and Company, 1910), ch. 3. Available at: http://www.gutenberg.org/ebooks/132.

confusion'.[34] That gives you some idea of the calibre of these documents. If we want them to be better, maybe we should pay teaching assistants more for what they do.

Anyway, I'm looking at profiles from good pupils in Year 8. One says, 'I do not like it when I'm challenged by staff'. Erm, well that's too damn bad, isn't it? I teach this pupil and his behaviour is usually excellent, except for the one time we all saw a squirrel climb into a bin and he shouted 'Dirty little fucker!' in his inimitable rasp. He really does find it 'hard not to call out'. Another profile says, 'I sometimes say things that might upset people'. Again, I've taught this pupil and his mindset is slightly babyish. He upsets people occasionally but it's because he's been mothered[35] and needs to be held to account for his behaviour. Meanwhile, I know that other teachers will read these documents and conclude that calling out is OK for that child or they shouldn't challenge their pupils. But, honestly, do we really want to give a kid a permission slip for saying things that 'might upset people'? We should only look at pupil data that is statistically valid, such as their diagnoses, test scores, and income brackets. Everything else was probably clattered out by underpaid and overworked staff, and are generally so slipshod as to make monkeys and peanuts look state of the art.

Next, ensure that you have worksheets as a back-up for whatever task you have planned. Most educators have heard of the Bill Rogers policy of forced choices.[36] An example from my career was when a boy named Kaçper started kicking off because another pupil had called him 'Worzel Gummidge'. Hmm, I thought, niche reference, before telling Kaçper that he could either be isolated or sit down. I dealt with him after the lesson. But did you know you can also use forced choices with an entire class? This is where the worksheet comes in. I call it The Sheet, since it's more foreboding – like something from Edgar Allen Poe. Make them simple, easy-to-monitor, and with clear word limits for each answer section. When pupils try to mess you up, simply wave The Sheet at them. 'No, sir,

---

34 William James, *The Principles of Psychology* (New York: Henry Holt and Company, 1918) p. 488.
35 I use the word 'mothered' here, but interestingly, the members of staff most guilty of this are men. The teachers that pupils are most in awe of are almost invariably women, often short ones. Don't ask me why.
36 Killian, My 5 Favourite On-the-Spot Behaviour Management Strategies.

not The Sheet!' There are many types of activity that you can put on The Sheet. I would recommend mostly short-answer questions that are easy to monitor. In 'How to Take on a Cover Lesson – and Win', I unveil a bullet points activity that would fit well on The Sheet.

Your school might lack a point-and-click detention system. If so, you have a few options: you can ask the pastoral managers or the head of year to collect the child, you can do it yourself if you have a free period, or you can ask departmental colleagues to help – providing you return the favour in future. The problem with these options is that they belie the term 'one-person behaviour unit' since you're relying on others. Plus, if you teach a larger proportion of difficult kids, you'll soon be neck deep in social arrears.

What to do then? Ask pupils to turn up voluntarily? If you like slim probabilities, sure. Maybe you could also pour a two-litre bottle of Pepsi all over your laptop, since, according to the second law of thermodynamics, there's a non-zero chance the contents could vaporise and reconstitute themselves back inside the bottle. Across an infinite timescale, it might happen once, but you need a sure strategy.

This is what I do: I set the detention for the next day and find out who has that pupil for period 5. On the morning of the detention, I email the class teacher and ask them to keep the child behind. This is better than asking other teachers to collect the child, since most teachers stay for five minutes after class anyway. It doesn't inconvenience anyone (other than the child, of course). At 3pm, you can take a leisurely stroll to collect your detainee.

Now, my opinion on consequences is that they come after the lesson. You never tell a disruptive child, 'You have a fifteen-minute detention', because that allows them to make a cost–benefit analysis of how naughty they should be, like an investor sizing up a portfolio. Instead, you either take a note of what they've done or you merely say that they're 'in trouble' and catch up with them later.

The rationale for this is twofold. Firstly, disruptive pupils are not themselves. They have been deindividuated. They're like the woman on Black Friday who lamps a pensioner over the head with an espresso machine. This means that for the sake of their group

– their tribe – they will want to act up, especially if there is a conductor at hand (a charismatic child who rivals your authority).

Secondly, whenever you make punishments fuzzy or uncertain, they are more effective. I spoke about this in 'Salience: How to Tell Off a Child the Scientific Way', and it is one of the areas where Bill Rogers and I agree: he recommends preventing children from asking 'why' questions.[37] If you don't know the punishment, you can't question it. Uncertainty works best because a 'period of anticipatory dread increasingly [activates] the amygdala', the neural pathway most correlated with feelings of fear, guilt, and anguish.[38] How better to induce contrition?

You may question whether it is right to induce guilt in a pupil who has misbehaved. You need to understand that as a teacher you have only a few cards to play. In some of the toughest and most violent schools, it's like having four Uno cards and a Top Trump in a game of Texas Hold 'Em. So, they'd better never call your bluff. The only way to do this is to add mystique to the sanction.

Besides, what I've seen in classrooms without clear rules and routines is infinitely worse. You'll hear racial slurs, threats of violence, a pupil quietly marvelling at his teacher's 'great personality' while groping the air like he's weighing a pair of water balloons. If you find that comment offensive, then reflect that it's not a whim of the author but something witnessed in an out-of-control classroom. Any kind of social, emotional, and mental health problems your pupils have will be amplified by a disruptive environment. I'm sure that Billy, who's just stabbed Rashida with a compass, can deal with a little guilt.

In terms of the consequences, as I've said, you just have to do what you feel and commit. Please do not try to be overly fair. You'll just wind up in some kind of Jarndyce v Jarndyce-style legal dispute, the kind of case that becomes over time, 'so complicated, that no man alive knows what it means'.[39] Children in trouble have an ability to negotiate that would put a Yale law grad to shame.

---

37 Killian, My 5 Favourite On-the-Spot Behaviour Management Strategies.
38 Sapolsky, Behave, p. 34.
39 Charles Dickens, Bleak House (London: Penguin, 2003 [1853]), p. 16.

Believe it or not, you can give a pupil a detention every day of the year and it still may not work. Remember Chihuahua? I once detained him for two weeks. Break, lunch, and after school. The experience was far more harrowing for me than it was for him. Some kind of Stockholm syndrome intervened in what should have been a straightforward disciplinary measure. Next thing you know, he's calling me 'daddy'.

The truth is that, yes, you really can decide on any punishment for any misbehaviour and, yes, it is slightly arbitrary, but what else are you going to do? Read his palm? Or maybe his horoscope says something about the conjunction of Mars and Neptune? No, your intuitive reaction to the misbehaviour should be calculation enough, but if you insist on a horoscope, try this: 'Today will be a day of isolation, good for reflection and calming the spirit. Later, you will find yourself sitting in a room when usually you would be outside. By home time, the sky will be darker than normal, with many omens such as the shops being shut. Amen.'

Similarly, pupils like Barry could not give a decimal fuck about a breaktime detention. In fact, he'd be grateful for the opportunity. Why go to the trouble of setting a frothing, tubercular badger on an Airedale terrier when you can simply stick it to Mr Elliott on his lunch break? 'Why'm I in a DT, sir? This is bullshit. Oi, how much you get paid, sir? Bet it's a dead ting, ennit.' All blared at you listlessly in a single, near-bottomless exhalation. The alternative? Ring the parents and set an hour. Why not?

I think the surest way of getting what you want involves a degree of confidence in your own judgement. And when you think about it, it isn't actually arbitrary at all. If they disrupted you, then that is significant. In sum: sanction misbehaviour consistently while keeping the specifics of the punishment undefined.

THE FLIPSIDE OF DEINDIVIDUATION

As stated earlier, deindividuation tends to happen when there is a conductor – a charismatic individual who can sway the group. The best part about this is that 'if … in a deindividuation situation and there is a tendency towards prosocial behaviour … the person tends to act in a prosocial manner'.[40] What this means is that by instilling certain values within the classroom, you can use deindividuation to create a positive learning environment. Much of this has a hormonal basis and is regulated by oxytocin, a hormone/neurotransmitter that 'binds us to our partners and groups, so that we can effectively compete with other groups'.[41]

The operative phrase here is 'compete with other groups'. If the children do not see you as part of their group, as well as the leader of it, then they will not follow you. Teachers should be more like prime ministers than presidents, in that they arise out of the parliament that is the class and are not imposed upon them externally like presidents upon Congress. This does not mean you should be *primus inter pares* or first among equals, either. Instead, it means that you need to either (a) show them that you have similar aims and ideas or (b) create a shared culture for the class.

In terms of (a), I am very lucky because I now teach at the school I used to attend. For my pupils, this makes me relatable – I'm definitely not from Little Dunthorpe or Harrogate or wherever. However, as I've said in the introduction, it doesn't mean I turn up at school in my Air Max trainers, pull my board pen out of my man bag, and regale them with how I 360 no-scoped some noobs on *Fortnite*. If you're 'down with the kids' then you're easily trodden on. Save it for the midlife crisis.

All it means is that I occasionally use local areas in the course of my instruction or I tell them stories about living in Coventry. It's odd but it gets them listening. Here's one I use for immigration. In some schools, a large proportion of pupils are anti-immigrant. The

---

40 Vilanova et al., Deindividuation, p. 12.
41 Jonathan Haidt, *The Righteous Mind: Why Good People are Divided by Politics and Religion* (London: Penguin, 2015), pp. 270–271.

moment you introduce the topic, prepare to be enlightened: 'Romanians are drug dealers. Albanians prefer human trafficking. Don't even get me started on those bloody Gypsies.' Ever met any? 'No.' 'But you've been watching those Liam Neeson documentaries, haven't you?' Look, I like *Taken* as much as the next geography teacher, but the lesson is about a very particular set of skills, and xenophobic ranting isn't an assessment objective.

I tell it how it is: 'I'm from Willenhall,' I say. Shudders all round. They know the area. For an equivalent, think Knockturn Alley for the wizards and little house elves of the Harry Potter universe. I tell them the story of Millie, the neighbour who, if I'd said she was from hell, would have Dante thrusting out of his coffin after half a millennium of slumber. 'At last, the tenth circle!' The woman was seemingly sponsored by the Ministry of God-Awful House Music. Her front lawn looked like a car-boot sale hit by a tactical nuclear missile. And once, at 3am, I was treated to a knock on the door. 'Scuse me, mate,' said a toothy bloke in a snapback. 'Could I borrow some milk and sugar to feed the littlun?' Milk and sugar? What are you feeding, a fruit fly? I don't want this book to be serialised by the *Daily Mail*, so I'm leaving it there.

Anyway, as I tell the kids, do you have any idea how thankful I am that the four other neighbours I've had in the last decade were all first-generation immigrants? The week after Millie was evicted by seventeen of the landlord's hard Irish cousins, a new neighbour, Innocent, moved in. We never heard a peep. Until one day, the dog was barking. 'What's going on!' I ran out of the house and Innocent – an *immigrant* – was in my front garden. But guess what? He was mowing the lawn. 'Thought I'd do yours while I was at it,' he said. Not exactly something you'd see on a UKIP poster, is it?

If you're not from the area you're teaching in, maybe try to make yourself relatable by creating your own culture. The best way to do this is to use humour. There are no blanket rules for this. Sue Cowley suggests '[treading] very carefully with sarcasm',[42] but it all depends on whether it's funny or not. If it's funny, you can say whatever you like – within the bounds of professionalism, of course. But it has to make the majority laugh.

---

42 Sue Cowley, *Getting the Buggers to Behave* (London: Bloomsbury, 2014), p. 14.

Here's an example. One boy I teach has this habit of walking into lesson as if he's trying to balance a pint glass on his chest. I could never figure it until one Monday morning he told me that he was 'hench'. Quite a unilateral declaration, I thought; so far as I could tell, he was just a little boy. Anyway, I decided to mess with him a bit. At the end of my blockbuster lesson on glacial erosion land-scapes, he remarked that I looked like I did a few press-ups myself. Meanwhile, he was puffing up his diaphragm like a Big Bad Wolf about to take a scuba dive. 'Trust me, Vincent, I learned from the best,' I said. 'Been at them little pink dumbbells, haven't I?' 'Ahh, those are so heavy, sir. I dunno how you lift 'em.' I'd then explain that he just needed to watch the Davina McCall workout DVDs 1–5. And this became our thing. There were so many variations on it that I can barely keep track. Barney the Dinosaur squat machines. Hello Kitty protein shakes. Vigorous workouts at the Purple Planet Play Centre. This was strictly during 'dead' lesson time – that is, while everyone was still settling down or packing away. Still, it was fun, and I've missed it this year.

It is important to give a counterexample since Cowley is right that humour can occasionally backfire. As a trainee, I taught a Year 10 boy named Johnnie. This boy had very bushy eyebrows and would joke that he was the 'Indian Mr Elliott'. Over time, he grew too pally and started to misbehave. One lesson he turned up in an odd frame of mind. He had sprained his leg and arrived on crutches, adding one of those weekly pill organisers to the rest of his stationery. Johnnie announced that he'd been staying up all night watching Babestation. Also, that his pills were making him too woozy to work. He was bantering me and I made the mistake of responding. All fun and games, right? Then, when he told me he couldn't write because his wrist hurt, I slipped up: 'Need to lay off the Babestation, Johnnie.' And I believe I made a Dr Feelgood quip in relation to the pills. There was no stark reaction to the comments; Johnnie found them hilarious, as did everybody else. However, later on I had to speak to my mentor about it, since somebody had taken offence and complained. You will make gaffes like this in your career. To limit them, keep any banter short and sweet. Don't overdo it because that is when you become complacent and slip up. Try to limit irrele-vant chit-chat to the beginning and end of your lessons, and if you wish to inject humour into your instruction, keep it subject specific.

Once you understand what constitutes appropriate behaviour, the biggest component of charisma is to jettison any worries you have about what your pupils think about you. There are pupils I've taught who quote me and steal my best jokes. I take it as a compliment. Why do they do it? Because I couldn't care less what they think so I say whatever absurdity pops into my head. If you can really, honestly, and thoroughly distance yourself from giving a damn what the kids think, you'll be funny.[43] It reminds me of my compulsory basic training for my motorbike. We had to ride a figure of eight around two yellow cones. If you looked at the cone, you would drive too far towards it and overshoot. Comedy is the same: never look at the cone.

THE LITTLE RED BOOK: SALVAGING POWER FROM IMPOTENCE

Teachers have about as much power as a solar panel in a sensory deprivation tank. You're only able to give out a certain number of detentions. The more you give out, the less of an effect they'll have (as outlined in 'Salience: How to Tell Off a Child the Scientific Way') and, furthermore, there are many children who don't even turn up for detention. Threaten them in class and they'll squint their eyes proudly, announcing that they have 'better things to do', as though you're merely some charity-mugger who's just pounced on them from behind Greggs.

As you'll remember from its supporting role in Wormwood School, the Little Red Book works. But why? And why Little? Why Red? It's a shame that Chairman Mao has a monopoly on this particular item of stationery, since I find it both convenient – it fits in your pocket – and conspicuous, as it draws associations with red cards in football games.

It is important to understand that the Little Red Book is simply a bluff, and I use it mainly because it allows me to reprimand in private

---

43 Read back through Chapter 2. I never made anyone laugh. I was too hung up on what they thought about me. Hint: it's eight letters, starts with w, and ends in -asteman.

– a phrase that spells RIP to bad behaviour. When you tell off children, you have to be careful not to take on the whole class at once. But how is one to rebuke individual instances of bad behaviour, without taking on the class as a whole?

Clearly, writing names on the board for C1, C2, and C3 is not going to help you.[44] All that will do is establish a kind of league table for bad behaviour. C4s, meanwhile, are so incendiary that they might as well be called 'plastic explosive'. Conspicuous punishments will allow pupils in class to transform themselves into the most unbearably pedantic jury since the European Court of Justice banned cheaper car insurance for women. Pupils will always have a prior allegiance to each other over their teacher. They will also use your attempts to discipline them as opportunities to show solidarity with each other. For instance, you might tell Ibrahim not to shout out. Jenna might then comment on your behaviour management, 'What did he *even* do!' All aboard, ladies and gentlemen. Next stop: Attitude City.

How to tell off one, without telling off all? A question that sounds positively Confucian in its obscurity and about as straightforward as the attainment of nirvana. Is it even possible to tell off one child while standing in front of an entire class, without drawing the righteous anger of the wannabe Clarence Darrows in the room with you?

It is, and this is what to do. If it is your first lesson with a class, and you notice them trying to terrorise you, you must do two things. Firstly, establish a clear monopoly on speech – in other words, one person speaking at a time.[45] The boundary has to be as stark as this, since otherwise pupils will terrorise you while professing ignorance, and thus with impunity. Pupils should respect the rules and each other.

Low-level disruption is obscenely out of hand in British schools. Many teachers have acclimatised to it, seeing it as a quirk of our education system. Tell them about China and you'll hear something vaguely xenophobic like, 'Yeah, but they're not creative enough.

---

44 Also known as the consequence system.
45 'Rule 6 – One person speaking at a time. This rule is cardinal really. It's where new teachers can really struggle': Phil Beadle, *How to Teach* (Carmarthen: Crown House Publishing, 2010), p. 17.

Here, we educate the "whole child",' whatever that means. This moving of goalposts inadvertently lowers our standards. I don't even know what a whole child is, as I've never seen a percentile or decimal one.

The aim of education is to have pupils know things – that's it. Don't excuse behavioural faults for charming idiosyncrasies. As Cowley puts it, 'if you give up, and let the students talk over you, you are basically saying: "Go ahead and talk; I don't mind." '[46] I couldn't agree more.

I was once told to drop lesson plans when they failed to secure engagement. Is your lesson plan so worthless that a little disruption can divert you from your learning intentions? Maybe this would work for Mr Chamberlain, who could stroll into class waving an engaging starter on a yellow sticky note. PEACE paragraphs in our time. But for teachers with integrity? No. By all means, adapt your learning when pupils are struggling, but adapting on the basis of entertainment value is setting kids up to fail. How do I know? I've done it. Many times. All they'll learn is that they can protest until you stick on YouTube or Kahoot! You may think, 'Oh, it's just once, and it was a rainy period 5 lesson. We'll make up for it tomorrow.' Let's take the same comment and apply it to a smoker: 'Oh, it was just the one, and I'd had a tough period 5 lesson – you know what the rain does to the kids. I'll quit properly tomorrow.' At least with the cigarette you're only harming yourself.

Back to the monopoly on speech. Once you've secured this, you need to explain that you know everything that is going on. Make it clear that, although you will not write names on the board, you *will* arrange time after school to catch up, if necessary. If I were in a more needlessly complicating frame of mind, I might call it omniscience for learning. Pupils need to understand that you know what they're up to, even if it's a smirk or a note pass. They need to know that even the most subterranean altitude is well on your radar. If I notice that a pupil has untucked their shirt, I may decide to forget about it. They're potentially challenging, but they're on task and so I'll overlook it. After they've worked for a good while, I might speak to them quietly and observe that they untucked their shirt forty-five minutes

46 Cowley, *Getting the Buggers to Behave*, p. 38.

ago and would they mind tucking it back in? This lets *them know* that *I know* what they're up to. I'll say it in a bantery way, and it tends to raise a smile; a little cat and mouse between teacher and pupil. Knowing everything that's going on, and saying out loud what you know, is a kind of power play.

Once you have established a monopoly on speech and omniscience for learning, you can then begin to implement the Little Red Book. But first, we'll need an instance in which to apply it.

Let's say that Michael is sitting at the back of the room. His legs are sprawled in front of him, arms crossed like a malignant genie, and he is chewing in a slow and cud-like manner as he considers you with the lazy disdain of a barnyard animal. His gum probably lost its flavour half an hour ago. And if you were to ask him why he was chewing, he'd just shrug like you'd asked for the capital of Burundi.

The reason, however, is that he is testing your boundaries. Chewing gum is merely the gateway drug to the more intoxicating behaviours of low-level disruption and answering back. If he's allowed to chew, he might start tapping his pen while you speak. Once he's exhausted that particular dopamine hit, he'll start shouting out, and then … he can do whatever he likes. He will then have the gall to complain that he isn't learning anything. Either he quits it cold turkey or you're a sitting duck.

If I saw Michael behaving like this, I would take out the book, look him in the eye, and then write his name in it. If he doesn't grasp the significance, I might raise an eyebrow as I do so; the kind of expression an interviewer would level at a candidate with his fly undone.

Midway through the lesson, and Michael alone is aware that something has happened. I might then announce to the whole class: 'You're all doing really well. Just remember, anyone who is unable to work will be dealt with later on,' and I'll wave the book. Funnily enough, Michael might thrust his hand in the air for a perfunctory nanosecond before shouting out, 'Are you gonna give me a detention, sir?' Don't rise to this: he is trying to drag the private punishment that you're levelling into the public arena, where his little juror friends can cast judgement on you. Just smile and wave the book; as Cowley says, 'it is best to use non-verbal, rather than verbal, techniques'.[47]

At the end of lesson, tell everyone except Michael to stand behind their desks, and the class is dismissed. You'll now notice that a peculiar change has come over him. It is as though in the few moments since his buddies left the room, he's reached for his pocket bible and discovered that, yes, the meek really shall inherit the Earth. And then it's all: apologies for this temporary blip, sir; yes, I really have behaved awfully, haven't I?; oh shucks, shan't happen again, sir; yes sir, no sir, three bags full sir.

If he tries spinning you a nursery rhyme, just remember that whatever barnyard animal product his three bags are full of, it isn't wool. Make sure that in the course of this discussion, you ask him (a) does he play video games and (b) did he not get enough sleep. He'll say yes to both since the only thing a naughty will ever own up to is his own blamelessness.

As for the punishment, set an hour's detention (since he wasted the hour) and then ring his parents. Tell them about the hour but then express concern about his Xbox, how he's not getting enough sleep, and how you're worried for his academic record. Next thing you know, the Xbox is in the attic with the camping equipment and it won't be back down until Julember.

The following lesson, when you wave that Little Red Book at Michael, the rapidity with which his head hits the textbook will be like somebody snipped his puppet strings.

You may be thinking to yourself: Michael only disrupted one lesson, wasn't this going a little too far? My answer is, no. Try not to take the expression 'handle with kid gloves' too literally. It refers to baby goats, not children. Michael is ruining his own education. Undoubtedly, his Xbox will have something to do with it. And, worst of all, if you did not come down on him, he would corral others into disruption and potentially ruin the learning of twenty-nine other kids.

It's a fair price to pay.

---

47 Cowley, *Getting the Buggers to Behave*, p. 38.

Chapter 4

BEHAVIOUR MANAGEMENT
IN ACTION

How does one go from a wasteman teacher to an effective one? Simple, by using the principles of behaviour management. These principles are in the background of this section, like the twangling of an ice-cream van on a hot summer's day. But they are there, nonetheless. The biggest take-home message is the one that's never left after the beep: phone calls. They need to be honest, forthright, but respectful. This is the key to helping pupils help themselves. What else? Prepare to meet some unusual characters. The bandits and marauders of the 'failed state' education system. Dalton McFlurry, Ryan Pudsey, and Hulk Jenkins. Realise that these pupils can only exist in the absence of authority. Like Ezekiel: a little phone call is all it takes to expunge bad behaviour from the narrative. Anyway, buckle up, knuckle down, and get ready for some serious next-levelism.

CLASS 9CBA

Before taking narrative flight from Wormwood, however, I'd like to begin this section by looking at the various successes I enjoyed during my time at the school. The first such success was Class 9CBA. Named after Caroline Bamford, a geography teacher who'd run off after thirty-five minutes with these delinquents, bequeathing them a very appropriate acronym.

'Right, Sam,' my boss said. 'Caroline's gone. We've got a supply in for the rest of the week. After that, are you OK to take over?'

'Sure,' I said. Aside from my Year 10s, I've got a strict reputation, so I was glad of the opportunity to have my mettle tested. 'Books?'

'We threw them in the skip,' he said. 'They were full of lighthouses.' A code word for penis drawings as there was a child in the office with us. 'And pictures of Caroline. Some of them, y'know, together.'

'Oh, Christ,' I said.

'It was bad,' he said.

During Caroline's final lesson, I stood at the door and peered through the glass trying to discern what was happening. She looked like somebody trying to play charades with gloves made of lead. She turned around and a big lad named Carlson got up, drew a 'lighthouse' on the whiteboard and sat back down again.

'How'd that get there?' she mimed to herself. Hmm, a real head-scratcher.

Next, I saw Mason tear a page out of a geography textbook and fashion it into a 'bugle'. He held the bugle in his mouth for a few seconds and blew air in Carlson's face. *Nobody* touches my textbooks. I opened the door and looked at every single one of them. Death stares all round. I had the Little Red Book in my hand and they all knew what that meant. I gestured to Mason and stood him outside by the plug socket.

'You're all doing so well,' said Caroline. Oh dear, had she been at the bugles too? How could she possibly stay so upbeat?

I was speaking to Mason: 'Did your mum raise you to vandalise school property? I've spoken to your mum – she's lovely – and how's she gonna feel when I ring home tonight and ...'

There was a whoop and a piercing shriek from the classroom. And then, 'JUST SHUT UP – SHUT UP, SHUT UP, *SHUT* UP. YOU STUOOOPID LITTLE BOY.'

Carlson bustled out of the class. I peered in the doorway. 'I can't deal with this, sir,' said Caroline. 'I'm done. Have the class. TAKE IT! I'm done ...'

My boss came in and tried to reason with her, 'Calm down, Caroline, we'll ...'

'No, I'm done. I expected to be teaching sixth form. I *told* you I only taught sixth form.'

'Did you read the job application?' he asked.

Caroline whisked her highlighters into her wicker stationery basket and blew past us like motorway traffic. By the time we'd turned around she was gone.

Monday morning, the following week. I looked at my timetable – 9CBA stamped indecorously in three separate timeslots. Good grief. My first lesson was period 5 that day. The other two hours melded together like clots of phlegm into a double period on Friday morning. Hallelujah!

I knew what I'd do for the first lesson. This class was far behind the rest of Year 9. I needed to quiz them until they understood the key concepts. I went in. No, 'Hi, how are you?' I didn't even introduce myself. What's the point? They knew my name, and I know how kids feel about all that *Balamory* rubbish: 'Hi, kids, I'm Mr Elliott. My favourite colour is bright purple. What about you? Tee-hee.'

'Look,' I said. 'You've driven one teacher out of her job. Vandalised countless textbooks – we have to replace those! And now you're so far behind that you'd need a GPS to rediscover the learning journey. You're going to …'

'You our new teacher?' said a stroppy little girl called Asia.

'Yeah, I am. Shout out again and watch what happens.' My tellings-off were deliberately blunt but ambiguous. 'The rules are simple: no talking unless it's a discussion, and raise your hand if you have a question. Violate these and you stay, but guess what … I won't necessarily tell you that you have a detention. You'll find out later. Might be I'm outside your class at the end of the day. Could be that one of my colleagues collects you. Whatever the method, just know I have *plenty* – more than triple science GCSE.'

Fifteen minutes pass and who should stroll in but Abdul. He'd got his arms out beside him, swaying absurdly from side to side. He reminded me of a wine-bottle opener when you spin the metal arms around. He sat down and I didn't make a fuss. He doesn't realise it, but if he disrupts me again I'm going to punish him severely.

The pupils complete the quiz as well as they can. I explain to them that it's OK if they lack knowledge, since we're going to green-pen the answers and they can do better next time. Asia's trying her best and even Abdul's still working on his attempt. I put the answers up on the board and begin questioning. We talk about rivers. Do they flow from the sea or from the mountains? Why? What is a waterfall and how on earth could one happen? I spoke about sediment, explaining that it was material transported by a river or, for our purposes, sand.

'Hey, here's a question: if a river floods and deposits sediment, why would the land become flat?' I drew a picture of a cat on the board. It was deliberately crude. It had long fangs like the vampire in *Nosferatu* and swirly eyes to suggest insanity.

'Oh no, sir, what's that!?' said Abdul.

'Your cat, Abdul. Dirty little critter. Found him in a skip, didn't you?'

The class exploded with laughter. Even Abdul was creasing up.

'Take a look at this silly little cat.' This is how I tell my stories in lessons and it always seems to work. 'This dirty animal soiled the litter tray and now we have to clean it. So, what do we do, Abdul?'

'Change the litter, sir. I don't want my cat getting dirtier – he's way too grimy as it is.'

Laughter again.

'Precisely, Abdul, now … what about this. If I pour litter in one side of the litter tray, is it going to keep piling up on one side?'

'Hmm, maybe a little, sir.'

'But it's not going to form a near-vertical mountain, is it?' I asked.

'No, it'll flatten out.'

This single exchange taught the class why a floodplain is flat. Sediment and alluvium are deposited and gravity ensures that it flattens out. It accomplished a secondary goal too. The kitty litter image was a kind of mnemonic. Whenever they heard 'floodplain', they always thought 'Abdul's cat'. So, they never forgot. Over the course of my practice, I've acquired thousands of these.

That's not to say things were plain sailing. There were more bumps and jolts than a white-water rapid, but they were learning. Two weeks later and Carlson was back from his stint in the SEN department – where modern schools dump their naughty children to sweep them under the rug. But, hey, at least the sensory deprivation room now has more brooding lighthouses than a Nordic detective drama.

'Wagwarn, sir,' said Carlson, tipping Abdul's book on the floor.

'Outside.'

'Whaaahhh, I haven't done anything?'

'You threw Abdul's book on the floor. I'll speak to you outside,' I said, picking up the book.

'Wasteman,' he muttered under his breath.

Yippee! I thought, Carlson's done it. He's called me a 'wasteman' and that's the smoking gun I need. When you have kids who are 'school-wide issues', the best policy is the just-give-me-that-chance mentality. It means that instead of worrying about being insulted, you actively look forward to it, since you can then enforce whatever sanctions you see fit. Part of why Luka was so unusually difficult was because of his shape-shifting temperament. Every time you thought you had a grapple hold, a shoe would come loose or he'd vanish in a cloud of fog, and, hang on, hadn't he always treated you so nicely? It's called gaslighting; Luka was very good at it and it drove me mad. Carlson couldn't hold a candle to Luka, let alone a gaslight, so he was dealt with very easily.

'Do you think it's right to call me a wasteman?' I said, when we sat in the office later.

'No, sir,' he said.

'You realise I saw you kick a football at the spotlight earlier?'

'You did?'

'It's broken.'

'No!' said Carlson.

'On the corridor yesterday, I heard you shout "spakker" at Ahmed.'

'You remember that?' He said. 'Look, it's just our joke, sir. You wouldn't understand.'

'It's always a joke, isn't it? Like you calling me wasteman. Let's see what your mum thinks.'

Carlson sat there, ashamed, and I dialled his mum. No reply. 'Don't worry,' I said. 'I'm here until 5pm. It's only a matter of time.' I tried again. There was a crackle at the end of the line.

'Hello?'

'Hi, is this Miss Szary?'

'Speaking.'

'Hi, Mr Elliott from Wormwood School here – Carlson's geography teacher.'

'You alright?'

'I'm good, thanks. I've got Carlson here in detention ...'

'What's he done now?'

'Look, Miss Szary, I'm afraid it's very serious. Carlson's been bullying a boy with special needs. He called him a "spakker". Now, I've just googled the word, Miss Szary, and it's a pejorative term for a mentally disabled person. It's similar to the word "retard", only with far worse connotations.' God knows what those connotations are – the computer's not even on.

'Oh, my God.'

'He's also committed vandalism.'

'WHAT!'

'Yesterday lunchtime, Carlson kicked a football at one of our spot-lights, before yelling, "Fuckin' leg it, lads!" It's been broken ever since.'

'Look, Mr Elliott, I'm absolutely mortified.'

Carlson looks almost comically repentant. 'Miss Szary, I wish that was the end of it. Not only will we need to get a contractor in for the light – it's a German company and quite a rare bulb, so the nearest servicing depot is in Rotterdam.'

'In Germany!'

'No, sorry. Rotterdam is in the Netherlands; the company's based in Germany – I should've made myself clear. Anyway, there's that, but there's also what he said to me earlier today.'

'Ooh, wait till I see him, I'm fu – I'm fuming – sorry. Sorry, Mr Elliott. I didn't mean to swear.'

'It's alright, Miss Szary.'

'What did he say to you?'

'He came to my lesson late, threw a pupil's textbook on the floor ...'

'Oh no.'

'Then he referred to me as a wasteman. You may be unfamiliar with the term. It's a gang phrase. It was coined by the Yardies in Jamaica and it's highly aggressive. In Jamaica, if somebody calls you a was-teman, it's usually an act of violence.' Can you see what I've done here? Mountains and molehills.

'Mr Elliott, I'm coming right away, and we're going to sit down and make sure that this never, *ever* happens again. God, I'm so embarrassed.'

'Don't worry, Miss Szary. We'll make sure Carlson starts getting it right, don't you worry.'

Now, that, ladies and gentlemen, is how to do a phone call home. In order to get to this level, you need to see phone calls as a kind of skill. The number of times I hear teachers ring a parent and lackadaisically go through the motions. 'Hello, Georgie was bad today. He did no work. He did X, Y, and Z. Georgie was mean to me. Waaah, waaah. My fault? What do you mean, my fault? Please. Please help me. Help me help your son! Help me help you. Help me … help you,' as Jerry Maguire would have put it.

The point is that parents have no idea that their child isn't a darling little cherub who drifted down from the ceiling of the Sistine Chapel. At school, things are different, and you have to make your case like a barrister. If you don't, well, the kids will make *their* case, and once they've told mum you're useless and couldn't teach your way out of a wet paper bag, the parents will assume that you're the problem and they'll never support you.

I messed up badly with Luka. And when it came to his mum, she thought *I* was the problem, since I hadn't conveyed the full extent of Luka's bad behaviour. If you look through the above, I didn't say anything false. I may have embellished it slightly for literary purposes, but if a pupil damaged a spotlight, that's vandalism – a crime. If a pupil calls someone a 'retard', well, in the United States that would be a hate crime. I am using these terms to point-score, in a sense, but that doesn't mean I'm wrong. We need to stop holding kids to woolly moralities, since when we do, our authority dissolves like cotton candy.

As you can imagine, I never heard a peep from Carlson again. Abdul worked hard for the rest of the year, despite having the worst conduct record imaginable elsewhere, and Class 9CBA became some of my hardest workers. Can't be arsed? Yeah, right.

THE CURIOUS CASE OF DALTON MCFLURRY

As far as Year 10 were concerned, things at Wormwood were as bitter as gall. But this one blasted rock was merely an island in an otherwise flourishing archipelago of learning – could that be a book title? As a tutor, I'd really come into my own.

'Books out. Where's your Five?' The 'Five' referred to their pen, pencil, ruler, calculator, dictionary, and planner. Look, it wasn't a maths initiative, OK?

Miss Zoolander from the Year 8 team popped her head in: 'Everybody got their Five?' she said. I nodded. 'Oi,' she swaggered in. 'What's this?' The pencil she picked up belonged to Dante. It was stubbier than a big toe in ballet shoes. 'Sir asked for your Five, not your 4.9 recurring.' Dante laughed. 'Sort it out, you scruff,' she said, tousling his hair.

'Right then,' I said. 'Yeah, got your Five? Yeah – pencil? No, OK. Forget again and it's detention at break. OK, right. Ajla, hand out the sheets. Brogan, take half. So … *this* is our PRIDE sheet. Anyone know what PRIDE stands for?'

Kieran put his hand up. 'P stands for Pride,' he smirked, 'then R is Respect, then Independence, Determination, and Excellence.' As a tutor, I knew how vital it was that pupils had this acronym memorised – especially the P, which is doubly important. Among professionals, this is known as Educating the Whole Child.

I banged on about what a Proud tutor I was for considerable time. The kids affirmed that they too were ready to exhibit some serious Excellence. And Miss Zoolander couldn't help herself – she had no choice but to remark upon their Respectfulness. We were that good.

But like the authors of the late-eighteenth century, we soon tired of speaking in capitalised nouns, and thankfully the bell went. The tutor group scattered and I marched back to the office.

'Ooh,' my boss said, looking at my timetable. 'Interesting group.'

'Naughty?' I asked.

'Not exactly. They're mostly high-attainers. Billed for level 7s at GCSE. You've got Dalton McFlurry, though.'

I remembered Dalton from a learning walk lesson I'd observed as a trainee. He was sitting in the corner of Mr Mayhew's class, and I was struck that he'd added so copiously to his Five. Indeed, it was more of a Twenty-Five. From the shuriken spinner toys through to the cubes with the clicky buttons on the side, he'd barricaded himself in with so many toys that he looked right out of a Fisher-Price catalogue.

'Here's Dalton,' said our guide, the Year 7 feelings for learning coordinator. 'Say hi, Dalton.' He grunted in our direction. 'Dalton has autism spectrum condition, so we've provided for his needs as well as we can.'

'What's this?' I asked, pointing to a lavender card on the edge of the table.

'Toy pass,' grunted Dalton.

I thought back to primary school, where 'Toy Day' had been an annual event we always looked forward to. Meanwhile, here was Dalton, with half of the foreclosed inventory of Toys 'R' Us installed on his desk.

'Dalton,' asked the coordinator, 'do you have your action pack?' Dalton shuffled on his chair and retrieved a plastic envelope with a label that said, 'Action Pack: Dalton McFlurry' on the front. The coordinator took it, we sat at a desk beside Dalton, and out came several pastel-coloured brochures. They looked like the water-based section of the Dulux colour chart. On closer inspection, they weren't brochures at all, but reports.

'These are part of Dalton's pack. This one' she held up a sea-foam-green one, 'is his Happiness Report.' She opened it and there were demarcations of fifteen-minute intervals for each lesson. 'What Dalton does is he marks how he's feeling on a scale from "Slugs, snails, and puppy-dog tails" through to "Sugar, spice, and everything nice" on the other end. Since Dalton is a visual learner, we felt this would be more appropriate for him. At the end of the lesson, Dalton will sit down with Mr Mayhew and fill out the report. If a teacher gets three "Slugs" ratings in a row, Dalton can choose to switch classes.'

Mr Mayhew began expounding on the Peasants' Revolt. Meanwhile, Dalton had taken a curly plastic twizzle stick and inserted it into a fidget cube, and was now engaged, with a neurosurgical level of focus, on extracting it. As yet, the jury's still out on Bop It for Learning (BIfL).

One year later, Dalton is in Year 8, and I am now teaching his class. But he hadn't arrived yet. We're learning about the Great Pacific Garbage Patch; incidentally, the topic that made Greta Thunberg drop out of school to pursue climate change activism.

'So,' I asked, 'if it's not larger plastics that are the problem, what are we worried about?'

'Could it be microplastics, sir?' asked Michael. 'The marine animals might be consuming these microscopic pieces of plastic?'

'Good,' I said. 'Now, Justyna. In science with Mr Beaker, you learned about food chains – what did he say was being transferred in food chains?'

'Energy, sir,' said Justyna.

'And can you remember what happens as we move higher up the food chain? To higher trophic levels?'

'The energy becomes more … concentrated?'

'Exactly,' I said. 'Now, Afdal, what will this mean for microplastics?'

'Maybe they will become more concentrated as well?'

'So, the higher up we go, the more microplastics we'll find – and who's at the top of the food chain?'

At that moment, the door thwacked open, hit the wall, and shuddered back on its hinges. Dalton stood in the doorway. 'Beep, beep, I'm a sheep. BEEP, BEEP, I'M A SHEEP. Meow, meow, I'm a cow. MEOW, MEOW, I'M A COW.' Dalton joggled into the room. He knocked Michael's book to the floor, took off a backpack that was big enough to trek the Cairngorms with, and disgorged all of his fidget toys onto the three adjoined tables where Michael and Afdal sat. Curly plastic snakes, glittery twizzle sticks, and countless shurikens: the stationery was engulfed in the deluge, and could just as well have been on the bottom of a ball pit play area. Michael picked up a toy mobile phone and advanced on Dalton. 'Slap!' It sounded like a fly swat on wet concrete.

'Ow!' said Michael, retracting his hand.

'Hands off my fidgets!' said Dalton.

'Look, Dalton, let's make sure there's enough space for everybody, shall we?' I proceeded to move some of the toys, but I wish I hadn't.

'BEEP, BEEP, I'M A SHEEP!' Dalton whirled round on me and began to rampage about the classroom. Workbooks were picked up and scattered, riffling down through the air. Dalton was punching pupils in the arm. 'NOBODY TOUCHES MY FIDGETS!' he said, gnashing his teeth. I went to the door, looked out, and saw Miss Champion coming towards me. Thank God. Dalton, meanwhile, was near the computer.

'DALTON, PUT THAT DOWN THIS INSTANT,' bellowed Miss Champion. Dalton had the computer monitor clasped to his chest and was tearing it away from the desk like he was uprooting a sapling. 'IF YOU DO NOT PUT THAT DOWN, RIGHT AWAY, YOUR MOTHER WILL BE PICKING YOU UP!'

'NO!' said Dalton, dropping the monitor onto the floor and then ripping the keyboard out of its socket. He made off to the back of the class in a scurrying lope, and hefted himself onto the gunmetal filing cabinet. The only thing missing from the scene was a squadron of paper aeroplanes.

I'd hardly noticed the door open but Miss Zoolander tapped me on the shoulder. '2E05's free,' she said.

Taking my cue, I said, 'Right class, pack up your stuff; we're moving to 2E05.' All the stationery was whisked from the tables, leaving only the plastic menagerie on Dalton's desk. Changing rooms took five minutes. I had to improvise a seating plan. Finally, it took an additional five minutes to boot up the computer.

'Where was I?'

'The consumption of microplastics, sir,' said Afdal.

'Right, so ... who's at the top of the food chain? And how might the consumption of microplastics affect ...'

The wall vibrated like a drum skin: 'GET YOUR HANDS *OFF* MY FIDGETS!!!'

'... them? Michael, what do you think?' At the doorway, members of the SLT were clopping down the corridor in high heels, then came the feelings for learning coordinator, and, finally, a member of the site services team.

'Dalton,' we heard through the wall. The coordinator was the self-appointed child whisperer in this scenario. 'Can you remember what we said to do when we're feeling icky?! Can you calm down for me, Dalton?'

'I WOULD BUT THAT *BITCH* TOOK MY FIDGETS.'

'Dalton, that's icky language – remember, we have to resolve our issues sensibly. I'm sure Miss Champion didn't mean to ...'

'Justyna,' I asked. 'What did we mean by the word "sustainable", and how might it apply to this topic?' I could tell that she wanted to answer the question, but it was like asking her to perform long division in an air raid. I decided to wrap it up. 'Let's leave it there, folks. Pack up,' I said.

I looked into the corridor and saw Miss Champion dialling Dalton's parents. She didn't even have to look at her computer. It was the fourth time this week he'd been sent home.

LESSONS FROM MY TUTOR

Luckily for me, Dalton's tutor, Mr Mayhew, had been given three 'Slugs' in a row and therefore Dalton could change group. Miss Champion asked me if I wanted him in my tutor group. 'Could make him easier to handle in geography,' she said. It was worth a shot.

I rang Dalton's mother to inform her of the change. When she picked up, she was on the defensive. 'The school doesn't understand my son's needs,' she said.

'Look, Mrs McFlurry,' I said. 'Dalton's been aggressive towards members of staff. He jabbed one pupil in the eye with a glittery twizzle stick the other morning and sent him to the school nurse. We can't go on like this.'

Mrs McFlurry sighed. 'In all honesty,' she said, 'he's been abusive at home lately with his little brother, Kaidon. He keeps pinching him and giving him nuggies.'[1]

'My theory', I said, 'is that Dalton's been given too many privileges. I'm aware of his needs, Mrs McFlurry, but he has a toilet pass, a time-out pass, and probably a pass for Area 51 if he rooted around hard enough. In his Learning Action Pack, the reports mostly specify his own level of happiness and there are no obligations for Dalton to meet. Here's what I propose: I'm going to make Dalton a Favours Report. He can do chores and help you out around the house, and it'll give him some understanding that life isn't a one-way pleasure portal from which he can take, take, take … but that he has to give in return. What do you think?'

'It sounds like a good idea but I won't hold my breath,' she said. 'You speak to him about it.'

'OK,' I said. 'Thanks for the support, Mrs McFlurry. I'll get back to you as soon as I can.' Click.

The Year 8s were in assembly and Dalton sat across the desk from me. He regarded me languidly, as some kind of lesser being – one

---

1   A nuggy is when you rub someone's head with your knuckles.

who was far removed from the Platonic realm of plastic cubes, squeezable rubber dinosaurs, and magic rainbow puzzle balls. More to be pitied than acknowledged. But, boy, did I have a surprise for him.

'Dalton,' I said, fixing my posture. 'I'm assuming the coordinator told you that you're hereby restricted to one fidget toy.' A gruff nod. 'To gain access to the toy, which will be kept in my desk drawer, you have to fill out a Favours Report.'

'Another report?' he said. 'I have five already.'

'This one is different,' I said as I took out the report – no fancy colour scheme, just a table I'd drawn on the back of a sheet of scrap paper. 'It works like this, Dalton. You're going to help your mother out. In this column, you need to do the washing-up, and you have to do it three times a week.'

'Three times!?' he groaned. 'Look, I'm sorry I called Miss Champion a bitch.'

'In the second column, you have to vacuum at least twice a week. Your mother says you enjoy this so it shouldn't be too tough. Finally, and you can do this on either Saturday or Sunday, you're to take your little brother Kaidon to the park.'

'NO,' he said. 'Not him, sir. I *hate* Kaidon. Please, sir, anything but that.'

'He's your brother, Dalton. Besides, he's a lot younger than you, and you should be looking out for him, not giving him nuggies. How would you feel if I gave you a nuggy?' I reached out to the matted clump of hair on his head like I was knocking a door.

Dalton was chuckling, 'No, sir. Staaahhhp,' he said.

'See, not fun is it. Now, the report's due on Tuesday, and it has to be signed by your mother – every slot. If you miss one, then guess what?' The drawer was full of fidgets and I extracted a Magic Cube Stress Reliever like a fairground claw-machine. 'Little Magic Cube here won't see the light of day until your first day of uni. Are we clear?'

'Clear, sir,' he said. Unhappy but resigned.

'Off you go,' I said.

Dalton kept to his Favours Report. He washed up, vacuumed, and became much closer with his brother Kaidon. He was even less abusive and nicer to be around, according to Mrs McFlurry. As for me, I found him a model student. One piece of research he conducted on the Great Pacific Garbage Patch was so in-depth and articulate that I almost considered sending it off to Greta Thunberg herself, but I had second thoughts when I saw he'd scrawled 'BEEP, BEEP, I'M A SHEEP' on the reverse. Some habits die hard.

Overall, Dalton became a studious, diligent, and somewhat bearable young man – a testament to the necessity of obligation as well as incentive. The strangest thing? When I presented him with his Magic Cube Stress Reliever one Monday morning, he said, 'I'm OK, sir, that stuff is for babies.' And I never saw him with another toy. He'd still lash out occasionally, and I'm pretty sure he still thought Miss Champion was an all-caps BITCH, although I never pressed him on this. Whatever it was, Dalton had taken several lumbering strides in the right direction, and that's what matters most.

WHERE'S YOUR TROUSER PASS?

'Sam, listen to me,' my boss said. 'You've got to be *on it* with this class, do you understand? They get nasty if they're given too much freedom.' Bullying had been a major problem. One girl called Amelia had been called 'Big Nose' with such remorseless frequency that she was now a school refuser, and a boy named Mudather had been christened 'Popcorn Chicken' after some boys had dumped a ramekin of chicken gravy over his head and filmed it on Snapchat.

This is what people don't understand when they criticise isolation or detention systems: the bullying that occurs in disorderly classes is far worse than any amount of discipline enforced by the teacher. I wonder how those nice people from the *Guardian* Opinion column would feel if their child came home from school crying because they'd been called 'blick' or 'freshie' – racist slang terms for dark skin and first-generation immigrants.

Several years back, I read a book called *The Blacker the Berry* by Wallace Thurman, a 1929 novella about racism among African-Americans in Harlem, New York. In it, the protagonist laments her 'face as black as her father's, and a nose which, while not exactly flat, was as distinctly negroid as her too thick lips'.[2] Almost a century later, I still hear this level of physiognomical insult bandied between kids in the corridor. Pupils who have self-defined as members of the lesbian, gay, bisexual, and transgender (LGBT) community are similarly victimised. The same is true for English as an additional language (EAL). And anyone standing out. Children in classrooms lacking authority can be subject to psychological abuse so severe it makes Dante's *Divine Comedy* look like the Edinburgh Fringe Festival. Which is why it's so important for teachers to be assertive in lesson. The flipside of 'a safe and stimulating environment for pupils' is the teacher's capacity to punish inappropriate behaviour.[3]

My first lesson with this class was on a rainy Tuesday morning. Small raindrops stippled the broad windows and the corner desk hung heavy in the gloom. One pupil shambled to his seat as I arrived. I was ready to go.

'Morning, class,' I said. 'Today, we're learning about the Holocaust …'

'Ahh YES!' said Langston, nudging his partner. 'This topic is SICK. We get to learn about how the Jews got gassed and bun in the oven.'[4]

'Langston, that's incredibly inappropriate. Speak like that again and you'll spend lunch wiping down the windows in the humanities office. Understand?'

'Sorry, sir,' he said. 'Sir, can I ask a question?'

'OK, Langston.'

---

2   Wallace Thurman, *The Blacker the Berry* (New York: Dover Publications, 2008), p. 8.
3   Department for Education, *Teachers' Standards*, p. 10.
4   This isn't a typo. Langston is using the word 'bun' in the slang sense meaning to 'smoke weed' or 'get burnt'.

'Actually, no, I don't think I should.'

'Right,' I said with mild exasperation. 'Why don't we start with how ordinary Germans perceived Jews in Hitler's Germany. You've probably seen movie depictions or read on the internet about what ...'

'Sir, my question's this,' said Langston, grinning. 'Did the Jews ever – y'know – with each other?'

'Pardon me?'

'On the trains to Auschwitz, did the Jews ever fiddle with each other?'

I excluded Langston from the remainder of the lesson. What he'd said was obscene. There was no bartering. I simply sent him to the office. The rest of the class handled the topic with great maturity. They listened, I told stories, and I tried to keep as many of them on their toes as I could. It was still a difficult class, but I had my techniques, storytelling being the go-to. One anecdote I always use for this topic is that, before the concentration camps, SS Officers used vans with 'Kaiser's Coffee Shop' written along the side. Jews would be loaded into the vans and the exhaust hooked up to the interior. Hundreds of thousands of Jewish people were murdered by carbon monoxide poisoning before Auschwitz was even thought of, let alone built.

'Sir,' asked Lucy. 'Why were most of the Jews killed during the war? Why weren't they killed earlier?'

'Well,' I said. 'Martin, you spoke about Russia earlier, didn't you? What did the war with Russia mean for Germany?'

'That they would have to make more trains, tanks, and – what was that word you used – ammunitions,' he said.

'Munitions,' I corrected. 'Good. And we know that Adolf Hitler lost this campaign, don't we, Gabriella?'

'Stalingrad,' she said.

'Explain,' I said.

'In the video, it showed soldiers fighting in Stalingrad, and the Germans lost and were forced to retreat.'

'Good. Now, clearly everything's going wrong for Hitler and, knowing his personality, we know he's unlikely to take responsibility for this – so what's the solution?'

Martin raises his hand so high I'm worried about his ligaments, so I let him answer: 'A final one, sir. His solution is the Final Solution. He blames the Jews and because of this they have to be punished.'

'And there we go. We can refer back to Hitler's "prophecy speech" of 1939 where he predicted that either Germany would be victorious or the Jews would be annihilated. He'd failed in the former objective so had to plump for the latter. See?'

The bell rang, the pupils scurried off, and I took my equipment box back up to the office. Langston is sitting asprawl on my office chair. The punnet of grapes at my computer now contains only a barren sprig. The boy has wrecked my lunch as well as period 1, I thought.

'I'm about to sort this,' I said, logging on to SIMS.

'Ooh, what ya gonna do, ring my dad?'

'Yeah,' I said, writing the number on a torn sheet and swivelling round to the Airfix-plastic telephone. There's a click at the end of the line. 'Hi there, Mr Elliott from Wormwood School speaking – Langston's history teacher.'

'What is it this time?' he asked.

'Unfortunately, it's quite negative. Langston's made some highly inappropriate comments about Jews during the Holocaust. He asked me if they'd fiddled with each other on the trains to Auschwitz.' Never euphemise a pupil's conduct. Always quote to them what the pupil has said.

'Oh Christ,' he said. 'Look, Mr Elliott, that's horrendous. He's always had a bit of a nasty streak. No idea where he gets it. And we've tried everything. I've spoken with the head of year; she'd set detentions, he went, and then we're back to square one the following week.'

'I understand, Mr Bluck,' I said.

'Call me Keith,' he said.

'I understand, Keith, but here's my proposal. Langston's got a lot of things he enjoys doing. At school, he does football, rugby, and is keen to leave on time to get on the number 13 bus with his mates. I'm presuming he has a game console of some kind?'

'Xbox,' said Keith.

'Right, and then we've got break and lunch during school time as well. That's a lot of cards to play with, Keith. Looks like a full house, if I'm honest. The problem so far is that he's not been inconvenienced enough for his behaviour. If we coordinate, we can solve the problem.'

'What are you thinking?'

'I'm thinking that he goes on report.'

'He's been on report before …'

'But this time we enforce it jointly,' I said. 'Any crosses, and we'll make it an hour *and* you take the Xbox for that day. Each cross will be equivalent to a very clear sanction. As for this Holocaust incident, I've already spoken to PE and cancelled his extracurricular for this week.'

'Tell you what,' said Keith, 'we can take the phone as well.'

'That's the spirit. Look, if he persists in this rubbish, he'll wind up staring at a blank wall when he comes home. He really needs it. His grades are in freefall right now.'

'Fair play. I agree with you, Mr Elliott. Let's make it happen. Drop us a text if you're planning on keeping him.'

'Will do, Keith. Cheers for the support.' Click. 'Langston, you ever heard of John Steinbeck?' I asked. He scrunched his face at me. 'No?' I looked over at my empty punnet. 'Oh well.'

Langston soon became a reformed pupil. He asked sensible questions, completed his homework, and even became noticeably less malicious. There was a time when he used to giggle maniacally whenever somebody used their laminated toilet pass, muttering 'Spakker, spakker' and clasping his shoulders with his hands as he stuck his tongue out and went cross-eyed. But now, while I could still see the urge, he thought better of it. Things were going wonderfully until around April, when I'd rung Keith to inform him of Langston's progress.

'Ahh, that's mega, Mr Elliott. I'm glad it's worked out. Yeah, he's great at home too. Keeps doing the vacuuming and washing-up. Have you spoken to him about this? Look, just to let you know, I'm going to Jamaica this week to visit my sister.'

Shit, I thought.

'But I won't be gone long – only a couple of weeks.'

Oh NOO, I thought, the receiver beginning to slip in my clammy palms. But what could I do? Who knows, maybe Langston would be fine if Keith left – he would be coming back and then there would be hell to pay. If he messes about while Keith's on his holiday, he'll return to a bedroom so barren he'll need a straitjacket to accessorise. So I just said, 'OK, Keith, enjoy! Again, thanks for the support.' Click.

Tuesday morning. Rainy again. I'm on the second-floor balcony and who should I hear below me but little Langston Bluck.

'Not gonna lie, I'm so happy my dad's gone Kingston,' he said.

'Why's that?' a friend asked.

'*FUCK* MR ELLIOTT, that's why,' he started doing that strange maniacal laugh again: 'HEEE HEEE HEEE.'

'Aren't you scared of getting in trouble?'

'Look, my Xbox been took up, plus I missed football for like …' he counts in his head. 'Three weeks. Fuck Mr Elliott, man. That wasteman's gonna pay. Watch.'

I'm back in the class. Langston has not arrived yet. We're studying the outbreak of the Second World War.

'When I talk about appeasement,' I said, 'remember the lollipop analogy. Can anybody recall?'

'You said, sir, that if a teacher tries to give lollipops to naughty kids, it just makes them naughtier, which relates to …'

'HEEE HEEE HEEE,' I look out and see who it is … Langston, looking positively demented. His shirt is untucked and billowing in the draughty corridor. What's more, he's taken off his blazer and, inexplicably, he's wearing a pair of tracksuit bottoms with trainers. 'WAAASTEMAN!' His tongue's out and he's shaking his head. He looks like he's doing the haka.

'Oh dear, Langston, where are your trousers?' I asked. 'Did you have an accident?' The class guffaws.

'You were an accident,' he says. 'HEEE HEEE HEEE. Did I ever tell you, sir, what a wasteman you are?'

'Yeah, about two seconds ago. Listen, Langston, you're already in a lot of trouble so why don't we sit down and call it quits? Hang on …'

'There's only one person doing any quitting here, and that person is *you*! Wait, what?'

I pointed to Langston's tracksuit bottoms. 'I see your three stripes but where's the Adidas logo?'

'Oi, Langston's got his trackies on back to front,' shouted Ryan Bleasdale, a naughty boy and Langston's arch nemesis. 'What a fucking *goon*! Langston, where's your trouser pass?' Ryan crumpled into hysterics, impersonating Langston's 'spakker' impression.

'Ryan, office,' I said. He may have insulted Langston but it was still unacceptable.

'Right, sir,' he said, wiping away tears of laughter. '*Worth it.*' He took his stuff and left.

Langston was almost breathless with embarrassment now. 'I'M FUCKING SICK OF YOUUU.'

'Langston, calm down, please. You're getting yourself into trouble. Just take a seat. You should've worn your uniform to lesson. I don't know why you've put on a pair of tracksuit bottoms – back to front as well. Is this a new style? Whatever, I'm sure it's very "peak", Langston, well done. Now siddown.'

'Peak means bad, you *wasteman*.'

'Whatever.'

After the lesson, I sat down with Langston and we discussed how he'd managed to 'get it wrong' this time, and how I could help him in this matter.

'Sir, look,' he said. 'I dunno why I do it. I guess my dad went Jamaica and I got excited. You guys have been so hard on me.'

'Hard on you?'

'Making me obey rules 'n' stuff.'

'Langston, everybody obeys the rules here. That's what school's about. If you grow up, get a job, and start calling your boss a wasteman, you'll be sacked. Turn up to work in some backwards trackies and you'll be doubly sacked. Get the point?'

'Maybe. But look, sir, it's my birthday tomorrow.'

No bloody way. 'Tomorrow?' I asked.

'Yeah, my thirteenth.'

'What a coincidence, that's my birthday too. Langston, did you know … not only were we born on the same day as Albert Einstein but our birthday is International Pi Day?'

'Einstein is boring,' he said. 'And why have pie when I can have cake – cake's peng!' He made some kind of 'nom nom nom' sound.

'Pi as in 3.14. Y'know, the number?'

'Number pie? Sounds dead.'

'Doesn't matter. Look, Langston, I'm putting you in iso for that little stunt. If it's your birthday, too bad. Learn to play by the rules. Consider it a gift to me, why don't you?'

'Dead ting,' he said, getting up to walk around the office.

'Siddown,' I said.

'Why?' but he did it. 'Look, sir …'

'Nope, I'm done now, Langston. As far as you're concerned, I may as well be in Jamaica right now, OK, because I have work to do – a lot. And I'm trying to have a nice life right now, not argue with you.'

And so Langston remained quiet, and when he came into school the next day, he was cajoled into iso, despite tearful protestations that 'MR ELLIOTT IS A PRICK.' Keith came back from Jamaica and we returned to the halcyon days. Strangely, as Langston improved, he began to really enjoy history. Sometimes he'd answer a question and I'd go to say, 'Well done, Martin,' before realising that the eloquent gloss of Winston Churchill's 'Iron Curtain speech' had come from none other than young Langston. I even had him into Year 9, which was funny because he used to boast that he'd be able to escape me at the end of Year 8, not realising that I'd been put down for every Year 9 class the following year, both history and geography, so there really was no escaping me. He returned to the Mr Elliott fold and continued to produce excellent work, which culminated in a stunning Year 10 mock result where he obtained a high level 5 – two grades above target.

Above all, the story of Langston is also a story of parent–teacher collaboration. Without Keith, as his holiday in Jamaica shows, I couldn't have done it; together we turned around the fortunes of one of the naughtiest of all naughties. Is that 'peak'? I don't know, you'd have to ask Langston, since he says it's a bad thing. But then he would say that, wouldn't he?

ANNUS MIRABILIS

In the summer of 2019, I had a phone call from the head of humanities at Willenhall School asking if I'd like to teach history and geography. I thought about it. The memories of the ASBO years could finally overlap with my teaching career, perhaps tending towards some kind of unified field theory. I would merge a deeper understanding of pupil disruption with the sustained exercise of teacher authority – all in the school I grew up in. An opportunity to close the circle like this rarely comes around. Of course, I said yes.

The Year 11s at Wormwood School were now winding down. I spoke to one boy I knew, Ricardo, who'd been targeted a level 2 in his geography GCSE – this at a school where target grades are meant to be 'aspirational', and thus one to two levels higher than even the most ruthlessly clinical assessment. Looking back, that Ricardo could paddle so furiously against the current of expectations reveals to us the powerful riptides lurking beneath the surface of even an 'outstanding' school such as Wormwood.[5]

The boy weighed, at a conservative estimate, around twenty stone, and sported a thick afro that reminded me of Sideshow Bob from *The Simpsons*. For a doppelganger, google a rapper named Big Zuu.

'Y'alright sir,' he said.

'I'm good, Ric,' I said. 'How's geography?'

'Awful, sir. I'm gonna fail.'

I thought back to a Year 10 lesson I'd taught where Ricardo had turned up at the door. He'd been late for his own lesson with Miss Burley. I told him so and he replied that I was a 'dickhead', that he

---

5   I've worked in 'outstanding', 'good' and 'inadequate' schools. There's little to no correlation between Ofsted rankings and good behaviour. Incidentally, Wormwood was last inspected a decade ago and this was flawed for two reasons: (1) it was in the summer so Year 11 had left and (2) Year 10 were on work experience. Had the inspection been a valid one, then there were the ancillary concerns that (a) the building has since changed and (b) 80% of the staff are now gone. Reminds me of Trigger's broom from *Only Fools and Horses*.

'had bare gyal dem'[6] (*way* more than I did, in fact), and proceeded to raise his shirt and wobble his belly at me. He got on all fours, shuffled under a table, and his pants slumped to reveal butt cleavage big enough to lose a remote control down. The class were cheering. I'd had to guide him out of the room by the scruff of his neck, since he had his shirt over his head like Fabrizio Ravanelli's signature goal celebration. He'd then marched around the school, throwing plastic chairs around in the Heart Space, which reverberated with hollow booms and thwacks.

'No wonder,' I said. 'You've been an idiot.'

'I know, sir. I'm not making excuses.'

In a way, Ricardo had been a nemesis of mine in the corridors, always commenting either that I was on steroids,[7] had fewer gyal dem than he did, or that I was a battyman. This last occasion was truly stunning. I'd been carrying a box and he'd said, 'Sir, you're a battyman.' I said, 'Who on earth do you think you're talking to? Get in the office.' 'No,' he said. 'I was talking to my friend Lee. Oi Lee, you're a battyman.' I said, 'Oh, so that makes flagrant homophobia OK now, does it? Since when is Lee a sir, anyway? What's he done, cashed in his behaviour points for an MBE?' Ricardo shrugged. 'Office.' He was isolated for two days.

He had a little spray bottle to spritz his afro. He sprayed it and shook his head like a wet dog. I felt sorry for the kid. 'Look,' I said. 'I'm here until 5pm most days. If you want any tuition, stop by the office.'

'Thanks, sir,' he said. 'I may do.' He had no intention of doing so. 'I'm sorry for calling you a battyman that time,' he said. He meant it.

'Yeah, you're a big boy now, Ric. Say it again and we'll deal with it like the big boys do.'

---

6   I have to defer to Trinidadnic on the definition: 'Gyal dem is a coolie-made slang term for indicating one or more girls ... "Eh yo look, gyaldem coming this way."' See https://www.urbandictionary.com/define.php?term=Gyal%20Dem.

7   Any teacher who's even slightly in shape is automatically 'on steroids'.

'I may be fat, sir, but I'm *quick*,' he swung an uppercut through the air and his belly flew up and down. Water sprayed from his mangy afro.

'Right,' I laughed. 'I was more traumatised by the truffle shuffle, to be honest.'

'Yeah, I was an idiot, sir,' he said. 'Soz.'

'It's fine,' I said. It was like the *Tom and Jerry* cartoons. In the few episodes where Tom actually caught Jerry, he always let him go, since the thrill of their rivalry was more valuable to Tom than seeing Jerry permanently vanquished. Ricardo was caught in the trap, twitching, but it wasn't possible for me to spring it. I'd offered him the tuition but it was simply too late.

At that moment, the rugby boys strutted into the Heart Space.

'Yes then, sir!' said Raleigh. 'Dunkno,[8] sir's gone for the map tie. Check it!' He took a knee and framed with his hands the world map tie I'd worn ironically since becoming a geography teacher.

'Sir's a Learned Geographer,' observed Cain. I'd taught these boys history the previous year. It was back before I'd taken up geography and they found the transition hilarious. 'Sir, can we do geography?'

'Geography's a dead ting,' I said. 'Only wastemans can do geography.' They laughed. 'How's history going, lads? I want level 7s!'

'Should get a level 5, sir,' said Cain. Raleigh nodded, affirming a similar prospect for himself.

'Level 5! Jeez, maybe you should've done geography. C'mon, you've survived a year with Mr Elliott,' I said, doing my 'strict teacher' routine while jabbing my finger at them. 'The exam's nothing compared to that.'

'He's got a point,' said Raleigh. 'Sir's truly next level.' Raleigh performed a salute.

---

8   Raleigh is going by the secondary definition – 'an expletive to celebrate something, in the same way you'd say "get in"' – at: https://www.urbandictionary.com/define.php?term=Dun%20Kno.

'History was such a mad ting,' said Cain, wistfully. 'Remember when sir told Kacey he was the Annihilator-in-Chief?' We all laughed.

'Look, boys, level 7s – that's what I want. Anything less and you will be annihilated, just like poor old Kacey.'

Ricardo had wandered off. For all their banter, Raleigh and Cain had a life path set out for them, and the same wasn't true for Ricardo. I'd been happy to speak to the boys since I hadn't taught them for a year, but I should've been more tactful. There's me banging on about level 7s and meanwhile Ricardo hasn't got a chance of even scraping a level 1, not unless the AQA mark scheme stipulates that 'higher-level scripts must fill every answer box with "I DON'T KNOW" scrawled on successive pages. Full SPaG marks awarded to candidates who consistently omit commas and full stops.'

A PILGRIM'S PROGRESS

When the summer term ended, I continued swotting up on geography and prepared myself for the following year. I sat looking at the plant pot and drinking glass my tutor group had gifted me. The pot said 'Best Geography Teacher' and the drinking glass said 'Best History Teacher'. Both were written in italics with gold marker pen, although the words on the latter had smudged.

Like the glass, my record at Wormwood was blurred. Although I'd improved drastically since my first placements at Chelmsley Wood and Leamington, I'd never conquered the class with Luka and Ezekiel. It meant that while I was delivering good outcomes and firm discipline for the majority of my pupils, there was always that niggling holdout. This bled into disruptions around the school and meant that I had to keep my gaze averted from Year 10 altogether, since my reputation with them was less Annihilator-in-Chief and more Terror Time target.

I decided to remind myself why I'd stayed in the profession. Chelmsley Wood had been the most onerous point of my career so far. Computers that wouldn't log in, corridors that didn't calm down, pupils that never shut up – it makes a regular baptism of fire look like the ALS Ice Bucket Challenge. I'd relive that Shackletonian commute, jog some painful memories, and remind myself how far I'd come. I got on a train to Marston Green and took the walk – three miles there and three miles back – to Chelmsley Wood Academy.

The tower blocks loomed against clouds heavily contused by storms, with lightning jags marbling their craggy underbellies. As I walked down the road, a dirt bike hairdryered past before pulling into a drive, and was swiftly followed by a gold Renault. The man leapt off his bike and started yelling. 'Fuck off,' he shouted, waving his helmet at the men in the car. The car reversed and it became apparent that they were trying to run him over. He moved back between a protruding bay window and doorway. 'Fucking low it, blud!'

An elderly couple peered out of the door. 'We're ringing the police!' she said. The men in the gold Renault – I could see them clearly: a couple of thuggish Phil and Grant types, hilariously shoehorned into the vehicle like an ugly stepsister's toes in a glass slipper – reversed and charged again. The man with the helmet swearing, the old lady squawking into the telephone, and the old man looking dumbfounded. Shortly after, sirens … and the Renault retreated. The man hopped back on his bike and sped off as well. I'd thought he was the elderly couple's son but apparently not. I don't know why drugs are so popular in Chelmsley Wood. Seems like the reality's exhilarating enough.

Standing by the school, I thought of Macaulay and his blustering insults; of Little Alfred and co. stampeding across from the Nisa Local; of Dalton McFlurry with his squeezable plastic dinosaurs; of Luka's subtle manipulations – 'I wish I could have big muscles like you, sir'; a phantasm of Chihuahua romped across the road in one of his feral rampages; and, of course, Ezekiel's words echoed back – 'Just think how much *stronger* you'll be.' I was sick of failing kids. I wanted every single class I taught to be on point. From a selfish perspective, I knew it was better for me too.

Teacher workloads are unmanageable. I think the biggest burden currently is that we're expected to behave like CBBC presenters rather than professionals. Well, guess what, I'm not lowering my expectations by pandering to pupil preferences. I never did it for

Raleigh and Cain, and I was their favourite – not that it's even relevant. Furthermore, I bent over backwards so far for my Year 10s at Wormwood that I'd only be lacking a pinch of salt to become a fully fledged pretzel. Fortunately, I don't take anything with a pinch of salt. I'll teach in the manner recommended by research and nothing more. I'll teach in Times New Roman, let the subject speak for itself, and bin off the Comic Sans. No frills, no gimmicks, no fuzzy-wuzzy.

On my walk that day, a storm had broken out in my mind: once I'd returned to my old school, I would never have a bad lesson again. It was a universal law. Science could posit equations to prove it, and this new outlook became vital if I was to improve the conditions of difficult kids. I would go in, get the job done, and get out. A homecoming to reverberate through the annals of Willenhall School. Mr Elliott, Annihilator-in-Chief … ready to take on the naughties.

A CRISIS OF CONFIDENCE

Willenhall School was an old-fashioned, brick-built, school. The only PFI building on site was the sixth form. This was my first day and I had to succeed. Some maths boffin somewhere was already jotting down the equations for this. The first lesson with Year 11 was strange. There were four boys and twenty-five girls. 'Don't give them an inch,' my boss said. 'No group work or gimmickry. Just teacher-led instruction.'

Yet another insight into the teaching profession. If you're an Ofsted inspector, you probably don't realise it, but inspections are rigged to impress you.[9] You simply can't observe a school without altering the very nature of what you're observing. If it holds for photons and neutrinos, then it holds for Miss Milk Tray's 'US Presidential Electron', where pupils use a double-slit ballot box to vote for their favourite elementary particles. The reality is that when teachers want results, they revert to the teacher-led methods of quizzing, questioning, modelling, scaffolding, and independent practice.

---

9 'Often the compromise had been for teachers to perform the Monkey Dance when observed and revert to "what works" when the classroom door is closed': David Didau, *What If Everything You Knew About Education Was Wrong?* (Carmarthen: Crown House Publishing, 2015), p. 96.

Then, again, we've come a long way since Ofsted criticised teacher talk and highlighted instead fizzy drinks, party balloons, and wedding cakes in lessons as features of exemplary practice. I wish I was joking.[10] I searched for those kinds of gaffes in reports from 2018 to 2020 and could only find the one about the topic of caves which 'started with a darkened classroom devoid of all adornments'.[11] It's still absurd but it was an anomaly. And I looked *really* hard. The following is typical of more recent Ofsted reports: 'teachers use their expert subject knowledge to plan and deliver activities in a logical order that helps pupils build on what they have learned before. They use probing and often very challenging questions to make sure pupils know and remember what has been taught.'[12] Amen to that, brother. Ofsted and the school system still have their fair share of marshmallows, but with sufficient focus on 'what works' the British education system should become more teacher led.

Back to Year 11. From the start, it was clear they didn't know very much. I'd put it down to the summer holiday, but I'd wager it had more to do with a legacy of group work. At first, some of the girls were quite resistant to the Mr Elliott style of questioning.

'Carla, when we say that one country is more developed than another, what do we mean?'

'Dunno.'

'Think. When we think of what we have in this country, and what people don't have in countries like, say, Afghanistan, what could we mean?'

'Erm, roads?'

'Good.'

'Wi-Fi.'

---

10 Daisy Christodoulou, *Seven Myths About Education* (Abingdon and New York: Routledge, 2014), pp. 34–35.
11 Inspection Report: Abbey School (9–10 May 2019): 'Outstanding'. Available at: https://files.ofsted.gov.uk/v1/file/50083727.
12 Inspection Report: Maiden Erlegh School (11 February 2020): 'Outstanding'. Available at: https://files.ofsted.gov.uk/v1/file/50148748.

'Yes.'

'Wait, that's right?'

'Sure.'

'Erm, I just dunno.'

'Don't tell lies, Carla – you've given me two answers. So, roads and Wi-Fi – two examples of things we have in this country that the denizens of Afghanistan may lack. What about this? We watched a video about the slums in Rio. What did we notice? Claire, you tell me.'

'Erm.'

'Water, electricity, tell me about these.'

'Oh, erm, well, the wires were all tangled and bunched up. This could be dangerous, since people might be electrocuted.'

'What about the materials – what were the favelas built out of?'

'Favelas?'

'The shacks on the hillside.'

'Oh … like, wood, boards … some had bricks – could they catch fire, perhaps?' she flinches like she's afraid of getting it wrong.

'Yes, exactly,' I said. And this was how the questioning proceeded. It was excruciating. They had no confidence at all. Often, when I'd asked a question, I'd be met with that flinching response – the fear of making a mistake. Claire even came up to me after the lesson to ask if I could leave her out of the questioning.

'Sir, it's not you. I'm just dumb,' she said.

'How's that, then? You had a lot to say when I pushed you?'

'Yeah, but it was difficult, and I was worried about getting it wrong. It gives me anxiety.'

'Look, Claire, it's my job to push you. We'll keep going until it's automatic. You say you're "dumb" and that it makes you feel "anxious".

Well, get used to it because there are more questions where that came from.' Claire pouted and walked off.

Two months hence, however, and Claire's smashing it. She gives answers to questions I've not even asked yet. And she's so confident on the slums topic (mainly because I've asked her around 200 questions on it), that she's got her hand up like a traffic conductor and period 5 is rush hour – in spite of my cold-calling policy.[13]

As for the other girls, I found an excellent trick. If you ever have a class that lacks confidence, try this. Do a quiz with them at the start of the lesson: six to eight questions on a PowerPoint. They will answer these in their books. Then, don't just reveal the answers but question them in class before you have the answers animate in. It's a dual strategy. By doing this, you've ensured that they have all quizzed themselves in their books and also that the pressure of being cold-called is still there. But this is only the first step. Next, you have them green-pen the answers so they match the PowerPoint precisely.

Now, if they struggled (i.e. the majority couldn't answer 50%), you say, 'OK, close your workbooks' and hand out sheets of lined paper. Put up the blank quiz. They do it again straight away. Explain to them the rationale for this: 'We're acting on immediate feedback.' As neuroscientist Stanislas Dehaene argues, 'By providing rapid and precise feedback on errors, teachers can considerably enrich the information available to their students to correct themselves.'[14] Finally, do the quiz once more at the end of lesson. Throughout the entire process, reiterate the importance of making mistakes.

For kids who lack confidence, you will be shocked at how happily they take to this, especially when they see how good they become. A word of warning, however: do not become too enamoured with

---

13 Cold calling is a questioning technique which involves calling on a random pupil to answer a question.
14 Stanislas Dehaene, *How We Learn: The New Science of Education and the Brain* (London: Penguin, 2020), p. 209.

performance in lessons. It is not the same as learning.[15] There is evidence that 'delaying, reducing, and summarizing feedback can be better for long-term learning than providing immediate, trial-by-trial feedback'.[16] Moreover, this is a salutary delay, since the consequent increase in retrieval effort 'produces longer lasting learning and enables more versatile application of it in later settings'.[17] So, while transferable skills are as much of a fantasy as my ASDAN certificate, it is likely that 'versatile knowledge' exists.

The problem is that if you always delay feedback, progress is not obvious to the kids. As Daniel Willingham says, 'it is pretty boring to practice something if we're not getting any better at it'.[18] Good teaching requires marketing: if you can't show the pupils they're getting better, they'll begin to disrupt, and then cognitive psychology is reduced to nothing more than a laboratory fiction. If there's a trade-off between performance and long-term learning, it happens because either (a) material is insufficiently spaced or (b) pupils become too fluent with the material and cease to consciously retrieve and analyse it. There is a danger of facts becoming part of the furniture, so to speak. To get around this, repeat quizzes to demonstrate fluency, but alter them subtly each time. Pupils will at least have the sense that they 'know it', even if they get it wrong on a technicality: 'Oh sir, I've just noticed. You changed the question!' Subtlety is key.

With Year 11, this quizzing approach worked. Some of the pupils were difficult. Occasionally, one or two would turn up late. And at the start they wanted to break me. One girl had lashed out when I'd asked her a question. Another claimed that with her old teacher they had made volcanoes with baking powder and vinegar. I'd

---

15 'Performance is not the same as learning': Mark McCourt, *Teaching for Mastery* (Woodbridge: John Catt Educational, 2019), pp. 82–83. Interestingly, McCourt claims that performance is replication, so that while it may be important for pupils to replicate Pythagoras' theorem in lessons, the aim is for them to replicate across extended time intervals and between contexts (i.e. to learn it). To my mind, this suggests that performance is a prerequisite to learning – you have to replicate the material at least once. Obsessive replication, and not replication in itself, is what will degrade learning.

16 Didau and Rose, *What Every Teacher Needs to Know About Psychology*, p. 84.

17 Brown et al., *Make It Stick*, p. 4.

18 Daniel Willingham, *Why Don't Students Like School? A Cognitive Scientist Answers Questions About How the Mind Works and What It Means for the Classroom* (San Francisco, CA: Jossey-Bass, 2009), p. 124.

asked, 'When, Year 3?' and she stormed out. Yet these two girls became some of the best pupils in that class. One earned a level 5 and the other a level 9. I'm not a neurosurgeon, but I know how to perform an attitude transplant.

THE GEOGRAPHY AMBASSADORS

'Here you are, sir,' said my colleague, Maria, handing me a zip-lock bag full of golden pin badges. The words 'Geography Ambassador' swirled into the centre as though going down a plughole. In the words of Langston Bluck they looked 'kinda dead'.

Nevertheless, while teaching my new Year 10 class, I find myself telling them, 'Look, I'm about to create the most elite group of geographers this school has ever known.' This is the sort of stuff you come out with after teaching for five hours straight. 'You are going to be part of an elite task force, and you will help me in my various endeavours. Who's with me?'

Two lads, Jake and Atik, raised their hands. 'Right, lads,' I said. 'First mission is to take this box down to the humanities. Chop, chop. Let's go.'

'Yes, SUH!' said Jake. Atik helped him with handling the box, and they were off.

'Sir, you can't just trick people into doing jobs for you, y'know,' said Savannah. 'That's mean.'

'Savannah,' I said. 'This Geography Ambassadors thing – it's gonna be big. Just you wait and see. Pretty soon, you'll be wanting to join yourself.'

'Yeah rrright, sir,' Savannah laughed, tossing me a glue stick.

The next lesson, we were learning about deserts. 'Listen up, class,' I said. 'I need more Geography Ambassadors. The Year 9s are about to pick their options and I need some of the most *hardcore* individuals to get out there – boots on the ground.' Savannah was laughing.

'I'll do it, sir,' said Andre.

'Me too, sir,' Rosie stood up behind her desk.

'Nice! Come and get your badges,' I said. Savannah wasn't laughing any more.

'And me!' said Josh. 'Y'know, when I first met you, I thought I was gonna hate geography but it's actually alright.'

'Innit,' said Brady. 'I dunno what it is but I always remember the stupid stuff he says.' It was like a crap version of *Dead Poets Society*.

One of the most important lessons came a few months later. I had Year 10. It was Friday, period 5. My boss had given me the revision materials for the weekend, but I'd forgotten to give them out to Year 11 that morning and they were still in my box. The Year 11s were dispersed throughout the school in a number of subjects far inferior to geography, like science, English, and maths.

'Geography Ambassadors,' I said.

Rosie, Andre, Jake, Atik, and Josh all stood up.

'I've got a mission. We've got ten minutes.' I'd logged on to the system while they finished their work independently and compiled five lists, each corresponding to a different portion of my Year 11 class. If they didn't get their revision materials, they wouldn't know what to revise over the weekend, and all the inroads I'd made into their lack of confidence would be buried in drifts of despondency. 'List A – Rosie and Josh. These pupils are in science. Take the list and cross off those who accept it. Andre, hit up maths and do the same for list B. Jake and Atik – you have to head to English. If Miss Willendorf sees you, tell her it's official Geography Ambassador business. Orders of Mr Elliott. She'll know what it means.' I had no idea if this was true or not. I gave each of the Ambassadors a list and they took to the corridors.

In the five-minute interval, a boy came in with a Meet Me At McDonald's haircut, otherwise known as a short back and sides with a perm sat on top, like a Heston Blumenthal attempt at a taxidermy soufflé. He was about six foot, built like a brickie, and demanded of me, 'Where the *fuck* is Rosie?'

'Excuse me,' I said. 'Where's your manners, little boy?'

'I said where the FUCK is Rosie, that scraggy little BITCH?'

This was Hulk Jenkins. I'd met him a few weeks back in the office, where he'd told me my lunch was shit as he placidly picked at a bag of Haribo Starmix.

In that moment, Rosie returned to class, brandishing the ticked names of Year 11s like a voter so enthusiastic she'd chosen every-one. She took one look at Hulk, her expression dropped, and she muttered, 'Oh no.'

'Yes then, you fucking little rat ...' he said, squaring up to the girl. As he drew nearer, I interposed myself between them like I was looking for a pen I'd dropped.

'Where did I put my *pen*?' I said.

Hulk stood behind me, mouthing off at Rosie, and was about to make a Mr Elliott sandwich as he drew nearer to her.

'Why you been spreading shit about me? Why you been chatting to Donnie about me and Cassie?'

'I dunno what you mean!' said Rosie.

'It's gotta be here somewhere,' I said, stroking my chin.

'Oh my days, don't fucking lie,' he said. 'It's on Snapchat and everything.'

I'm in-between them but I'm behaving in a non-confrontational manner. In situations like this, a pupil could easily switch on you, but you can't just stand by either. If you do, it will signal to other pupils that they can play-fight and confront one another, and since you're stuck with the class you may as well change your name to Mr Jeremy Kyle for the remainder of the year. Nevertheless, you should always have a play-within-a-play. This was mine.

'Hulk,' I whispered to him. 'I'm giving you the opportunity to leave this room. No one can hear me. Only you. Either you leave or I'll pull every lever available to me to get you expelled. Do you understand? You've already brushed against me – you've physically assaulted a teacher …'

'I didn't *touch* you, sir.'

'You did, Hulk. To be honest, I'm a big boy and I'll happily take one for the team. Try to move me and you'll only be moving yourself, out of that door and down to the Job Centre. Understand?'

'Sir …'

'I've said all I'm gonna say,' I said.

Hulk shook his head in disbelief and his chest collapsed like someone had let out all the hot air. With his silly haircut and his slumping posture, he reminded me of those inflatable tube men you see flailing outside car dealerships. He jabbed his finger once more at Rosie, like a Disney villain in the death throes of dissolution. 'Wait till I catch you,' he said. 'LUCKY!' he laughed to himself. 'Jeeez, you are *fucking* lucky.' As my remaining Ambassadors came shuffling into the classroom, Hulk barged past, elbowing them into the walls one by one, 'MOVE! Out my FUCKING WAY.'

'What was that all about, sir?' asked Josh.

'I'm not sure,' I said, eyeing Rosie with suspicion. 'Whatever it is, it's getting sorted.'

NEMESIS

Towards the end of the autumn term, my colleague who taught Hulk Jenkins geography had had enough.

'They just don't *listen*,' he said.

'What's the matter?' I asked.

'The room! It's always unlocked. Whenever I go to 2B08, the Year 10s are in and it looks like they've emptied a skip in there.'

I knew what he meant. The pupils were being allowed to run around the design block where he was being forced to teach geography. The door didn't lock properly, which meant that a deft ruler swipe was all it took for a determined pupil to gain access to every saw machine and power sander in the entire school. Why it was allowed I'll never know. That pupils weren't walking around with lopped off fingers and hooks for hands was miracle enough. What it meant for my colleague was that the pupils had established a territory. He could never set up without instigating some kind of turf war or challenging pupils who stood gouging lighthouses into the solid oak desks with a steel framing square. It reminded me of *The Warriors*, the 1979 movie where rugged street gangs battled with melee weapons like crowbars, shovels, pipes, machetes, and sledgehammers. In the case of my colleague, it meant taking on a Hulk Jenkins equipped with hand files, hacksaws, and partially lathed table legs.

My colleague was a second-year Teach Firster. He had an admirable obsession with getting it right with the Hulk Jenkins class. In spite of the difficulty, he repeatedly affirmed his desire to keep plugging away at it. Unfortunately, I knew from my experiences at Wormwood that once you've forfeited the respect of a class, you've irretrievably lost them. Counteracting the impression is like the punishment of Sisyphus, the King of Corinth, who was condemned to push a boulder up a hill for eternity, before watching it roll down again as it neared the top.

'I can take the class,' I said.

'No,' he said, blinkingly. 'That's fine. I think I've almost got them. Besides, they only act up when we go over exam stuff. Maybe they'll be ...'

'Stop rationalising it,' I said. 'I've been where you are. You can turn it around, but you'll strain all your ligaments and pop a few discs before you're even close to getting them to heel.' He tried to object. 'I know you want to get it right. It's commendable. But you're not doing the kids or yourself any favours.'

'Shit,' he said. 'Maybe you're right.'

'Mate, I'm so right that I've gone off the screen like Pac-Man and come back on the other side. You just gotta trust me.'

He sighed – half relief, half resignation. We spoke to the boss later on that day and made the switch. But, in a final twist, during his last lesson with Year 10, my colleague gave a detention to ten of them. They were brought to sit it with me in humanities. The kids were still unaware of the switch.

One little boy – Farhan – had a grin wide enough for a dentist to check his wisdom teeth. Beside him, Mario fiddled with the windows, looking over his shoulder to regard me with languid contempt as he did so. At the head of the table, his perm like a deep-pile bath mat and a litter of snapped biros forming a mound around and in front of him, sat Hulk Jenkins.

'Oi, why we even here, sir? Yo, can I open the window?' he asked.

'You know why,' I said.

'Where's sir?'

'He's busy. He'll be here shortly.'

'Oh, so we get a detention for being late and sir can't even follow his own rules. Bait geezer.'

If someone is bait, it means they've committed a mistake through some kind of oversight, or drawn undue attention to a misbehaviour you were planning on getting away with. An example would be: 'You're so bait: I can't believe you got arrested for shoplifting a Cadbury Creme Egg' or 'I can't believe you mentioned wagging it in front of my mum. That was bait as fuck.'

'Alright, question time's over,' I said.

'How long we got, sir?' said Mario.

'All break.'

'What, why!?'

'Your teacher explained,' I said, logging on to the computer. 'The head of humanities explained. How many more explanations do you want?'

'Can we open the window, sir?' said Hulk.

I shook my head. While checking my PowerPoints, I heard a snapping, crunching sound, like twigs trodden underfoot.

Hulk was looking up at me. In his hand he had five green biros – all snapped. Under his foot, he was twisting the remains of the biros into slender plastic shards. 'Mad how they do that, sir,' he said. 'Just get all crunched 'n' that. Why?' He seemed pensive. Farhan and Mario laughed. The girls covered their mouths, eyes smiling.

'Right,' I said. 'Let's get this sorted. You wanna play games with Mr Elliott then you'd better learn to lose them.' I made a phone gesture with my hand and started waggling it beside my ear. 'C'mon, into the office.' I asked a colleague to take over the detention, marched Hulk in and sat him down. The following patter is how any aspiring Annihilator-in-Chief takes care of business.

'What would your mum and dad say if they knew you'd damaged school property?'

'The window, sir,' said Hulk, trying to parry.

'Yeah, I saw you mouth to Farhan to shut up when he told you to take your coat off, and I know the windows game, lad – better than Bill Gates does. "Open the window, close the window – can I open the window, sir? Oh, now I want it closed again!" It's just an excuse to be out of your seat. As for me, I'm ringing your dad. I've heard that he's taken your Xbox. I shall have to lend you some first-class stamps and some envelopes, since that's the only way you'll be speaking to your online buddies ever again.' I picked up the phone and started dialling from memory.

Hulk is stunned. He gets his way in every pupil–teacher confrontation. I've heard it countless times in the corridors: 'Now, now, Hulk … we don't use words like "retard", do we? We're better than that.' Always in first-person plural, like he's part of the royal family or something. But now he sees that I'm all about bottom lines. Getting the job done and simple instructions. That's the beauty of bottom lines – there's nothing to read in-between.

'I get it, sir,' said Hulk.

'Yes?' I stopped dialling but held on to the receiver.

'I get it.'

'Tell me what you were doing. Don't lie to me. When I came to Willenhall School, I used to sit in that room right where you sat. I'd wear my Air Max trainers and Lacoste tracksuit on Fridays. Teachers would have to put up or shut up. We used to pelt teachers with snowballs in winter and rotten fruit in the summer, and even on Halloween the teachers wouldn't say boo to us. So, don't kid a kidder. Tell me the truth.'

'Jeez, sir, I dunno. Winding teachers up – it's just funny, innit. You said that thing to me about how you were gonna get me excluded so I just thought, "Oh, I'll wind him up about the window – he doesn't like that so I'll keep doing it." You know a *lot* though, sir. I can't lie. How'd you know about my Xbox? And my dad's number?'

'It's my business to know these things,' I said, recalling how I'd spoken to the Year 10 team the moment I'd taken the class.

'Fair play. I guess I'm lucky you're not teaching me, innit,' he smiled.

'Why's that, then?'

'Couldn't mess around. Or maybe I could,' he smirked, 'but it'd be more difficult.'

'What about your grades?'

'Yeah, I'm failing geography anyway.'

'It's only Year 10 – you've got plenty of time.'

'Nah, I can't be arsed,' he laughed.

'Hmm,' I said, finally putting the receiver down, which I'd been gesturing with throughout the entire conversation. You're in for one hell of a week, I thought, looking forward to Monday. One hell of a week.

ANNIHILATOR-IN-CHIEF

Taking on this class was undoubtedly the toughest moment of my career. What I'd seen in that detention was barely a snippet. My first day with the class and I headed to 2B08. It was a narrow galley classroom with no windows and long fluorescent strip lights that cracklingly emitted a sickly yellow glow. The dimensions of the room seemed to amplify gloom and modulate hope to an inaudible frequency. I remembered having my design lessons in here. Mr Tudor would scream until he was red in the face – like Violet Beauregarde from *Charlie and the Chocolate Factory*, only with cherry gum instead of blueberry. In this very room, I'd taken a sleeping pill from my mate for a dare (look, we didn't have smartphones back then). Mr Tudor had yelled at me while my head sagged and my eyelids fluttered between the no man's land of the class, with its paper-plane sorties and sawback-bayonet battles, and the never-never land of chemically induced stupor.

The absurdity of these flashbacks didn't divert me for very long, since at the end of the galley I heard the sound of plastic scraping, along with a click, and a gang of Year 10s were now standing in the class.

'Yo,' said one.

'Outside,' I said, walking towards them, but keeping my arms open to signal non-aggression. They were out of the class and I went back to setting up the computer.

Then, 'BOOM, BOOM, BOOM'. I approached to see what was going on. I heard a plastic thwap sound, like a CD case hitting the wall, and then a 'NYEEER, NYEEER, NYEEER'. The fire alarm. Luckily, it was only the alarm of the fire alarm, a high-pitched buzzing noise triggered by lifting the plastic lid; a kind of screeching prelude to triggering whole-school evacuation. I closed the lid and it shut off abruptly. Then, back to the computer again, that plastic thwapping noise again, and then 'NYEEER, NYEEER, NYEEER'. These Year 10s did *not* want me to have a nice life.

I'd shut the door again but the pupils admitted themselves with a shatterproof ruler.

'You our new teacher, sir?' a couple asked.

'Let's siddown,' I said, setting up the PowerPoint. They arrived in sips not draughts. I couldn't wait any longer so I began my patter at ten past with around 70% of the pupils. 'Here's how it works. Talk over me and I will keep you. Break anything in this room and I will keep you. You stick that pen in that plug socket, Travis' – he jolted, shocked that I knew his name – 'and what'll happen?'

'Will I be kept, by any chance?' he asked.

I gave him a thumbs up. 'You're one third of the way through Year 10, so get the message: you will fail this GCSE. You'll have spent three hours a week in this dingy tech room, and for what? Level 2 grades? How pathetic is that?'

'It's not our fault, sir,' said Kaley.

'No, it's not anyone's fault,' I said. 'I'm not blaming you because I don't know you, do I? I don't know you, so how can I form a judge-ment? You have one chance, and this is what you have to do – *all* you have to do, in fact: you listen to every single word that comes out of my mouth. That's it. If you can do that, you will earn at least a level 5, and if you can do more than that, a level 7 or above. But for now, I want to set aside issues of homeworks, mock exams, and whatever other admin nonsense. I'm not here to bore you with the details that for Article B, Subsection D, you must know X, Y, and Z. We're focusing on knowledge. That's it.'

The pupils seemed vaguely inspired by this. I knew they would be. It's the kind of message I wish I'd received in my ASBO years. A firmer foundation of concrete knowledge and fewer of those bouncy-castle spit-balling sessions that some have the temerity to call teaching. Lesson after lesson, year and year, I'd followed the mouldering paper trail of reports and resources: 'Samuel needs to understand key skills like not getting a U grade.' Then, the triumphant cavalcade of abstraction: analysis, evaluation, synthesis. The kinds of words that cause confusion in pupils and lead them to think they know far less than they actually do. Within the profession, terms like differentiation and Assessment for Learning have a similar function, causing student teachers to overthink, denigrate knowledge, and rear kids on an enervating diet of empty nutrients instead of the bolstering proteins of no-nonsense instruction. Why tell a person to prime their glutes, flex their quadriceps, and explosively contract their calves, when you simply want them to jump?

Then, from the back of the galley I heard 'BOOM, BOOM, BOOM' at the door again, before the inevitable 'NYEEER, NYEEER, NYEEER', and in came Mario, Hulk, and a boy I'd never seen before. 'Ahh,' I thought. 'That must be Ryan Pudsey.'

Ryan was better known by his surname, Pudsey, although he had far less charitable intentions than the blindfolded-bear mascot. Absent parents, violent uncles, alcohol abuse; never mind raising money for Children in Need, he *was* one. Set this Molotov cocktail against one of the most deprived wards in the country – Wood End in Coventry – and you have a rapidly combustible mixture.

'Yo,' he said, standing at the back. 'Where do I sit?' I pointed to the seating plan I'd projected onto the board. 'Sir, that's peak! I can't be arsed to sit next to Gavin.'

'Right,' I said. 'Siddown, we'll speak later.'

At this, Pudsey started touring the classroom, picking up pupils' biros, snapping and shoving them into the yellow plug sockets that had originally served soldering irons.

'HEY!'

'SIR, STOP HIM!'

'Fuck you, gimme your pen,' said Pudsey, towering over Farhan.

'Tramp!' he was grinning. 'Get your own; they're only 25p. Get your mum to go Wonga.com.'

Hulk had been quiet, but Pudsey's disruption served as a catalyst. He'd moved from his seat and was now sitting with Mario. They were talking loudly to try to block me out. From there, everything became a battle. Suddenly, none of the kids could see the starter, despite a font size large enough for a desert island castaway. And, thanks to Pudsey, nobody had any pens.

Right, I thought to myself. You've been here before. This is Chihuahua with his snarling disruptions. It's Luka, only with a perm so voluminous it would have your Auntie Carol speed-dialling an appointment at Curl Up and Dye. Ezekiel too: Hulk's scared of his dad. You can use that. You need to not only nip this in the bud, but rip up the seedlings, sow the soil with more salt than a grit truck, and snip off these tentative germinations before they can embed any further.

'Pudsey,' I said, 'come here.' I spoke so that only he could hear me. 'One chance: sit down.' I looked him in the eye – no emotion, only the calm but inexorable tidal force of conviction. He sat by Gavin. 'Now,' I said, 'we're learning about hydroelectricity. Does anyone know what a dam is?'

'What Pudsey's mum says when she stubs her big, fat, hairy toe?' said Farhan.

'Oh no, Farhan! Where's your neck, you fucking Minion?'

I looked at both of them. No speech. No expression. Only the infinite resonance of a vast emotional flatline. BEEEP. Inscrutable. What should I do? There was no telling, but I was confident. This radical surgery I was performing braved the impossible. They couldn't see my PowerPoint? Oh well, I'll improvise. We're about to lose the patient? Fine, just pass me the plastic cutlery and the anaesthetic throat spray, since that's all I have. Insurmountable odds, and yet I think I'm about to effect a recovery. And I've no idea how.

'In Scotland,' I said. 'I'd gone on a hike. Just me and my little brother.' The pupils were listening silently, their eyes wide. 'I was about your age and my mum had said not to go on this twenty-mile hike. "Don't go," she said. "You might see a goose."' The kids laughed.

'A goose!' said Hulk. 'Just chin it! Ain't about having some goose tinking he runs tings.'

'Trust me,' I said. 'Any goose that wants to tussle with Mr Elliott is getting more than just iso. But, yeah, I ignored my mum and went out on the twenty-miler, and since I was something of a Bear Grylls back in the day, I brought a small bottle of Powerade to last us the journey. Despite being in Scotland, the trek was boiling. We made it to the summit of Mount Cardigan, and on the way back the Powerade disappeared. We lasted a few more miles without water but he took the last few drops and we needed a refill. I was so thirsty. In the orange glow I was hallucinating Irn-Bru waterfalls and creeks bubbling with Guinness froth.'

'Guinness is Irish, sir,' said Kacey.

'Yeah, I forgot,' I said. 'Anyway … we came upon a reservoir. Enormous body of water that was so clear you could see the rocks at the bottom. And I wanted a drink. So, I held on to a tree branch and lowered myself down the side. Now, I can't swim …'

'You can't swim, sir?' asked Farhan, smirking at Mario like, 'Who is this guy?'

'Yeah, I tried in Year 5 but I can't float. I'm negative buoyant. In your first lesson, they teach you how to float, but if you're unable to do so then you can't proceed. Plus, I was made to wear Speedos. Not only did I have to sit in the shallow end with rubber-ducky arm-bands, I also had people commenting on my skimpy swimming pants.'

'Did the "S" peel off, sir?' asked Mario.

'Nah, luckily not, but it was very traumatising all the same. Now, when I went to dunk the bottle in the reservoir, the branch snapped. I fell in. It would've been OK but the reservoir had steep, slippery sides. I couldn't get any purchase. I was flailing out of the water like a salmon up a stream but I just couldn't get up the side. In the end, I pinched my fingers together and threw out my hand like a grappling hook, embedding it in the sludge on the bank. Then I asked my brother to get a stick to haul me out. Once out, I had to take my shirt off and wring it dry, or at least drier – it was sopping. There was a road beside the trail – we were near the bottom now – and a coach full of old ladies pulled up along the lay-by. Some laughed, others threw their heads back and guffawed. They were laughing at me! And that, boys and girls, was my first ever experience at a reservoir.'

This story, so seemingly irrelevant, had somehow worked. A pitch-perfect melody. I was stunned. How could such a crummy story evoke such disproportionate impact? It was like cracking a safe by playing 'Chopsticks' on a toy xylophone. Scratch that. With a class this naughty, it was like I'd managed a casino heist with nothing more than a Tickle Me Elmo and a Fisher-Price getaway car.

From here, I launched into questioning pupils about the reservoir, about the benefits of storing water, the mechanics of hydroelectricity (turbines, generators, and so on), and the utility of renewable energy. I have stories and narratives of this kind for every new class I take and they generally revolve around personal mishaps and misadventures, with myself as the protagonist lurching hopelessly between plight and predicament.

Since this lesson, I've always used stories like this. I think the point is that they are only obliquely relevant. This keeps them low-stakes, since you're setting the scene for the topic and not immediately quizzing them on GCSE content. It also allows them to know you as a character and establish various class memes and in-jokes. With my stories, I set up the Mr Elliott character as someone who is irreverent and heedless of authority. A no-nonsense individual. A renegade – but by God does he get results.

LOOSE ENDS: TEACHING IS MY SPORT

The beginning of a first lesson with the naughtiest class might seem like an odd place to conclude this autobiographical section, but that's because the end of the beginning is often nine-tenths of the story. When the United States entered the Second World War, the downfall of Adolf Hitler was implicit and Winston Churchill was already penning the war's epitaph. Teaching is the same. Once I'd

told my story, the interactions in lessons took on an automatic quality; interactions that were no less thoughtful for feeling effortless.[19]

My one holdout was Pudsey. Again, again, and again. Unfortunately
for him, the Groundhog Day of pupil disruption is quite the learning
curve. I remembered my failings with Luka. Chalked up my success
with Ezekiel. Recalled how I'd variously punished and been punished by Chihuahua. And I dwelt on what I'd lacked over at
Wormwood. At Willenhall School, the teachers were backing me.
Year 8, Year 9, Year 10, Year 11 – every single year head was backing
me. Every time Pudsey sacked off the work, I rang home and collected him for detention. Meanwhile, every other teacher filed their
complaints with the head of Year 10, who did the same. The Key
Stage 4 head finally offered Pudsey an ultimatum: one wrong move
and he'd be packed off to Wormwood. I told him myself that he'd
be eaten alive if a managed move like this went ahead.

'Listen to me, Pudsey. Remember when you threw that chair?'

'The one I dropped on the floor?'

'Dropped … threw. It's all semantics. Now I've got that class on track
– do you understand? The course is permanently set. Like a river
flowing through a gorge. The walls are so high that they can't even
see any alternative on the horizon, yet you're still attempting to
scale that sheer cliff. I'm at the top, Pudsey. Big bucket of water.
You're getting doused every time, brudda. Splash canyon.'

'Yeah,' he said, eyeing me determinedly.

'Teaching is my sport, Puds. Roger Federer. Mike Tyson. Michael
Jordan. I'm on their level. Hell, if MJ could dunk like I teach, he'd
have been invalided from the NBA with repetitive strain injury. You
will never outclass me. As for the chair … you threw it, you dropped
it, it spontaneously got up like a *Beauty and the Beast* furnishing –
whatever. The point is, you broke the rules. And now you're being
punished. In this school, teachers are backing me and you should be
grateful,' I said, smiling. 'And at the end of Year 11, when you've got

---

19 That is to say, the interaction was effortless, not the learning. As I've said
    elsewhere, learning needs to pose challenges to be productive.

that level 5 in geography GCSE, just think … how much *stronger* you'll be.'

At that moment, there was a perfunctory knock at the door before it swung open and bonged off the metal bin, and in came Savannah and Jake.

'Sir …' she said, eyeing me nervously.

'Here,' I said, opening the zip-lock plastic bag before passing her a Geography Ambassador badge. 'Wear it with PRIDE.'

She laughed and Jake saluted, 'Yes, SUH!'

'Annihilator-in-Chief,' I corrected. Even Puds cracked a smile.

Chapter 5

THE NUTS AND BOLTS OF LESSON STRUCTURE AND FEEDBACK

Sling on that leather tool belt and prepare to build the most empowered learning community since Plato nailed that 2x4 to the door of his garden shed: 'Let no one ignorant of starters and plenaries enter here'. We'll inspect the vaunted gables of assessment: 'It's draughty, the tiles are falling off, and can we take down the gargoyles while we're at it?' As for the marking – even if we could turn our red and green pens into Black+Decker drill bits and switch the setting to 'teeth-chattering mania', we would still fall far short of our workload. But as another esteemed philosopher, Bob the Builder, once put it: 'Yes we can.' With the odd trick and workaround, we can chuck the marking in the skip along with the shattered breeze blocks and scraps of loft insulation. Finally, homework – as with most home work, the solution is a bit of DIY – put the onus on the kids. Anyway, enough skiving. Back to work …

TAKING THE REGISTER

'Michael.'

'Here, sir.'

'David.'

'Here.'

'Erm, Nee-am. Is there a Nee-am, here?'

One pupil has a knowing smirk. 'It's pronounced NEEVE, sir.'

I look back at the register: N-I-A-M-H. That spells Neeve. Bit of the old Irish phonics working their magic there, I think. 'OK,' I said. 'Is NEEVE in?'

'Here, sir,' she says, embarrassed but inured to the misunderstanding.

Some registers are so tricky they could go in the *Telegraph* puzzles section. Even when they're not difficult to read, pupils will have their preferred intonations. God help you if you see Mia and confuse a Mee-yah with a Mie-yah. There's a vast world of difference. Erm, hello, it's clearly *Mee-yah* – are you like, stupid? Yeah, well, it's not exactly Fred, is it? Whatever happened to all the Freds, with their lovingly un-mispronounceable names? Extinct, I suppose, along with all the other Flintstones.

Now, I understand Mia's frustration. It's not her fault that her name is phonetically ambiguous. It's not her fault that nobody had the good sense to call her Fred. And, indeed, it must be frustrating to be called Mie-yah lesson after lesson. If my parents wanted me to be called Mie-yah, they would've, like, named me Maya, y'know? Sheesh.

So, for our sakes, then, as well as that of every child who flinches before their name on the register, how do you solve a problem like Mee-yah? First off, don't make the register a big deal. When the pupils arrive, there should be a starter on the board. They should be concentrating on the title, the date, and getting their stationery out. In most schools, Windows and PowerPoint are the default. Some schools use Macs, but unless you're some hipster writing dystopian epics about a world in which retro has once again become mainstream, I'd stick to Windows. Besides, using a computer that doesn't even have a right-click function isn't quirky; it's downright irresponsible.

To show a starter while taking the register, click 'Slide Show' on your PowerPoint. Every computer will have an option that allows you to minimise the PowerPoint so that you can take the register while simultaneously displaying the starter. If it's a Windows computer, click 'Extend'. If it's a Mac, simply wear your red Doc Martens to work, douse it with a pumpkin-spice latte, and whirl the mouse around like a nunchuck until something happens.

It is a safeguarding requirement for every pupil to have their photograph on SIMS, so you should learn to match faces to names before you ever set foot in the classroom. You will struggle to remember names if you attempt to learn them in the course of your instruction. As with chess champs, who've memorised the best parries and moves, you should already know who's who before you ever set time on the tournament clock.[1] If you're teaching properly, your working memory will be overloaded, which makes it difficult to learn names on the job.[2] Better to set time aside and learn the names in advance.

The best way of taking the register is the low-key approach of ticking off the names silently. Do pupils gain anything from you shouting out their name? Other than distraction, no. As Phil Beadle says, 'You don't need to call out the names, Victorian style. Just take a look around and see who's there and who's not.'[3]

Next, you're going to want to learn how to pronounce their names. Here's my advice: do it through questioning. If you want to question a pupil whose name isn't Fred, try this. Point to them and say, 'Sorry, what's your name again?' and they'll tell you. It's better than asking Axolotl, whose parents are clearly inveterate MacBook users: 'I'm sorry, erm, boy, but how do I pronounce your ridiculous, crazy name?'

ON STARTERS

Some teachers don't like starters. I understand why: learning styles, Brain Gym, along with the four-part lesson structure of starter–guided–independent–plenary. The starter was conceived in the 2000s, an era rife with educational gimmicks and impostures. Phil Beadle summarised Department for Education and Skills' expectations of the time as follows: 'Starter: word search. Guided: how to copy off the board. Independent: intense copying off the board.

---

1   Willingham, *Why Don't Students Like School?*, p. 39.
2   Willingham, *Why Don't Students Like School?*, p. 20.
3   Beadle, *How to Teach*, p. 85.

Plenary: how might we improve copying off the board?'[4] I like this guy already.

Beadle recommends sacking off starters altogether. Instead, he suggests either setting homework at the beginning of the lesson or introducing the learning objectives from the board. His rationale is two-fold: firstly, creating starters places strain on teacher workloads and, secondly, starters are too cognitively demanding for pupils – and 'cognitive means some kids not being able to do it: non-cognitive means you get a calm lesson start'.[5] He has a point.

I've never read Das Kapital. Have you? When you consider the opening chapter, it's little wonder: 'THE TWO FACTORS OF A COMMODITY: USE-VALUE AND VALUE'.[6] Imagine the conversation with the publishers.

'Karl, we were thinking, and this is a really nice heading ...'

'Yes, I wanted something quite technical but also very accessible. COMMODITY – the word just grabs you, doesn't it?'

'About that. Have you considered something a little less ... clunky?'

'Clunky? How is it clunky? It's such a crisp image. The readers will die for it.'

'And the capitals, Karl, do you not think they come off quite – aggressive?'

'This is Das Kapital and you want me to use lower case? This book is fierce, it's bolshy, it's ...'

'We've been floating some ideas to really grab and inspire the reader.'

---

4   Phil Beadle, Four Steps to Being Chucked on the Scrapheap, The Guardian (24 October 2006). Available at: https://www.theguardian.com/education/2006/oct/24/teaching.schools.

5   Beadle, How to Teach, p. 91.

6   Karl Marx, Capital: A Critique of Political Economy [Das Kapital] (Moscow: Progress Publishers, 1887). Available at: https://www.marxists.org/archive/marx/works/1867-c1/ch01.htm#S1.

'Inspirational? What about one of my later chapters? I'm telling you, Chapter 7 is a real humdinger – all your doubts are going to wither away. "THE LABOUR PROCESS OR THE PRODUCTION OF USE-VALUES" – intellectual, but relatable, y'know?'

'Hmm, yes. What do you think about "Live, Laugh, Love"?'

However, while I agree with Beadle that lesson starts shouldn't be too cognitively demanding, I do think starters have a place. As we shall see, they're easy to make, they give pupils something to do while you're setting up, and they can provide a foretaste of the lesson ahead.

I don't agree with colleagues who say that copying down is a useful strategy. I doubt even Hitler's Napola schools went so far as to have children copying the 25-Point Programme as a starter task. Yet this is exactly what I have observed a colleague produce for a 'difficult' Year 11 group. Copying can seem like the answer, but it seldom is. Nine times out of ten, it is going to get you into trouble, so unless you have 'indoctrination' among your success criteria, I would avoid it.

To prevent disruption, base your starters on prior knowledge. When we talk about a task being 'cognitively demanding', it largely depends on whether we know it or not. Pupils in Year 7 won't know what 'democracy' means, whereas Year 10s will. Similarly, if you use a technical term like 'respiration' in a Year 9 starter, it isn't going to be cognitively demanding if they studied it last week. Don't see knowledge as something that is either inherently easy or difficult. Knowledge is an imprint that fades gradually. The earlier we arrest the regression with recall, the easier the task.

For my starters, I do a quiz. It doesn't require much effort since I recycle quizzes I've used before. I don't think it's an unduly onerous task. I don't always do quizzes, though. Often, I put an image on the board with an open-ended question. For instance, it could be a medieval tableau of plague doctors and flagellants, asking, 'How does medieval medicine differ from today?' Pupils will be hard pushed to make a mistake. The boy with the perm might opine that, 'Yo, mandem's got a beak, innit. Looking like Zazu from Lion King.'

Meanwhile, higher-attainers might draw a contrast between medieval superstition and the scientific method.

In ITT sessions, open-ended questions are offered to trainees like a precious commodity. The problem is that they only work when pupils have knowledge about the question to tap into. Asking a random open-ended question and expecting it to work is like constructing an oil rig in the middle of the Atlantic, slapping a British Petroleum logo on the side, and expecting the good stuff to obligingly gurgle into your pipelines. My advice is that you can use virtually any resource as a starter, providing you can leverage prior knowledge and you have a willingness to *commit* to it.

If you are taking on a new class, or wish to foreshadow the topic of the lesson, try the following. Put a picture on the board with 'What might this be?' underneath. You can do it with vocabulary, if you like, but use etymological hints. For instance, if I wanted to cover the word 'democracy' in my starter, I could have on the board, 'In Ancient Greece, *demos* meant "people" and *kratos* meant "power". What might the word democracy mean?' Ensure that the word or picture is sufficiently mysterious to keep pupils guessing. Timings? Give them five minutes to think, pair, share. Then, launch into a remorseless bout of questioning.

Both of these starters are backed by evidence. There is so much evidence for the efficacy of quizzing that I'd only overrun my word count by citing it here. Meanwhile, Peter Brown cites multiple studies in support of the notion that 'trying to solve a problem before being taught the solution leads to better learning, even when errors are made in the attempt'.[7]

---

7   Brown et al., *Make It Stick*, p. 11.

ON PLENARIES

I've never done a plenary in my life. In my training year, it was always one of those things I was getting round to, like recycling or being more polite to strangers. You might decide you want to do a plenary; perhaps you think you can crystallise what you've taught your pupils. Then again, which episode of *EastEnders* are you more likely to remember: the one where Peggy and Phil lose the Queen Vic, get it back, and then resolve to never lose the Queen Vic again, or episodes from the infamous 'Get Johnny Week' where Phil and Grant set off in a Range Rover to lay the smackdown on crime boss Johnny Allen, only to be captured at gunpoint? What a glorious week for television. Every day there was a new cliffhanger, and I kept thinking, 'Man, those Mitchell boys are gonna kick some serious ass. No way he's getting away with this one.' I felt Johnny was let off the hook quite lightly when his daughter simply rang the police and had him arrested. Hmm, why hadn't anyone thought of this before? Anyway, my point is that the suspense kept me thinking about this utterly ridiculous plotline. Imagine the alternative: 'Well, on Tuesday, Phil and Grant gave Johnny a bloody good kicking – now he's in jail. Right, pass us the remote, will you? Gregg Wallace is telling poor people how to shop.'

Clearly, while *EastEnders* is often praised for its realism, 'Get Johnny Week' is not actually evidence against the value of plenaries. As Didau notes, it comes down to the distinction between learning and performance: '(1) Performance in the classroom [what we are measuring with a plenary] is extremely dependent on the cues and stimuli provided by the teacher, and (2) performance is a very poor indicator of how well pupils might retain or transfer new concepts.'[8]

Furthermore, as Peps Mccrea points out, 'the most beneficial time for someone to retrieve a memory is just before they forget it'.[9] It's counterintuitive, but by attempting to reinforce core knowledge with plenaries, you are actually delaying this point of optimal recall.

---

8   Didau, *What If Everything You Knew About Education Was Wrong?*, p. 277.
9   Peps Mccrea, *Memorable Teaching: Leveraging Memory to Build Deep and Durable Learning in the Classroom* (London: Peps Mccrea, 2017), p. 83.

Teachers have become neurotic about what their pupils know at any given point in time.

'Jaiden, I want you to write what you've learned in the lesson on this sticky note before leaving.'

'Yo, we just did this.'

'Yes, but I need to check. It's for my exit ticket.'

'Your exit ticket,' he kisses his teeth. 'Why you need an exit ticket?'

'LOOK, I'M TRYING TO BUILD A BRIGHTER FUTURE FOR YOU, SO JUST DO YOUR EXIT TICKET, OK.'

Another opportunity cost is that time spent on plenaries could be spent on a simpler, less gimmicky activity. An opportunity cost is an economics concept meaning that by choosing one option, we often lose out on other alternatives. There are only so many hours in the day, after all. The reason I never got round to plenaries was because the pupils had so many questions about the actual content of the lesson. My theory is that we only insist on them because it satisfies some deep desire for symmetry and the rule of three. Starter, main course, dessert. Reduce, reuse, recycle. Catch it, kill it, bin it. The problem is that although it's an intuitive notion, good things don't invariably come in threes. *The Matrix Revolutions* went straight to DVD for a reason. And while the *Lord of the Rings* trilogy was excellent, don't even get me started on *The Hobbit*. I didn't realise it was possible to fall comfortably asleep in a cinema chair without several years of contorting yourself into a Perspex box for a living.

But hang on, what about starters? Aren't they gimmicky? No. They serve a purpose. They give the pupils something to do while you take the register. Plenaries could feasibly serve the purpose of crystallising knowledge, but as we've seen, they fail in this regard. Therefore, gimmick.

LEARNING OBJECTIVES

Should we tell our pupils what they are going to learn before they set about learning it? Here's what Phil Beadle thinks: 'telling the kids what they are going to learn is a fatuous piece of egotism on the part of the teacher'.[10] He then goes on to quote the results of a study where 'authors systematically deleted various elements of the lesson for a period of the time to see which elements of the lesson were crucial to optimise kids' learning'. It found that 'all that really counts is the process of practice and review', while 'not sharing lesson objectives at the front end made no difference to the kids' learning'.[11]

As a pupil 'expert' in a group discussion might put it, I partially agree with this statement. Having three learning objectives listed on the board and monotonously drawling through them is boorish and inept practice. They've always seemed fairly pointless to me. But we should consider the contrary evidence from John Hattie's *Visible Learning*, which synthesised over 800 meta-analyses, 50,000 independent academic articles, and encompassed around 240 million pupils.[12] The effect size of 'learning goals versus no goals' was 0.68 and for 'explicit teaching' it was 0.57, in a study where anything above 0.4 was above average.[13] One recent study also found that hearing a 'brief rationale of the lesson beforehand' could increase engagement by 25%.[14] Seemingly, learning objectives have some salutary effect.

Perhaps they follow the Law of Fun Boy Three and Bananarama: 'It ain't what you do, it's the way that you do it, And that's what gets results.' It's basing lesson objectives around skills objectives rather than knowledge criteria that leads to them being about as handy as a pair of Birkenstocks in an ass-kicking competition. Once you've done away with clearly defined knowledge checklists, all kinds of abominations become possible, as Beadle illustrates in his table of

---

10 Beadle, *How to Teach*, p. 91.
11 Beadle, *How to Teach*, p. 92.
12 Peal, *Progressively Worse*, p. 183.
13 See https://visible-learning.org/hattie-ranking-influences-effect-sizes-learning-achievement.
14 Busch and Watson, *The Science of Learning*, p. 26.

'useful verbs that you might want to use to set objectives': 'Evaluation – appraise, argue, assess, compare, conclude, contrast, criticise, describe, discriminate, explain, interpret, judge, relate, summarise, validate.'[15]

He provides similar lists for synthesis, analysis, application, comprehension, and knowledge. There is not a single teacher currently in the profession who has not resorted to one of these lists in the final few coffee sips before an NQT observation. To be clear, Beadle is not in favour of this kind of thing – is anyone? – but his list neatly demonstrates how lesson planning through a skills rubric quickly descends into the kind of frenetic synonym competition that would make Peter Roget wish his thesaurus had gone the way of every other -saurus. Or that he'd been visited by Blackadder and had it chucked into a nice roaring fire. Even the greatest minds can never know what posterity holds for their inventions.

Perhaps learning objectives should be mostly for practitioners. As Greg Ashman says, 'we need to be clear about what we want students to learn', and if I have only 'the vague intention of the students learning some science then there is a clear risk'.[16] Thus, learning objectives may simply help you to navigate your own lesson plan. For trainees and NQTs, they're worth the extra effort but they must contain meaning. It's best to have a simple objective with technical knowledge specified in brackets.

Here's one I made earlier:

Hot deserts – students must know the following:

1 Where we find deserts. (equator, degrees of latitude, atmospheric circulation)

2 The average rainfall and temperature in deserts. (mean and range)

3 The plants and animals we find in hot deserts. (water scarcity, sparse vegetation, animal adaptations)

---

15 Beadle, *How to Teach*, p. 186.
16 Greg Ashman, *The Truth About Teaching: An Evidence-Informed Guide for New Teachers* (London: SAGE, 2018), p. 106.

This is how I construct learning objectives. For myself, I put the key knowledge in brackets. When I share them with pupils, I simply remove the bracketed knowledge. This is because I don't want to gild the lily, as Shakespeare puts it; to over-egg the pudding; to do something to death. To be blunt, if you miniaturise your own lesson at the start of your own lesson, not only have you given it a peculiarly fractal structure that is going to confuse the pupils – 'Hang on, haven't we done this already?' – but you are also going to make yourself look like an idiot.

I also think that learning objectives should remain static. Please don't try to incorporate them into some kind of meta-activity unless it is very simple. There can be some benefits to this, since according to Hattie, metacognitive strategies have an effect size of 0.60.[17] But, even then, this is only where objectives are couched in simple, ordinary, pupil-friendly language.[18] Thus, I could share my first two learning objectives and ask the pupils to think about what the third one might be, and this would combine the strategies of pre-testing and metacognition. Would I do this myself? No. But you might want to, and that's OK. We can't all be ASBOs, can we? When doing so, just remember, this has to involve a medium difficulty inference to give pupils the illusion of participation that is so crucial to long-term memory storage.

When thinking about learning objectives, this gem from Hattie says it better than I can:

If I said to you, I'm gonna teach you what Australian Rules football looks like ... but I'm not gonna tell you what the rules are and I'm not gonna tell you how to score. But I want you to go out there and play it. For many of you, you'd give up very quickly.[19]

---

17 See https://visible-learning.org/hattie-ranking-influences-effect-sizes-learning-achievement.

18 David Didau, Why I Struggle with Learning Objectives and Success Criteria, *The Learning Spy* (6 December 2015). Available at: https://learningspy.co.uk/learning/8696/#_edn1.

19 John Hattie, John Hattie: Learning Intentions and Success Criteria [video], *Stem Learning* (2012). Available at: https://www.stem.org.uk/rxacud.

Only use lesson objectives grounded in knowledge, and not the empty kind Beadle warns against. Here's your success criteria. You must avoid: (a) boring pupils into a coma, (b) boring yourself into a coma, (c) visiting Thesaurus.com, or (d) instigating a strange kind of 'Guess what's in my head' game – aka shit-show charades (how's that for a synonym?) – where you have pupils formulate your own lesson objectives for you.

ON ASSESSMENTS

Assessment is incredibly tough. Picture every topic in teaching as one of those nut selections you get for Christmas. Differentiation is like some little hazelnut you can stomp on. Behaviour management? Like a walnut, it has a reputation for being tough, but apply pressure to the midpoint and you've cracked it – no problem. Then you root around in that mesh bag again and, hmm, what's this? Improbably, you pull out a coconut. It's big, rock solid, and you can bash your head against it repeatedly before realising the only nut you've managed to crack is your own. That's assessment.

Why is it so hard? Because knowledge is invisible, progress isn't linear, and everything we've ever taken for granted is simply a lie our parents told us so we'd shut up and eat our veggies.

Here's a thought experiment. Imagine that you were a driving instructor. But you're not going to sit in the front seat, oh no. No more narrowing your eyes in contempt at the simpleton foolish enough to stall the engine on his first go. You're going to stand on the pavement. The windows on the car will be tinted. And, guess what, here's some earmuffs. That's right, Mr Car Whisperer, I know how you love to pick up on cues from the engine. Well, sorry, that's cheating. Right. Lesson one. Teach this bastard to drive.

This is how it is in schools. We can never know what our pupils know – not precisely, anyway. By contrast, driving instructors can see what their learners are doing. If they stalled initially, it was because they took their foot off the clutch without putting their foot on the gas. Reversing into a bay? They turned too early. Spiral roundabouts? Stay in your goddamn lane, perhaps. To take the analogy of driving instruction to its logical endpoint – picture having two years to assist not one, not two, but thirty of these tinted-windowed learners with passing their driving test. Then multiply that by the number of GCSE classes you have. Finally, consider how much more content there is for GCSE than for your standard driving test. Now do you understand why assessment is so difficult?

Can't we just assess pupils on the GCSE exam – mock exams, past papers, and so on? No, we can't. There are two reasons for this. The first is due to Goodhart's law, which holds that 'when a measure becomes a target, it loses its value as a measure'.[20] When we use GCSE papers for practice assessments, they're invariably entered into a spreadsheet; this spreadsheet is then used to hold department heads to account. In other words, what should be a measure of pupil progress becomes the neurotic focus of head teachers who have a copy of Daisy Christodoulou's *Making Good Progress?*[21] on their desks but have never read the bloody thing. But can't it do both? Can't the mock GCSE paper allow us to see (a) how well pupils are doing and (b) how bloody inspirational teachers are – just look at all those level 7s! Again, no. Christodoulou gives two examples of target distortion:

1 In the British education system, the focus on pupils obtaining five A*–C grade GCSEs led to an obsessive focus on the C/D grade threshold.

2 In healthcare, a UK government target for A&E patients to be seen within four hours led to patients being held in ambulances outside hospitals in order to avoid 'starting the clock'.[22]

And you know what, I'm going to be honest. When I assess pupils on mock GCSEs, I'm so much more lenient, although I don't think so at the time. Give me some GCSE papers from the newly agglomerated Bell Green and Wood End academy (known as Wood Green, obviously), and I'll mark them normally. Ask me to mark my own

---

20 Marilyn Strathern's definition in Daisy Christodoulou, Assessment: High Stakes, Low Improvement. In Robert Peal (ed.), *Changing Schools: Perspectives on Five Years of Educational Reform*, Kindle edn (Woodbridge: John Catt Educational, 2015), loc. 1038.
21 Daisy Christodoulou, *Making Good Progress? The Future of Assessment for Learning* (Oxford: Oxford University Press, 2016).
22 Christodoulou, Assessment, loc. 1041.

papers, or any from Willenhall School, and you'll see me cheerfully tallying up the score before I realise – oh dear, this is going to be less than a level 5. Oh lord. I start flinching. No, this can't be. Wait! I turn back, riffling desperately to question 3.1 on climate change: 'It's gonna be, like, bare hot man. Plus, renewable energy – it's fully sick. Windmills n that.' At the bottom, a cone-shaped object emitting baleful fumes and a little glass jar with water in it. Y'know what, he's not wrong, is he? And the use of the word 'like', could it be that he's qualifying what he's saying? At the bottom, that diagram is clearly meant to represent carbon capture – but at a micro level, for environmentally conscious citizens. Hmm, a lot of thought went into this. I guess it is a level 5 after all. Smashed it, Wayne.

OK, so the case for GCSE practice papers has taken a hit. But what else? Surely, if they represent the exam that we're aiming for we should simply rinse and repeat until we get it right? Well, no. The other part of the problem is that if a pupil does get a level 7, for instance, it's very difficult to pick apart what specific items they need to work on. As Christodoulou says, 'what matters is not the test, but the inferences the test allows us to make'.[23]

Take this practice question from a GCSE geography paper: 'Describe the primary and secondary effects of a tropical storm. Use a named example and your own knowledge. (9 marks).' Right, let's say a pupil got a level 9. Great, full marks. Nothing to see here. Move along. OK, what if they got a level 5? There must have been some pieces of knowledge they didn't know – but *what* didn't they know? Had they forgotten that 6,300 people were killed in Typhoon Haiyan? Or was it that they neglected to mention the widespread flooding? But, wait, maybe they knew about widespread flooding but didn't mention it because they thought they'd earned full marks.

As for any pupil unfortunate enough to get a level 1 or a U, it's not even clear-cut that they knew absolutely nothing. For instance, perhaps they forgot the name of the case study – Typhoon Haiyan – or maybe it was that they didn't remember what a tropical storm was? Perhaps primary and secondary effects made them unsure? Or maybe it was something to do with the kind of carbon capture Wayne spoke about in his answer? The exam question is a small one

23 Christodoulou, Assessment, loc. 1063.

– it covers two out of 348 pages of the geography textbook – and still it's not targeted enough, since it doesn't allow us to infer exactly what our pupils know and don't know. Anything else? Yeah, it says nothing about how well they know the other 346 pages.

How do we tackle this? Forgive the pun, but Greg Ashman provides an insight with the following football analogy:

> Imagine a soccer coach who used a similar approach with her team. Every training would involve a practice game of soccer. At the end of every session she would then write a note to each of her players containing advice on various aspects of their performance and what to work on next. She would give these notes out at the start of the next training session. This is not, of course, how real soccer coaches work. They constantly intervene and provide verbal feedback. They gather players together and explicitly instruct them in some aspect of play ... This is important because real games are unpredictable. If you want your players to improve a particular skill then you need to develop a discrete activity that targets that skill. You do not wait for the need for this skill to occur serendipitously and fleetingly in the context of a game.[24]

Here, Ashman highlights both what assessment in schools currently is – a practice match every session – and what it should become – lower-level drills. If I were to apply this analogy to assessment in geography, I would test each item individually. This would be as simple as including in a recall test the following questions:

1 What is our case study? (1)

2 List four primary effects of tropical storms/hurricanes/ cyclones. (4)

3 Describe the following secondary effects in no more than two lines each: water shortages, and landslides. (2)

With this short test, I have still only covered a small section of that large question above. In the interests of symmetry, here is another test I could use to check the remainder of this content:

1 List three other names for a tropical storm. (3)

2 List four secondary effects of tropical storms. (4)

---

24 Ashman, *The Truth About Teaching*, pp. 124–125.

3   Describe the following primary effects in no more than two lines each: 6,300 people killed and 30,000 fishing boats destroyed. (2)

The point with this short assessment is that it is more reliable than longer answer questions. For questions 1 and 2 in both quizzes, I can gauge whether they have the discrete items of knowledge necessary to earn higher marks in the nine-mark question. For question 3 in both, you would earn one mark per description. For instance, if you explained that 'Typhoon Haiyan caused water shortages because the large sea waves (storm surges) polluted freshwater supplies', you would earn a mark. You would earn two for describing both secondary effects. The best thing about assessing discrete items of knowledge is that it's difficult for me to make a mistake. They either know it or they don't. I'm not going to be twitching and beading with sweat if they get anything lower than a level 5, am I?

Is there any place for longer, more summative forms of assessment? Yes, but only for putting the pieces together. The smaller assessments tell you what elements of knowledge your pupils have. But it's no use getting the 'London Calling' jigsaw out of the loft when you've only got enough pieces for half a red double-decker, three-fifths of St Paul's cathedral, and other landmarks so incomplete you have to tell the kids that you bought the 1941 Luftwaffe Edition. You might want to use them occasionally to ensure that the content you are teaching aligns with the end-point exam – whether at Key Stage 3, GCSE, or A level. Dylan Wiliam and Daisy Christodoulou suggest that pupils should perform 'regular retrieval practice on everything in the whole unit and then at the end of the six weeks, there should be an assessment covering everything in the unit'.[25] But when it comes to grading these longer assessments or using them as diagnostics, remember: it is counterintuitive but they cannot help us moving forward. On a larger scale, they can 'give you a way of comparing people to their peers nationally on a very broad domain of knowledge'.[26] This allows us to make an inference such as,

---

25 Dylan Wiliam and Daisy Christodoulou, Marking, Assessment, and Feedback. In Carl Hendrick and Robin Macpherson (eds), What Does This Look Like in the Classroom? Bridging the Gap Between Research and Practice, Kindle edn (Woodbridge: John Catt Educational, 2017), loc. 635.
26 Wiliam and Christodoulou, Marking, Assessment, and Feedback, loc. 611.

'Scunthorpe Academy is a bit crap' or, 'Oh look, that Michaela School where the teachers are really strict came fifth on Progress 8.'[27] That's about it.

There are many other kinds of assessment. Untold quantities of contending theories just waiting to be dredged up from whatever learning swamp they're currently wallowing in. My advice is to leave it for now. If you're a trainee or NQT, you can wade into those brackish waters later on, if you so wish. In the meantime, work on your subject knowledge – this will allow you to break down diffuse assessments into their component chunks.

MARKING

If assessment is the toughest topic in education, then marking is the most controversial. I'm going to consider it both from an emotional and academic perspective. Largely, in this book I'm trying to think about what works, so I'm going to start with the academic case.

Phil Beadle claims that marking 'is the most important thing you do as a teacher. All of the other stuff is no use whatsoever if you don't mark your books properly.'[28] Looks like that's half the profession out on the scrapheap already. What else? 'Where it gets more vital and difficult is when you move from geography (hard, but you can always get them doing maps) through to history (harder, but you can always get them doing historical maps) into English (nigh on impossible).'[29]

Before I go any further, let me just state that I am a geographer and I rarely ever do maps. I hate them. God knows where Cov is – I live here, isn't that enough? Neither am I some keen-bean for hiking who wears a Karrimor fleece and walking boots seemingly modelled on a camel's muzzle tied shut with a shoelace. I wear Air Max on every school trip. Full stop. Some geographers can't hack it; that's OK, I get it. You like your walking boots. Good for you. Just think,

---

27 See https://www.compare-school-performance.service.gov.uk/schools-by-type?s
    tep=phase&geographic=all&region=0&phase=secondary.
28 Beadle, *How to Teach*, p. 213.
29 Beadle, *How to Teach*, p. 213.

without your patronage of the outdoors section, Sports Direct might finally have discontinued their 'Not Even A Mother Could Love It' range. Anyway, I just hope people read this paragraph and think before stereotyping.

Now, I've just done the calculations and I think marking might actually take infinity long. Yes, you heard me. Infinity long. And that's only for each class. As Georg Cantor discovered, you can add together infinities to make larger infinities. By my estimation, all my marking taken together will actually be somewhat larger than regular infinity. And here I am selfishly writing a book. This is pretty irresponsible of me.

I just don't think marking can ever justify the amount of time spent on it. My reasoning is as follows: firstly, Ashman says that 'writing comments is time consuming and inefficient compared to simply speaking to a student'.[30] Speaking is around five times faster than writing. This means there is an inevitable opportunity cost. Time teachers could spend on planning or honing their subject knowledge is sacrificed to a task so monotonous it would have a medieval scribe longing to return to the monastery to copy out the rest of the collected works of Thomas Aquinas – only 7,000 pages to go!

Secondly, it has to do with what we mean by effective feedback. Dylan Wiliam says that 'there are much more effective ways of structuring feedback interventions than just marking students' work'.[31] Ashman outlines how this might look in English: 'Instead of marking, imagine selecting a key issue to address, such as the quality of topic sentences, then planning an episode where you intentionally and explicitly teach students how topic sentences work and what distinguishes good ones from bad ones.'[32] Yeah, Greg, that sounds great and all, but I still have infinity marking left to go. Maybe later, I dunno.

My contention is that marking is so onerous that nobody will ever do it properly. Although both Christodoulou and Beadle highlight the

---

30 Ashman, *The Truth About Teaching*, p. 124.
31 Wiliam quoted in Didau, *What If Everything You Knew About Education Was Wrong?*, p. 267.
32 Ashman, *The Truth About Teaching*, p. 127.

benefits of specific guidance,[33] the vast majority of feedback is going to be generic. Christodoulou explains why generic feedback is so ineffective. Broadly, the idea ties in to larger debates surrounding assessment, but I'm not going through that again, so here's the skinny:

> I can remember writing the target 'use more full stops' on a piece of work. On the surface, this seems quite a specific target which a pupil could understand and act on.
>
> If a pupil's understanding of sentence structure was very well-developed, and she had missed out full stops as a result of carelessness, then the target would be helpful. But if her problem was that she was using lots of run-on sentences because her understanding of sentence structure was very weak, then such a target would not tell her where she should be using more full stops.[34]

This illustrates the pitfall of even a seemingly sound written comment. I do this all the time in geography. I keep my books marked but I doubt my comments really help anybody. In my NQT year, I thought I'd stumbled on the solution. I called them 'mini resources'. You would see me in the office, reams and reams of little Nazi resources flying out of the printer, with checkboxes and questions formatted artfully beneath. 'I'd hold off on the patent, if I were you,' said my boss. But there was scarcely a day when I wasn't rubbing their perfectly guillotined edges in my colleagues' faces as I cheerfully ran down yet another Pritt Stick to a claggy nub. To give feedback, I read whatever work my pupil had produced, ticked the relevant question on my mini resource, and then bam – stick it! Job done. Well, almost. Better put a red tick in the corner as well, just in case.

The point is that the multiplicity of possible errors existing in any single essay is, again, infinite. This means that there is no simple solution to providing specific feedback. Other than through a slog so intense and ungratifying that, in a daze, you momentarily understand the problem of teacher retention, before doping yourself with

---

33 Christodoulou, *Making Good Progress?*, p. 93; and Beadle, *How to Teach*, p. 216.
34 Christodoulou, *Making Good Progress?*, p. 95.

yet another double Nespresso. What was I thinking about again? Oh yes, marking.

If we assume that the majority of written feedback is going to be generic, we then have to consider why this is such a problem. It's because 'generic targets provide the illusion of clarity: it seems like they are providing feedback, but they are actually much more like grades'.[35] And a grade is useless, since it merely 'summarises different sources of errors without distinguishing them'.[36] When we mark our books, it is as if we are continuously grading one never-ending summative assessment. Christodoulou expounds on the problems of descriptor-based assessment in *Making Good Progress?*, so if you want to know more, buy the book. And, look, I like the cover too, but please don't go leaving it on your desk just to show off.

Feedback is not invariably helpful. It is a double-edged sword. One study found that while 'feedback interventions, on average, significantly improve student performance', they can 'also be detrimental, with over one third of feedback interventions doing more harm than good'.[37] If we accept that a third of all feedback is actually harmful, my question is this: out of all the feedback you provide, in which segment is the bleary-eyed generic commentary you wrote on Sunday evening likely to end up?

Finally, let's turn to the emotional case, because I think Beadle makes several good points: 'What is the point of kids doing work if no one reads it? None. Not reading it sends all manner of negative messages to the child: effort is pointless, their work is of no value to you, and they could have got away with not bothering.'[38] He goes on to say that 'random ticking' – the current policy in bog-standard ~~comprehensives~~ academies across the country – 'is insulting to the intelligence of the children you teach'.[39] He also points out that your 'stance on presentation of work is pretty definitive: if you are lax with it, the students will take this as an incitement that they can take the mick'.[40] He's right. God knows I love a good lighthouse, but only

---

35 Christodoulou, *Making Good Progress?*, p. 96.
36 Dehaene, *How We Learn*, p. 211.
37 Busch and Watson, *The Science of Learning*, p. 25.
38 Beadle, *How to Teach*, p. 216.
39 Beadle, *How to Teach*, p. 217.
40 Beadle, *How to Teach*, p. 218.

when I'm visiting windswept Hebridean outcrops – not in the exercise books.

Christodoulou. The name continues to come up. But, yet again, she has the answer. If we want to deal with marking, we need to jettison the rather antiquated notion that pupils should write an essay every lesson because 'this is not the best way of working out how a pupil needs to improve'.[41] Tasks we can meaningfully assess – and thus, mark – will be ones where we have isolated the different components.[42] For an example, see my tropical storm test in 'On Assessments'.

In a nutshell – one only marginally less tough than assessment – my solution is that children should write fewer essays, more targeted assessments, and that, if you do mark, ensure it is specific.

HOMEWORK – SHOULD WE BOTHER?

I could just as well write, 'Respiration – A Load of Hot Air?' Whatever my thoughts on homework, like marking, it's here to stay. Nevertheless, it's worth delving into the research. If you're convinced of its efficacy, then you'll be more likely to set it and less fearful of those year-head planner trawls.

'You haven't been getting much geography homework, Kayleigh,' says the head of Year 8. 'Are you writing it down when sir asks?'

'Sir says I can think like a geographer so I don't need to do any homework.'

I'd had a stressful couple of months. Every time Year 11 did a geography mock, it turned out to be the wrong one, so I'd spent successive weeks marking GCSE papers. Saying Key Stage 3 was on the back-burner is an understatement. They were out in the coal shed.

---

41 Christodoulou, *Making Good Progress?*, pp. 93–94.
42 Christodoulou, *Making Good Progress?*, p. 93.

Homework is another one of those moral issues in teaching. Greg Ashman notes that many teachers 'see marking as some form of penitential devotional act',[43] but you may well be thinking, 'Well, I've never heard any evidence in favour of homework. So, why bother?' Phil Beadle relates the following:

'Y'know what son?' he exclaimed, no doubt brushing his slicked quiff back from his forehead as he did so. 'If they can't teach you all the stuff you need to know during the day, they can't be very good at their jobs, can they?' (Why-oh-why-oh-why did they not immediately make him education secretary?)[44]

Furthermore, I have to agree with Beadle that 'our workload is absurd enough without the existence of homework'.[45] As with marking, he notes that while feasible for the tick-and-flick marking of maths, it's impracticable for essay-based subjects.[46] In looking abroad, we may read that 'teenagers in Finland did less homework than Americans, but scored at the top of the world in international tests'.[47] All the while, I'm salivating and breaking out in goose bumps over the prospect of sacking off a metric shit tonne of work: 'Listen here, *boss*, they don't do homework in Finland, so you won't catch me doing it here. What's Finland got to do with anything? Erm, it's like, the most bitchingest, gnarliest education system in all Europe. PISA test scores? No? Sheesh, read a book for once. *The only homework they do in Finland is listening to death metal and going skiing.* Maybe *that's* what we need for our kids right now. Sure, it's counterintuitive, but it's *what works*, y'know?'

Sadly for me, the research is a little more nuanced. In his paper on Finland's PISA performance, Tim Oates has this to say: 'The children in PISA 2000 were 15 years of age … [most] educational tourists had arrived in Finland 2001 and made a serious error. They got off the plane and asked the Finns about the system in 2000 – not what it was like during the 1970s and 1980s [i.e. the period of sustained

---

43 Ashman, *The Truth About Teaching*, p. 126.
44 Beadle, *How to Teach*, p. 170.
45 Beadle, *How to Teach*, p. 170.
46 Beadle, *How to Teach*, p. 171.
47 Amanda Ripley, *The Smartest Kids in the World* (New York: Simon & Schuster: 2013), p. 39.

educational improvement].'[48] Well, there goes for death metal for learning (DMfL).

Far better to look at two countries which haven't seen a decline in their PISA test scores. Firstly, Singapore: 'every term, all the parents go with their children to the book store to buy practice books for all their subjects, and that it is totally normal for parents to set their children homework from these books once they've finished their school homework'.[49] And China: 'Angela had to do a maths paper that night, in addition to her English homework. These took her three-and-a-half hours, which Jenny told me quietly in the kitchen was typical of an evening's homework.'[50] Four hours a night sounds a little excessive. You might still be thinking, 'Isn't this rather anecdotal?' Besides, if we want to know what works, there's a decade-long lag, isn't there? How do we know that what's happening in Singapore currently will yield good results in ten to fifteen years' time?

When I first read in *Visible Learning* that homework had an effect size of 0.29 (0.2 being a small effect size, 0.4 average, and 0.6 large), I was ecstatic.[51] Now, I'm gonna tell my boss: 'Right, so I've read this "meta-analysis" over the weekend. You probably don't even know what that is, do you? Tell you? Well, it's very *scientific*, for a start. It has all these numbers. *Decimal* numbers. That's how you know it's legit. No fractions or percentages here. *John Hattie* made this, not some William Hill plonker. This is the real deal. Anyway, I've been doing some quantitative analysis of my own, and did you know that mobile phones, chess instruction, and mindfulness have effect sizes of 0.37, 0.34, and 0.29, respectively? I'm going to *aggregate* these findings. That's right. No more homework. My kids are playing *Chess Master 2020* on their phones while I stick on some good old-fashioned Mongolian throat-singing – to align their chakras, you see? Is chess really appropriate for history? Look, it's got knights in it. Feudal system and all that. What more do you want? Sheesh!'

---

48   Tim Oates, Finnish Fairy Stories, Cambridge Assessment (April 2015), p. 2. Available at: https://www.cambridgeassessment.org.uk/Images/207376-finnish-fairy-stories-tim-oates.pdf.
49   Crehan, *Cleverlands*, p. 120.
50   Crehan, *Cleverlands*, p. 149.
51   See https://visible-learning.org/hattie-ranking-influences-effect-sizes-learning-achievement.

Yet again, my hopes were dashed when I read *The Learning Rainforest*. As Sherrington puts it: 'Homework, taken as an aggregated whole, shows an effect size of $d = 0.29$' – that is, between small and medium. Oh, but turn the page and here comes an important detail: 'The studies show that the effect size at primary age is $d = 0.15$ and for secondary students is $d = 0.64$.' In other words, homework for secondary schools falls into the bracket of $d > 0.6$, and can therefore be considered 'excellent'.[52] And not only that: apparently, the kind of homework matters too. Thanks a lot, Sherrington, now what am I going to say to my boss?

The best evidence we have currently suggests that homework has at least some effect, and that the gains we're talking about are not even marginal but potentially life changing. Until homework is positively disproven as good practice, we ought to set it, which leads to my next point: how do we set, collect, and mark homework without burdening teacher workloads?

Ashman helpfully distinguishes between four types of homework: completely useless, mostly useless, school replacement homework, and high-quality homework.[53] Homework that is useless is often complex task completion. Ashman gives the examples of write-ups, posters, and research tasks. School replacement is that satirised by Beadle at the beginning of this section: 'if they can't teach you all the stuff you need to know during the day, they can't be very good at their jobs, can they?' Finally, high-quality homework is, quite simply, retrieval practice of taught material.[54] Sherrington, in his analysis of *Visible Learning*, puts it as follows:

The highest effects in secondary are associated with rote learning, practice or rehearsal of subject matter; more task-oriented homework has higher effects than deep learning and problem solving. Overall, the more complex, open-ended and unstructured tasks are, the lower the effect sizes. Short, frequent homework closely monitored by teachers has more impact than their converse forms.[55]

---

52 Sherrington, *The Learning Rainforest*, p. 95.
53 Greg Ashman, Homework, *Filling the Pail* (26 September 2018). Available at: https://gregashman.wordpress.com/2018/09/26/homework.
54 Ashman, Homework.
55 Sherrington, *The Learning Rainforest*, p. 96.

Incredibly, it seems that I've been following best practice all along through sheer laziness. One of my favourite homeworks is to give pupils a small postcard with three facts on it. I explain that I want them memorised. By the following Monday, there is an isolated desk at the front of the class. In register order, the pupils come to the front, write down the facts from memory on a sheet, hand it to me and return to their seat. The rigmarole serves a purpose. Pupils are submitting their homeworks at different times. While one is submitting, the others are working. In sitting momentarily at the front, the pupil is also separated from their peers. Together, these factors obviate the possibility of copying. Excellent. This homework really is astonishingly easy to produce and set. If it's a last-minute jobby – 'last-minute jobbies' are not an example of best practice, and neither does Hattie list an effect size for these, but they're an undeniable reality during the frenetic blur we call the five-hour day – simply write three facts on the board and have the kids copy them in their planner. Tell them you want them memorised by next Monday. The best part? You can tell your boss that you're 100% research led in this matter.

You can use any method you like providing that it involves the retrieval of something previously taught. At my old school, they introduced a Knowledge League. Each week, you'd give the pupils five facts on a sheet of A5. The following week they'd sit a test. Pupils earned a point for each fact. Then, you'd open up a spreadsheet and input the results. You could show the pupils while they were packing away how well each of them did in terms of knowledge retention – we put a little Premier League logo on the side of it as well to trick them into thinking it was cool. You know how kids are. Once they see that purple lion, it's game over, baby. OK, so it was a bit gimmicky … and did I ever do it? Hell no. I simply said, 'Remember all the facts or I'll keep you at lunch.' Then again, I was fortunate enough to have them in the period before lunchtime every day of the week – lucky them. Nevertheless, I'm giving you this idea because it's something that you might want to use. I was being thoughtful. Take it or leave it.

Finally, I want to address the collection of homework. To put it mildly, I'm not a schedule kinda guy. I somehow get to where I need to go and always at the right time, but don't ask me how. It's inexplicable. Like Boris Johnson. At the start of the year, Mrs Stabilo always asks if I'd like her to order a school planner for me: 'They come in two colours: Baby Vomit and Papa Smurf.' She takes my glazed expression as, 'I'll pass on that, thanks,' and then offers me a cup of tea.

Here's how I see it: 'take therefore no thought for the morrow: for the morrow shall take thought for the things of itself. Sufficient unto the day is the evil thereof.' Yeah, and that's in the Bible.[56] In spite of its many gaffes – unlike *Visible Learning*, there are no decimals in the Bible, which is maybe why they thought pi was equal to 3 – I think they were on to something. When you write too much in your planner, it just stresses you out. If you're stressed, your teaching is going to 'hit the fan', let's say. And at that point, homework has to take a back seat because if you can't get it right in the classroom, no amount of pupils copying and pasting off of Wikipedia is going to help.

Now, I don't want to sound like an infomercial, but did you know that you can set and collect homework entirely within the course of your lessons without ever having to write anything in a planner? As the inventor of the Slap Chop vegetable dicer put it, 'You're gonna have an exciting life now.'[57] Here's how it works. Imagine you're being evidence based and setting five facts for your pupils to recall the following Monday. Now, you've had a heavy weekend. You're in class and you don't even know if you've set any homework, let alone what. Worst of all, you've left your planner in the office. Why not make it part of your routine to check a pupil's planner while they're doing the starter activity? Simply turn to the previous week and see if you've set any homework. The best part? If you'd written it in your own planner, you'd likely have jotted something like, 'Homework: Year 10', whereas the pupil planner will have all the details right there on one page. You could do this all year if you like – I do. Sufficient unto the class is the planner thereof.

Finally, marking homework. Well, it's retrieval practice, isn't it? If they can't retrieve it, they've not bothered. Zero marks.

---

56 Matthew 6:34.
57 TheRealVinceOffer, Slap Chop [video] (6 July 2010) at 0.38. Available at: https://www.youtube.com/watch?v=UxGn2Egekic.

Chapter 6

SPREADSHEET NUMEROLOGY AND THE SEATING PLAN ZODIAC

Ever wondered what a *Mortal Kombat* fatality on an intellectual concept might look like? Look no further. Now, I want you to get a handle on data so you don't get the sack. But doing so requires me to disabuse you of the notion that data in schools is in any way valid or reliable. It might even be harmful. The sort of thing a guy in a trench coat might accost you about in an alley: 'Hey, kid, you wanna buy a spreadsheet?' Once data is out of the way, we can then make informed decisions about our seating plans. The tricks are very simple. No reading the runes. No visiting Stonehenge for inspiration. Merely a couple of seating constellations that you can remember as easily as Orion's Belt or the Big Dipper.

TARGET GRADES

In front of me now, I have a mixed-ability seating plan for Year 10. Apparently, Tom is on a flight path for a level 5, Marian is soaring towards the stratosphere of level 7, and meanwhile Zack is about to emergency land on the manure-laden paddock of level 1. Now, I'm not going to say, 'I teach Zack and he's a very bright boy,' because data isn't meant to be airtight. There will always be gaps in the data and this shouldn't lead to the explosive decompression of the concept.

What I will ask is, how were these targets determined? Was it through the kind of assessment I spoke about earlier? Well, I know that it wasn't through the functional assessment curriculum specified by E. D. Hirsch – 'to make tests fewer and better … and base them on well-defined, knowledge-based curriculums'[1] – since those are

---

1   Eric D. Hirsch, Jr, *Why Knowledge Matters: Rescuing Our Children from Failed Educational Theories* (Cambridge MA: Harvard Education Press, 2017), p. 15.

about as far away as the Andromeda galaxy. Some 4.5 billion years from now, when our galaxies finally collide, we'll probably still be wistfully sighing at the prospect of assessing knowledge in schools. By that point, it won't matter because we'll all live in the computer with Wreck-It Ralph and the Microsoft paperclip. 'Do you need any assistance?' 'I sure do, Clippy. These four-dimensional pupil-tracking sheets are doing my nut in.'

Forget target grades for a moment. Let's consider predicted grades. In essay-based subjects, these are always decided through what Daisy Christodoulou calls the quality model, where a pupil completes a task, such as an essay, and 'the marker judges how well they performed'.[2] The question here is 'how sure can we be that all markers are applying consistent standards?'[3] We can't. Assessing a piece of extended writing is as subjective as it gets. Google 'greatest American novel' and it won't be long before you see *Moby Dick* by Herman Melville. Has anyone actually read this book? In one chapter, Melville goes into the most painstaking detail about the many different types of whale – and believe me, they're all extremely 'prodigious'. Melville will remind you of this many, many times. Yeah, yeah, Melville, whales are big, I get it. I just wanna see Moby Dick, c'mon! What's this? 'Chapter 74. The Sperm Whale's Head – Contrasted View.' Jesus Christ, Melville, OK, but after this, no more of this bloody 'cetology' stuff. If I wanted to read about their anatomy, I would've taken whale studies at uni. 'Chapter 103. Measurement of the Whale's Skeleton.' Fuck it, I'm watching *Free Willy* instead.

Every school I've worked at has used assessment descriptors based on some kind of summative assessment to create pupil data. In the past two years, however, there's been a radical change. These days, I'm tasked with assessing pupils holistically, leaving whatever summative assessment pupils might have taken in an ill-defined hinterland.

'So, how heavily should the assessment influence the predicted grade?'

---

2 Christodoulou, *Making Good Progress?*, p. 65.
3 Christodoulou, *Making Good Progress?*, p. 64.

'Oh, just a tad.'

'A tad – isn't that a little low?'

'Look, these assessments have to be really rigorous, Sam. Somewhere between a tad and a smidgen.'

'What else should feature in the predicted grade?'

'I'm not going through this again. It was made perfectly clear in the meeting: assessment – a tad; behaviour – no more than a modicum; and participation in class should make up between a vestige and a morsel. Got it?'

Level descriptors are possibly the worst part of this process. They leave you woefully underprepared for anything approximating reality. Brace yourself for endless debates about whether Jayhem is 'able to see patterns in geographical data, making links with present-day concerns, such as climate change', or whether, as Mr Cavil asserts, he is 'able to see patterns in geographical data *consistently*, making *coherent* links with present-day concerns, such as climate change, mentioning *specific* issues such as the EU blocking our ability to speak out and protect polar bears'. Well, Jayhem never mentioned the protection of any polar bears in his assessment, but he *did* mention his dad voting 'leave' because of it during our class discussion. I crack my knuckles before weighing in: 'Listen up, guys. Clearly, this morsel outweighs the tad constituted by the assessment. Jayhem deserves to be a developing activated learner and not an activated developing learner. Now, let me get at that spreadsheet because I'm about to empower some young learners up in here.'

BUT WHAT IF DATA WERE MORE ACCURATE?

What if we could say with 100% certainty that our descriptors were accurate, our marking reliable, and that such grades could predict how well pupils might do at GCSE?[4] Imagine if grades could be as straightforward as the price of a tin of baked beans. Surely, then we'd have some predictive validity. Price them at £10 and nobody's going to buy them. Discount them to 10p and you've got a riot on your hands.

But I'd still be sitting here saying 'So what?' As marketing guru Rory Sutherland puts it, 'More data leads to better decisions. Except when it doesn't ... it's important to remember that big data all comes from the same place – the past.'[5] My favourite example of perfectly accurate data being misleading comes from *The Choice Factory* by Richard Shotton:

First is the experience of Tom Leahy who, when he was head of marketing at Tesco, analysed the performance of their gluten-free products. The sales data hinted it was an under-performing section – those that bought gluten-free goods only spent a few pounds on these items each shopping trip. A naive interpretation suggested de-listing them to free up valuable shelf space.

However, sceptical of the numbers, Leahy interviewed gluten-free shoppers and discovered that their choice of supermarket was determined by the availability of these products. They didn't want to make multiple shopping trips, so they visited whoever had the specialist goods ... Leahy used this insight to launch Tesco's hugely successful 'Free From' range long before the competition.[6]

The additional point is that a supermarket can always make changes to influence consumer behaviour. There's a single independent variable – price – and consumers either buy or they don't. Teachers

---

4   Dylan Wiliam certainly doesn't think we could ever say this about school data: '[Value-added measures] have almost no reliability. They're just basically noise. Progress measures for individual students are just not worth having, they're just a waste of time': Wiliam and Christodoulou, Marking, Assessment, and Feedback, loc. 493.

5   Rory Sutherland, *Alchemy: The Surprising Power of Ideas That Don't Make Sense* (London: Ebury Publishing, 2019), pp. 9–10.

6   Richard Shotton, *The Choice Factory: 25 Behavioural Biases That Influence What We Buy* (Petersfield: Harriman House, 2018), p. 121.

don't have a simple lever they can pull to manipulate an outcome. And we shouldn't confuse ourselves by eliding the enormous multitude of learning attitudes, behaviours, and domains of knowledge under a single number. Instead of a lever, we have a vast control panel with various buttons, dials, and oscillometers. The complexity of inputs makes a cryptic crossword look like it came out of a Christmas cracker. In sum, a pupil's grade is quite the opposite of what it says on the tin.

MAKING LINEAR PROGRESS?

Another problem is that progress isn't linear. Pupils tested at the same starting point can attain wildly different results. Moreover, the testing at Key Stage 2 (primary school) that determines GCSE target grades is clustered and doesn't foreshadow the kinds of extreme grades pupils are liable to obtain later on.[7] Sure, a high-attaining pupil at Key Stage 2 is more likely to get a higher grade at GCSE, but the truth is that 'more children get to the "right" place in the "wrong" way, than get to the "right" place in the "right" way!'[8] Even where it allows us to assess probabilistically what proportion of the cohort obtaining a middling grade is likely to gain a level 5 or above at GCSE, the question again is 'So what?'

Probabilistic assessments can be useful, providing they inform us about an intervention. A percentage of smokers develop cancer, for instance, just as a proportion of pupils obtain a U grade. However, we can simply quit smoking to eliminate what risk of cancer exists. There's no comparable intervention to avoid getting a U, unless you count quitting your GCSE, which is not quite what we mean. Meanwhile, the factors determining GCSE targets are various – lack of phonics instruction, undiagnosed special needs, paucity of knowledge-based instruction at Key Stage 2. Which do we turn our attention to, for which pupils, and for how long? Data obtained at the cohort level answers none of these questions. As Sherrington

---

7   Mike Treadaway, Why Measuring Pupil Progress Involves More Than Taking a Straight Line, *FFT Education Data Lab* (5 March 2015). Available at: https:// ffteducationdatalab.org.uk/2015/03/why-measuring-pupil-progress-involves-more-than-taking-a-straight-line.
8   Treadaway, Why Measuring Pupil Progress.

says, 'you can stare at the numbers and grades all day long and no child learns anything more as a result'.[9] And I'm sorry to trot this one out as well but 'weighing the pig doesn't make it fatter'.[10]

The final problem is that of expectations and the Pygmalion effect. In one study, 'researchers falsely told teachers that some of their students had been identified as potential high achievers'.[11] These students made larger gains in academic performance, regardless of whether they were higher-, middle-, or lower-ability students. Meanwhile, we know that ordinary assessments, such as those taken at Key Stage 2 to determine GCSE target grades, are biased against disadvantaged SEN pupils and ethnic minorities.[12] This is compounded by the fact that 'children with low initial attainment have particularly unpredictable future attainment'.[13] Often, we take an absence of evidence (lack of knowledge) at Key Stage 2 as evidence of absence (lack of ability). This does our kids a disservice. Imagine being predicted a level 3 at GCSE. I'm sorry, but unless you're an unusually resilient pupil, you're hardly going to work yourself into the ground to obtain such an embarrassing grade. Far more likely, you'll conclude that (a) geography isn't for you, (b) you're a visual learner anyway, (c) imagination is more important than knowledge, and (d) fuck this, I'm joining the army/navy/a Royal Caribbean cruise liner.

Does data actually serve any purpose, then? You know what, I think it does. On his blog, Didau shares a lovely collage of different secondary school data sets.[14] If you thought PowerPoint animations were impressive, you should see the kind of groundbreaking work people are doing on Excel. If the development staff at Atari had been this creative, maybe we'd still be sitting in arcades today playing whatever sequel to *Super Breakout* these wizards had dreamt up – Differentiation Quest, perhaps, or TLR Tycoon. Yeah, now I'm starting to appreciate why data is such a fetish in schools. You wanna

---

9   Sherrington, *The Learning Rainforest*, p. 116.
10   Sherrington, *The Learning Rainforest*, p. 117.
11   Busch and Watson, *The Science of Learning*, p. 9
12   Christodoulou, *Making Good Progress?*, p. 105.
13   Treadaway, Why Measuring Pupil Progress.
14   David Didau, The Madness of Flight Paths, *The Learning Spy* (23 March 2019). Available at: https://learningspy.co.uk/assessment/how-do-we-know-pupils-are-marking-progress-part-1-the-problem-with-flightpaths.

know the answer? Type in www.addictinggames.com on your school browser. Guess what? 'Access denied. Your account has been flagged.' You kidding me? I only wanted to play *Neon Tetris*, for crying out loud. What ever shall I do? It's at this point that you open up that Excel spreadsheet and start 'doing' some hardcore 'data', hehehe. Try stopping me now, SLT.

Except that they won't, and they never will, and this has to do with something called 'careerism', for which data is the precondition. Linear progress is for management, silly, not the pupils. Anyway, Phil Beadle puts it better than I can. Enjoy this one:

Data tells management which of the kids in Year 11 are likely to get the grades that will obtain management a promotion, and so we treat data with reverence, as it is likely to be the difference between a Lada and a convertible Audi with 'go faster' stripes for the deputy head.[15]

I really do wonder if Beadle has ever worked at KFC because, boy, can he serve up a zinger. Yowzah.

BLAGGING YOUR WAY THROUGH DATA

Again, I've got my spreadsheet open. My humours, chakras, and corresponding celestial bodies are all in perfect alignment. And now, in communion with the Pythagorean harmonies of nature, I am going to derive my top five things to say about data in meetings. Here we go:

1 'This class has a high proportion of pupil premium kids. Perhaps we should spread them around a bit. That way, in group-reading tasks, the PP kids can be helped by their peers.'

   I call this one Trickle-Down Education for Poor Kids. The assumption is that PP is a useful proxy, which, in a sense, it is. PP kids are likely to have a smaller vocabulary than non-PP

---

15 Beadle, *How to Teach*, p. 205.

kids.[16] Nevertheless, the jury's out on the implications. We know that peer feedback is far less useful than teacher feedback.[17] And wouldn't having all of the PP kids sitting together enable the teacher to target misconceptions more easily? Perhaps. But if you want to do well in a meeting, don't say any of this. Besides, if we have the PP names written in red, intermixed with the ambers and greens, it's way more visually appealing.[18]

2 'This class has a high proportion of white British boys. My feeling is that there is a high potential for disruption here. Perhaps we should spread them around a bit. That way, in assessment-style tasks, the WBBs are unlikely to distract one another.'

This one's known as Some of My Best Friends Are White British Boys. Now, disclaimer here: I am, in fact, a white British boy. In my area of Coventry – Willenhall – there are a lot of white British people and they're pretty disruptive, I'm not gonna lie. One time, the Co-op had to blast classical music from speakers by the door to get rid of the yobbos (Mozart being a well-known yobbo repellent). Anyway, the Co-op closed down and now we have a Heron Foods. My point? If my teachers had known that I was a white British boy, I might not be living in Willenhall right now. Perhaps I'd be a professor at Harvard University, studying the mating habits of wild pangolins, and during my studies have inadvertently discovered the vaccine for coronavirus. You never know.

3 'There's a fair number of high-attainers in this class. This means that, although we should be pitching to the top anyway, there has to be sufficient stretch and challenge for the most able.'

---

16 'From birth to 48 months, parents in professional families spoke 32 million more words to their children than parents in welfare families': Alex Quigley, *Closing the Vocabulary Gap* (Abingdon and New York: Routledge, 2018), p. 4.

17 'But in light of Nuthall's discovery that most of the feedback pupils get on their work is from each other, and most of that is wrong, it's clear that this is hugely unreliable': Didau, *What If Everything You Knew About Education Was Wrong?*, p. 283.

18 Red, Amber, Green, or RAG rating, is a system whereby pupils are given a colour code to indicate their current level of attainment. PP kids aren't necessarily always red. In fact, they are often the highest attainers. My problem is that, all too frequently, we lazily conflate low attainment with imperfect correlates, such as the income bracket of a pupil's parents

Good Will Hunting for a Starter Task. This one's tricky because you have to deploy some serious doublethink. No, I don't believe in stretch and challenge. Yes, we need to pitch to the top – when don't we? I know that whenever I teach the topic of beaches, I'm making it pretty bloody difficult. I mean, there are so many ways to teach beaches. The easy way: 'Hey, look, a beach.' And the hard way, as I do when pitching to the top: 'Look at this broad deposition of fine sediment. Avast, ye hearties, moor the vessel starboard side by the jetty and hand me my rum.' However, in my thorough analysis of this spreadsheet, I can see that there are a disproportionate number of high-attainers (i.e. more than seven). This is why I'm making the unusual case for stretch and challenge. In effect, I'm saying, 'Look, this class data is completely unusual. I've spotted it, unlike you amateurs. We have to take radical action.'

4   'The vast majority of pupils in this class are EAL. Do we have the support staff for this? I'll do what I can in terms of differentiated resources, but we have to be mindful of limitations. I'm glad they're in this class – it's important for them to be immersed in the English language – but my instruction is going to be quite tricky.'

Oh, look, it's Throw Every EAL Pupil in the School at a Newly-Qualified Teacher and See What Happens. My favourite. First off, English as an additional language covers a large spectrum. Some EAL kids are the best English speakers in the entire school. For others, saying they have English as an additional language is like me saying, 'My other car is a DeLorean with a flux capacitor.' Whatever in-house EAL expert you have will tell you that immersion is good for these pupils. But even as someone whose knowledge of languages ends abruptly at Duolingo Level 2 (*en français*), I can tell you that saying immersion is good for certain EAL students is like saying the boy in the wave pool with the rubber-ducky armbands should try out for the synchronised swimming team. Send me to France. Go on. I guarantee I won't learn anything. I'm white British, so maybe I'll learn to bellow football chants and throw crumpled cans of Carling at French people. But that's all. Anyway, don't point out any of this in a meeting and you'll be A-OK.

5   'In the last mock, Sundus got a level 3, but this time, she got a level 3.8. Her target is a level 6 so this is good progress. I think your idea of movement breaks might have helped, but I've also been trialling Socratic questioning. She may need some intervention – can I put her down? – but by the end of Year 11 she should get there.'

Here we have the Tom-Tom Go, also known as the Stating the Bloody Obvious. Unbelievably, just like everything else in this list, I promise you that it will work. It goes like this. Think of mock papers like stops on a roadmap. To make a good impression, simply name the level they got at each stop and give a plausible reason for the difference between each grade – examples I've heard range from 'He's absent a lot' and 'It was Ramadan', through to the classic 'His dog passed away after a long battle with gout'. You can say anything you like providing you find a way to exculpate your own teaching. Do the pupils matter? Of course, but not in meetings. For instance, if a pupil earned a level 5 in the autumn mock but only a level 3 in the spring one, tell your manager: 'We'd been focusing on _____ skills'. Insert whatever skill appertains to your subject, be it map skills, inference skills, whatever. These are suitably nebulous and unverifiable.

You can even blame the mock paper: 'Well, the mock didn't align with the teaching sequence we set out at the beginning of the year.' If the kids sat an easy mock in the spring term, then well done you. You've almost certainly made progress since the autumn. In this case, success was down to two things: (a) whatever departmental gimmick happens to be in vogue and (b) a unique strategy that you created after painstaking years of research, setbacks, and fist-shaking at a cloud-contused sky with tearful expostulations that you 'just wanna help these darn kids'. This way, credit is due to both you and your boss, and you can all go home with that warm fuzzy feeling. Finally, you need to cap off your exposition with a suggestion in response to the question, 'What do we do, going forward?' Just say 'some intervention' since it can mean anything the higher-ups want it to.

My problem with data is not data itself. I am not against quantitative analysis or research. Neither am I saying that 'Britain has had enough of experts.'[19] My issue is the *provenance* of the data in schools. Often, diagnostic tests are slung together with scarce consideration for how well they actually cover the knowledge domain or replicate the final exam. Worst of all, once a score is inputted into a spreadsheet, it is transmuted into a reality.

To take spreadsheets on face value is to become blinkered. Here is one example. I took on a Year 11 geography class and they sat a mock exam immediately after the summer holidays. The papers were marked and a process similar to money laundering occurred whereby those grades became a solid currency among the SLT. Then, the SLT issued the blanket statement that predicted grades, which were to be sent home to parents, could be no more than a grade higher than the performance in the mock.

Believe it or not, it is possible to get a level 2 in a geography paper right after the summer holidays. If you've been busy windsurfing in Malaga, it's quite unlikely that you've bothered learning much about sustainable traffic management strategies in Freiburg: 'Sorry, mum – I'm getting pretty sick of the beach. The sea is too blue and it clashes with my outfit. The sun? If I stay in it too long my skin's going to turn that nasty golden brown colour again. As for the drinks – look, there's only so much ice-cold refreshment a person can take. If you need me, I'll be at the hotel reading up on tram networks and vehicle registration fees.' We need to reconcile common sense with the findings of educational researchers.[20]

Later on, the grades that are predicted on the basis of that terrible mock paper will be sent home in the post, leaving young Kayleigh or whoever to think she's on course for a level 3. And what will that mean for her later performance? Moving forward, we need to ask ourselves the following: 'Are schools creating a kind of cognitive dissonance by holding assemblies telling students that a fixed

---

19 Henry Mance, Britain Has Had Enough of Experts, Says Gove, *Financial Times* (3 June 2016). Available at: https://www.ft.com/content/3be49734-29cb-11e6-83e4-abc22d5d108c

20 It's not as straightforward as saying 'we need more common sense', since many findings are counterintuitive, as with interleaving, spaced practice, the bean bag study I mention in 'Textbooks and Social Mobility', and much else.

mindset is bad but then giving those same students fixed target grades in the classroom?'[21]

SEATING PLANS: THE HUNDRED FLOWERS TECHNIQUE

I have left the discussion of seating plans to the end of this chapter because much of what I have to say – especially about mixed-ability seating plans – is contingent upon arguments made in 'On Assessments' and 'Blagging Your Way Through Data'.

This is one of those last-but-not-least scenarios, since if seating plans were software, they'd be your boot-up, your operating system, and your anti-malware protection all rolled into one. There are a number of philosophies on seating plans. Some say mixed ability. Others say boy-girl. Blind insistence on either of these is to ignore the more nuanced syntax of pupil interaction.

The creation of a mixed-ability seating plan is a mere box-ticking exercise. I would avoid it, or at least create one that is only ostensibly mixed ability so as to blindside SLT.

The problem resides with the very nature of the data itself. A human being cannot accurately assess another human being from words, categories, and qualifications alone. Just ask a recruiter: CVs don't tell you very much. Intuition conveys a much greater volume of nuanced information than crude labels like higher, middle, or lower, especially when the provenance, reliability, and validity of these labels is highly questionable. We have evolved over millennia to become uncannily accurate judges of character. Let's make use of this adaptive cognitive mechanism.

If you are a new teacher taking on a class for the first time, the best is the Hundred Flowers strategy. It works like so. Firstly, tell the pupils to stand behind the chair they want to sit at. When all pupils are standing behind their preferred chair, you can then shuffle them

---

21 Hendrick and Macpherson, *What Does This Look Like in the Classroom?*, loc. 1724.

until they are in a more sensible seating arrangement. The key to the Hundred Flowers technique is to keep the kids standing until you're sure they're in the right place. The best way to do this is to keep moving them until they stop smiling. Then they sit. It's that simple.

Why is this necessary? Because you have to capture the attention of thirty kids, continuously, over the space of an hour. And, for children, the opinion of their peer group is vastly more important to them than the opinions of parents and teachers.

If you're an emotional thinker, moving them until they stop smiling may sound harsh, but we need to remember the aims of education. Pupils are there to learn new information. You're not running a crèche. If we allow pupils to sit wherever they like, they'll mess around, since it's the path of least resistance. As Didau and Rose put it, 'our ability to self-regulate represents a key cognitive difference between young children and adults'.[22] Seating kids next to their friends and expecting them to behave is like telling them not to think of a pink elephant or a white bear – it has the opposite effect. Indeed, Wegner et al. found that 'trying to not think about something makes someone more likely to think about that thing. This is known as "The Rebound Effect".'[23]

You might think you've found a solution by clapping your hands together and saying, 'OK, little kiddies, today you can sit wherever you like – yay! But remember, you *have* to self-regulate.' Ironically, telling them to self-regulate will be more damaging than leaving it moot. To succeed, remove the temptation altogether.

BUT MIXED-ABILITY SEATING PLANS ARE WELL-SUPPORTED BY RESEARCH!

One piece of research frequently cited in favour of mixed-ability seating plans is the Montana State University study by Angela

22 Didau and Rose, *What Every Teacher Needs to Know About Psychology*, p. 176.
23 Daniel M. Wegner, David J. Schneider, Samuel R. Carter and Teri L. White, Paradoxical Effects of Thought Suppression, *Journal of Personality and Social Psychology*, 53(1) (1987), 5–13, cited in Busch and Watson, *The Science of Learning*, p. 24.

Hammang.[24] Tragically, it seems that educational bloggers are either unable or unwilling to use the power of Ctrl + F. In all 111 pages of research, there is no mention of 'mixed ability'. The three conditions were random, student-chosen, and teacher-chosen seating plans. Although the teacher-chosen seating plan saw 'increased outcomes' for lower-attainers with no impact on higher-attainers, this has nothing to do with mixed ability. One teacher even wonders how 'things would have been different had I paired kids up in a seating chart where one higher level student could help a fewer [sic] low performing students in his vicinity! I guess it is something to think about for next time.'[25] This is one of the final entries in the teacher journal for this study, suggesting mixed-ability seating plans were not even trialled once, let alone consistently, throughout the course of the experiment.

GROUPS OR ROWS?

If it were up to me, I'd seat pupils in rows rather than groups. But I do not insist on this because there is evidence that 'activities which require communication between students, such as generating lists of ideas, are best served by group seating'.[26] I have a hunch that rows are best for the majority of class teachers. This is because Ashman highlights the tendency for 'social loafing' in group activities, where one pupil does most of the work.[27] However, due to the volume of contrary evidence, I've had to moderate my own view. Indeed, from a cognitive standpoint, pupils could benefit from 'the greater variety of sight lines' offered by multiple grouped seating plans.[28] You wouldn't think that your ambient surroundings would have much of an impact on the knowledge you retain, would you? But as Didau states, 'we tie the acquisition of new ideas to what we

---

24 Angela J. Hammang, The Effect of Seating Assignments on Student Achievement in the Biology Classroom. Master's thesis (July 2012), p. 7. Available at: https://www.teachertoolkit.co.uk/wp-content/uploads/2017/05/HammangA0812.pdf.

25 Hammang, The Effect of Seating Assignments, p. 85.

26 Greg Ashman, Research on Seating Arrangements, *Filling the Pail* (12 October 2012). Available at: https://gregashman.wordpress.com/2016/10/12/research-on-seating-arrangements.

27 Ashman, Research on Seating Arrangements.

28 Didau and Rose, *What Every Teacher Needs to Know About Psychology*, p. 68.

already know in the visual and emotional contexts'.[29] Sitting in rows is unlikely to give pupils the varied sight lines they need in order to transfer knowledge between contexts.[30] But, then again, in Kevin Wheldall's research, 'children stayed on task for about 70 per cent of the time when seated in groups and for 88 per cent of the time when seated in rows'.[31]

You're right to feel disorientated by the research. I felt like a cuckoo-clock soldier with all the back and forth in that last paragraph. Maybe we should use group tables for discussion-based lessons and rows for written and assessment activities. The problem here is that a lesson is not solely one or the other. Then there is the practical matter of moving the desks. Plus, if you share rooms with other teachers you have to take their style into account.

GROUP-TABLE FENG SHUI

When arranging pupils in groups, you want to minimise disruption. To do this, consider who are the disruptive characters. Usually, these are the popular children. If you feel that your self-esteem is too high, and that you'd like to be humbled consistently by having children whisper swearwords about you, by all means seat them together. If

---

29 David Didau, What Every Teacher Needs to Know About … Seating Plans, The Learning Spy (9 September 2016). Available at: https://learningspy.co.uk/planning/every-teacher-needs-know-seating-plans.

30 'If students are regularly moved they encounter a greater variety of sight lines and thus a greater and more unstable range of visual cues. Their ability to transfer what they learned within the classroom improves': Didau and Rose, What Every Teacher Needs to Know About Psychology, p. 68. However, Didau also says the following: 'To be clear, the benefits of the order created by sitting kids in rows probably outweighs the fairly mild advantages of varied seating. Also, the research on the variation effect is more nuanced than this but is certainly not a justification for grouped seating arrangements … I can't really see how being in grouped tables provides additional sight lines' (personal communication, 27 October 2020). From my perspective, seating plans that vary across the course of the year provide a variety of sight lines since pupils could be facing the rear window in term 1, the whiteboard at the front in term 2, and so on.

31 Kevin Wheldall and Larraine Bradd, Classroom Seating Arrangements and Classroom Behaviour. In Kevin Wheldall (ed.), Developments in Educational Psychology, 2nd edn (Abingdon and New York: Routledge, 2013), pp. 181–195, cited in Ashman, Research on Seating Arrangements.

not, you want to set up a triage: high-popularity boys and girls, studious boys and girls, and children who fit neither category.

Remember, although school popularity is a stupid concept, it is a social reality for the kids. Don't go thinking you're exempt, either. How often do we accord somebody social status because of their job title, dress sense, or the car they drive? You can ignore it, sure. It's unpalatable. But don't pretend you've never witnessed promotion-seeking members of staff gravitate towards the deputy head in the smoking shelter on a staff night out. 'Oh no, I don't smoke. Just loving the al fresco vibe.' If you're looking to be canonised or buried in Westminster Abbey, feel free to pretend that arbitrary popularity doesn't exist. But I assure you that it does, and remember: it's no reflection on the children under your duty of care.

I was popular at school because I was an arsehole. I can distinctly remember the day I went from a middling level of popularity to becoming one of the most talked about pupils. I'd been terrorising Mr Campbell-Bannerman for weeks before hitting something of a disruptor's block. It was always the same. How many more things could I set aflame with a Bunsen burner? I needed to diversify my portfolio. The next breakthrough could make for a biopic starring Benedict Cumberbatch. One languid summer afternoon, I noticed a friend struggling to stack one stool on top of another. They should have collapsed together but these two stubbornly refused. Aha, I thought, they're the wrong way round. And, thus, an epiphany: you could stack the stools on top of one another to create a structure. All I had to do was wait until the teacher left the room and I would have one of the most viral disruptions in the history of Willenhall School.

Sure enough, ten minutes in and Mr Campbell-Bannerman had extracted Cain. Cain had brought in Lucozade bottles filled with vodka during lunchtime and was thus something of a 'madhead'. Incidentally, he was also popular. Members of the science department were soon standing outside the classroom looking concerned, each taking turns to remonstrate with young Cain in spite of his insistence that he 'couldn't give a fuck'. I stacked the stools. No one said a word. Three, four, and finally five. I clambered up the clanking, trembling structure before removing a fibreglass ceiling tile. I held my arm out and my friend Taylor passed me another stool. I pushed this stool up into the ceiling and affixed it to the wobbling tower. At last, with the aid of a boost, I climbed into the ceiling void.

With Cain sent home, the door opened, and out of curiosity the head of science looked in at the class. 'Remarkably quiet, sir,' said Mr Blowhard. The stools were trembling vigorously. 'What's this?' he said, walking towards the tower. 'Some kind of experiment?' One of the legs slipped and I came crashing through. The stools scattered, though one hung in the ceiling like a chandelier frame. I thudded onto the desk as fuzz from ruptured fibreglass drifted down like confetti. The class was in uproar. Mr Blowhard barely understood what had happened. And Mr Campbell-Bannerman looked very nervous indeed.

Fellow pupils would reminisce about this for years afterwards. And from here on out, if you'd ever sat me with my friends – well, 'Terror Time soon, my brudda.'

In terms of the seating plan then, the consideration of popularity can help you. For group tables, what's most crucial is not who is sitting next to whom, but which pupils sit across from one another. Any grizzled, veteran class teacher can tell you this. You want to have studious girls sitting across from high-popularity boys, and vice versa. But wait, isn't this a mixed-ability seating plan? No. Sometimes popular children are high-attainers and studious pupils can quite easily be middle- or low-attainers. Furthermore, mixed-ability seating plans take no account of *where pupils are looking*.

Remember, most pupil disruption occurs at the extremes. It is the high-popularity children, the ones most concerned with their social lives, who are most keen to terrorise. In each class, you should only have a handful of these pupils. It's the same for unconditionally studious children: they're a blessing but a rarity. Most children lie somewhere in-between. The point is to neutralise these extremes. When high-popularity children look around and see only pupils getting their heads down, they've no audience, and they'll set to work too.

Finally, the best way to use group tables is to have high-popularity children (annoying arseholes) looking away from the centre of the room. They can face the front, for instance, but only if they are sitting at the front. Otherwise, many other pupils will be in their eye line. Ideally, they should face either out of the window or towards the door. However, in some cases, these pupils may (rightfully) complain that they have to turn to see the board. This is another problem with group tables – somebody has to occupy these spaces. In this case, just make sure they're sitting at the front.

THE SIMPLICITY OF ROWS

This is going to be a very short section. Why? Because rows do most of the work for you. In a class of four rows, use the four corners strategy. Sit the most disruptive and popular pupils on the front row on the far left and right, and at the back row on the far left and right. Job done. We don't have to worry about pupils facing the centre of the room in this scenario because they're only looking at the backs of pupils' heads.

SEATING PLAN TWEAKS

If you're a stern-faced, neo-Victorian tyrant teacher with a photo of Michael Gove in a filigree locket, you might prefer rows. Similarly, if you're a fuzzy-wuzzy, flip-flop wearing vegetarian who campaigns for nuclear disarmament on the weekends, you probably prefer groups. Or … could it be that we stop allowing our political philosophies to bleed into our interpretations of what works? I don't like grouped tables. You can probably tell. But if I had the option to do away with them, I wouldn't, because there's a chance I'd be making a mistake. (Happily, COVID-19 has achieved this on our behalf.) If you find yourself having to put up with the table configurations of other teachers, then you won't have time to change the entire layout, but you can make subtle tweaks.

For instance, group tables create more fertile ground for disruption.[32] In this case, why not detach two of the smaller tables from the grouped tables and place them at the front? Don't do it straight away. By all means, let the pupil who wants to disrupt put his foot in

---

32 Ashman, Research on Seating Arrangements.

it first, and then tweak the arrangement. Moving two tables will take about ten seconds, if that. Just make sure to put them back at the end.

Similarly, rows are notably deficient in terms of group discussion. For this scenario, instruct pupils on rows 1 and 3 to turn around and face the rows behind them. They can discuss any topic in groups of four. It won't work for group *work*, since four pupils will be sitting at a two-seater desk. That said, I say elsewhere that group work is immoral, so maybe this isn't such a bad thing. Group *discussion*, by all means, once the pupils are sufficiently knowledgeable; but group work – yuck, no thank you. I'm sure it was a brilliant invention, once upon a time, up there with square pegs in round holes so far as giant leaps for mankind are concerned. Maybe I'm wrong. Far be it from the creator of the wooden drinks dispenser to pass judgement.

Overall, providing you use the Hundred Flowers and four corners strategies, in addition to considerations of where popular pupils are looking, you can create durable seating plans every time.

Chapter 7

CREATING RESOURCES

As Mahatma Gandhi once said, simplicity is next to godliness. The theme of this chapter is that a resource should only ever be a piece of paper or a textbook. By the end, you will discover that the only resource of any value is the one in your head. Inspirational, right? The sort of message you can imagine seeing on a beauty therapist's Instagram account against a rain-dappled window pane overlooking the sea, with palm fronds on either side. But far from being a quotation to pin up beside that woodcut wine-bottle ornament – 'Veni vidi vino' or 'Stop and smell the rosé' – I promise you that this is the truth. Please, for the sake of the environment, wean yourself off of that photocopier. As for the print credits, you can cash these in at HR. Make sure to barge in without knocking and thump your fist on the desk. They love that.

WHY OVER-PLANNING ALWAYS FAILS

This scenario should not demand too much imagination. You've spent your entire weekend planning a series of lessons. The textbook is now dog-eared, having been riffled abusively, and your PowerPoints have been formatted to within an atom's breadth. What could go wrong?

Ironically, I think this is exactly the point where everything can and will go wrong. Why? Because through all the frenetic keyboard clattering, you have merely built up battlements in your mind against your pupils – crenellations of confidence that are ripe for destruction. There is no script for reality, and lessons are no different. Worst of all, when you plan everything in a brittle sequence, your lessons become incompatible with the messy reality of learning.

Part of the problem here is the delusion that in education progress is linear. Evidence against this assertion comes from someone who probably wasn't very fun at birthday parties: Hermann Ebbinghaus.

He was a German psychologist who committed 'nonsense syllables' to memory. He chose these deliberately since items like 'ka' or 'li' would have few associations in long-term memory. At intervals, he noted how many he'd forgotten. Each time he reviewed the information, the curve tapered off more gradually (he forgot at a slower rate), but it was never permanently retained. Thus, progressive decay is the rule of memory.[1] This explains the summer holiday knowledge fade-out, also known as the windsurfing in Malaga (WSIM) effect.

Ebbinghaus taught us two lessons: (1) we can use spaced learning to help us forget more gradually (making learning more durable), and (2) progress is more two steps forward, one step back than it is linear.[2] Teaching is neither lighting fires nor filling pails. It's loading a bucket with hot coals that are smothered at the bottom and fiery at the top. The idea that a sequence of lessons could adequately track the idiosyncrasies of remembering and forgetting among pupils is the Laplace's demon of learning – the hypothetical creature that French scientist Pierre-Simon Laplace proposed could predict the future, providing it knew the location and momentum of every particle in the universe.[3] We cannot know the prior learning or minds of our learners,[4] and until we can, linear progress is illusory.

Let us take up the story, then, of the weekend warrior teacher on his first Monday back. It is 8.57am, he boots up the computer, and is now pacing back and forth. Oh dear, what's this? 'Windows is updating. 0.001% complete. Don't turn off your computer.' Immediately, his bowels turn to jelly.

It is 9.03am and the pupils have knocked on the door, waited a patient ten seconds for an invitation to come in, and are now at their chairs, peppering him with questions. 'Hi sir, what are we doing

---

1   Busch and Watson, *The Science of Learning*, p. 4.
2   Whether we review or test material, we are 'improving retention by lessening the rate of decay': McCourt, *Teaching for Mastery*, p. 86.
3   Pierre-Simon Laplace, *A Philosophical Essay on Probabilities* (New York: John Wiley, 1902), p. 4.
4   'Most students would already know about half of what they were being taught, but each would know a different half. If we were to assess students' prior knowledge before teaching each new topic, we would be unlikely to find out much to help us in our teaching': Didau and Rose, *What Every Teacher Needs to Know About Psychology*, p. 66.

today?' 'Sir, do bugs count as pets?' 'Hey sir, how come you have a beard in like two days?'

Meanwhile, he's at the computer, sweating bullets and waiting for that juicy PowerPoint to come; yet somewhere at the back of his mind, in confidential whispers, 'computer says no'. Because he spent so long planning it, he cannot let go of that bloody PowerPoint. And, at the base of his brain there is that single totem pole with the Microsoft Office logo, all thoughts dancing around it, illuminated against the impending darkness.

This is a very real phenomenon, similar to stage fright. How do you escape it? Sometimes it seems like teaching is a kind of quicksand: the more you struggle, the deeper you sink. The only difference is that the solution is not simply to do nothing.

There is only one way of planning for every eventuality. You need to know your subject back to front, inside out, round and round. When you truly internalise your subject, are passionate about it, and have crafted various stories and analogies inside your head to explain challenging concepts, you can teach with just a board pen. Better than, 'Technical difficulties. Please stand by.'

There is never a quick fix. You cannot try to input all of the effort for your lessons into PowerPoints during a convenient weekend slot and then expect to simply plug and play when you step foot in the classroom. You have to plan in order to facilitate spontaneity.

Here is how I would do it. First of all, I would think about my learning objectives. I would have a PowerPoint that has some pictures, a link to a video, and some tasks that correspond to my learning objectives. I do not know the shape my lesson is going to take. It could be that I have a starter question that keeps them engaged, which somehow mutates into something more, and I may spend my whole lesson on that.

As a trainee, I was told never to do this, but one starter I had was: 'If Protestantism and Catholicism were desserts, what would they be?' We had a very fruitful, hour-long discussion, with the cherry on top being that I was hired on the basis of this observation.

If you are a trainee, you'll be reluctant to have sparse text on your PowerPoint, but that's OK. Advice to wean you off text-heavy slides is available in Chapter 8.

PLANNING ON PAPER

When it comes to lesson planning, you should come up with the bulk of your ideas with pen and paper, and only afterwards make a PowerPoint. This is because computers are inherently distracting. Emails ping into your inbox like pinballs in an arcade machine, computer windows mass like a deck of playing cards, and there is always the persistent little voice at the back of your mind: 'Go on, google something irrelevant. You know you want to.'

Many years ago, I read a book called *The Presentation Secrets of Steve Jobs* by Carmine Gallo. Whatever you think about Steve Jobs, the man was a visionary who knew how to capture an audience. You might be saying to yourself, 'Hang on, I'm a geography/maths/history teacher, not a Silicon Valley CEO,' but it's irrelevant, I promise you. Pupils are far more vociferously critical of presentations than any amount of turtlenecked Apple fanboys. When you initially take on a class, you need to be able to hook your audience immediately, and thereafter establish your authority. In his book, Gallo observes that PowerPoint bullet points 'force you to create a template that represents the exact opposite of what you need to speak like [Steve Jobs]'.[5]

Think about it. For GCSE geography, I might plan a lesson on why some countries are rich and some are poor. I would end up killing the topic by having it readily dissected for my pupils. Instead, I need to tell the story. People are poor because the British Empire took over most of the developing world, plundered it for its resources, and left a slew of failed governments in their wake. They are poor because of malarial mosquitoes and the tsetse fly that kills their cattle. They're poor because a parasitic guinea worm coils up inside their intestinal tracts and lays its eggs, or because its cousin,

---

5   Carmine Gallo, *The Presentation Secrets of Steve Jobs: How to Be Insanely Great in Front of Any Audience* (New York: McGraw Hill, 2010), p. 4.

Onchocerca volvulus, lays eggs behind their retinas, causing river blindness. Hell, even global warming plays a supporting role, turning vast tracts of land into salt-laden desert. If I want my pupils to know all of this, will I display it on the interactive whiteboard for them to see? No. Bullet points can never tell a story. If they did, we could throw Jane Austen in the bin and reach for the CliffsNotes.

Don't get me wrong. I use bullet points. But they come in after the kinds of teacher-led discussion I consider in 'Crafting Narratives' (History and Geography). Here's how I like to think of it. Humans, at a visceral level, enjoy suspense. Whenever we say something is 'interesting' – lectures, relationships, *Game of Thrones* – we are always talking about the uncertainty of 'what's coming next?' In terms of presentations and tasks, think of yourself as a French waiter – the snooty kind who brings dinner to the table under a silver cloche before ceremoniously lifting the lid. The cloche is the presentation, the task is the spatchcock chicken inside. Even if your task is a turkey it won't matter too much, since so much of teaching is smoke-screened in suspense. Does this mean I ask specious questions simply to stall for time? No. Pupils will cotton on if they aren't learning. You merely use your time presenting information in the gradual manner demanded by Rosenshine's Principles of Instruction, and suspense is what enables you to serve bite-sized chunks.[6] It's why crafting narratives is so fundamental to planning.

If you're feeling sniffy about me referring to *The Presentation Secrets of Steve Jobs* – I think it's rock solid – then maybe the psychological literature can sway you. Cognitive bottlenecks are well-documented barriers to task completion.[7] Our working memory is limited, which is why so many research-based instructional systems now advocate 'presenting information in small steps' à la Rosenshine[8] or managing the amount of information to which we are exposed.[9] By closing down your computer, you are allowing your

---

6 Barak Rosenshine, Principles of Instruction: Research-Based Strategies That All Teachers Should Know, *American Educator* (spring 2012): 12–19, 39. Available at: https://www.aft.org/sites/default/files/periodicals/Rosenshine.pdf; and Tom Sherrington, *Rosenshine's Principles in Action* (Woodbridge: John Catt Educational, 2019), pp. 63–64.
7 Willingham, *Why Don't Students Like School?*, p. 107.
8 Sherrington, *Rosenshine's Principles in Action*, p. 15.
9 Mccrea, *Memorable Teaching*, pp. 23–25.

working memory to focus solely on the mechanics of the lesson, and not 'PowerPoint design issues like fonts, colours, backgrounds, and slide transitions'.[10]

Of course, this literature refers to pupils in classrooms, but does it not apply equally to professional teachers? Unless you have been teaching for decades, you won't have the entirety of the course content lodged in your long-term memory. You just won't. Memories are like sandcastles on a beach – the sea will gouge away their foundations, topple them, and demote them to slushy little gobs of sediment. As a teacher, I think it's important to be humble in what you know, because this is always receding, which means you have to consistently reinforce it.

If we're not experts, then we have to break down our own self-instruction, just as we do for the kids in our classes. What's good for the goose is good for the gander, so to speak.

I only say all of this because I've been guilty of it myself. When I first entered the profession, I remember spending hours and hours on formatting. I'd be fiddling with the little yellow dots on the text-boxes to give them bevelled edges. One time I went through a phase of having the entire PowerPoint on one slide, with a sequence of animations so complex they'd have made Alan Turing long for the days of the Enigma code. The formatting of my PowerPoints became so abstruse that colleagues would struggle to use them, pupils would struggle to follow them, and I couldn't plan any of my lessons coherently. 'But look, mum, no slides!'

How, then, should we plan with pen and paper? Here's what I do. First off, I start from the principle that I can never know my subject well enough. Why do I do this? Because I know that stupid people are stupid because they think they know it all. This is a real phenomenon.[11] It's called the Dunning–Kruger effect, but you might have seen it on a television show called *The Apprentice*, where the popular candidates studiously ignore the suggestions of the behavioural economics grad who doesn't sell second-hand cars for a living. I guess when you've tasted success in your spit that morning, it

10 Gallo, *The Presentation Secrets of Steve Jobs*, p. 6.
11 Busch and Watson, *The Science of Learning*, p. 77.

doesn't really matter if you think the Thames is the second largest river in London or that Big Ben is twenty diameters in width.[12] To avoid gaffes of this kind, simply take your degree out of the picture frame and slap a 'back to school' sticker on your pencil case. As with rescue dogs, learning is a lifelong commitment.

Once I know that I don't know, I will sit there with pad and pen and do a bit of retrieval practice. If I'm teaching a historical topic, I might have five facts written on a piece of paper, and I'll cover these and rewrite them from memory. This allows me to explicitly recall whatever I need to know in class the moment I'm put on the spot. Obviously, I will know more than these five facts – I'll have read around the subject at home. The point is that these facts are locked and loaded, and they'll give me anchor points for other narratives and analogies that I may want to introduce in my lesson.

When I have warmed up my mind a little, I will start to jot down vague storylines, and I will try to research the odd story with some human interest, perhaps as a hook. One time, I knew I was going to have to teach the topic of soil erosion to the most disruptive Year 10 class in the school. Riveting stuff. I sat there for half an hour thinking, 'How can I relate this to what they already know?'

When I finally had my lesson with those Year 10s, I asked them to imagine me dumping a bag of soil in the playground. Would it stay there? How would the head teacher react? But we know there's soil down on the field, right? Why will *that soil* stay, and this soil (that I bought from B&Q with my hard-earned money) disappear? Some found it funny, others told me the lump of soil would outlast my career prospects, but all knew intuitively that it was because the grass roots would bind the soil together like sinewy Velcro.

The story works for two reasons. Firstly, notice how I'm refracting a physical topic through an interpersonal lens. This hardly required much effort. The story was quite a stupid one. I said, 'What if I buy some soil from B&Q?' Not exactly *Finnegan's Wake*, is it? Still, it's hard for pupils to relate to Sub-Saharan Africans at risk from soil

---

12 Michael Moran, 10 of the (Unintentionally) Funniest Quotes from *The Apprentice*, *Digital Spy* (6 November 2018). Available at: https://www.digitalspy.com/tv/reality-tv/a869591/apprentice-quotes.

erosion when your only notion of subsistence is shopping at Aldi. Secondly, as Dehaene notes, 'learning is active and depends on the degree of surprise linked to the violation of our expectations'.[13] The idea of a teacher defiling the pupil environment is an unusual one. Besides, that's why we have displays, right? What might seem like a ridiculous story ticks two very well-defined psychological boxes.

Once you know the facts and analogies you're going to base your lesson around, you can think about the tasks the pupils will be doing. Personally, I always start my lesson with a quiz, since Rosenshine's Principles advocate daily review of past learning.[14] I'll think of some way of providing guided practice: for instance, writing a short paragraph with sentence stems.[15] I can shoulder surf and give immediate verbal feedback on these – although not always, since some commentators suggest that high levels of immediacy and frequency in feedback can degrade learning.[16] I will then try to build in an opportunity for asking lots of questions.[17] Finally, I will conclude with some kind of independent activity for my pupils – this can be marked or examined for misconceptions to be addressed in a subsequent lesson.[18]

TEXTBOOKS AND SOCIAL MOBILITY

I find it hard to get my head around the reluctance of teachers to embrace textbooks. It's as though they feel they are losing some of the magic of teaching by resorting to what is a perfectly convenient and utilitarian device. This is in spite of the fact that there is a noted correlation between textbooks and PISA test scores: 'the use of high

---

13 Dehaene, How We Learn, p. 203.
14 For a 'review of past learning', see Sherrington, Rosenshine's Principles in Action, p. 37. You may be wondering why I refer to this guide so frequently. It's because it is (a) research-based and (b) succinct enough to be implemented in schools without misinterpretation.
15 David Didau, The Secret of Literacy: Making the Implicit Explicit (Carmarthen: Independent Thinking Press, 2014), p. 42.
16 Didau and Rose, What Every Teacher Needs to Know About Psychology, p. 84.
17 Sherrington, Rosenshine's Principles in Action, pp. 27–31.
18 'Scaffolding should be withdrawn as soon as it is no longer needed': Didau and Rose, What Every Teacher Needs to Know About Psychology, p. 79.

quality text books most likely contributes to the success of these top performing education systems'.[19]

I love textbooks, and despite the almost universal bias against them, textbooks have influenced my career path. Geography departments are so desperate for staff that PGCE providers now offer a £17,000 bursary.[20] Tragically, I trained as a history teacher and was later roped into geography. I therefore had the worst of both worlds: for my bursary I got a history bus pass, and now I teach geography. Nevertheless, I often boast to my colleagues that I couldn't be happier about being a geography teacher, even though I'd had no interest prior to taking over from Caroline Bamford.

You don't have to look too far into the greatest hits compilation to be forgiven for thinking it's not a very interesting subject. 'Ooh, river erosion processes or coastal landforms at Swanage – so many options.' Then there was the fact of my ignorance. A pupil had once told me she'd been to Torquay over the weekend, and I'd observed that it was remarkable she'd been to Spain and back in such a short time. She was polite enough to correct me, 'No, sir, you're thinking of Turkey. *That's* in Spain.'

Why, you may be wondering, would I be happy about becoming a geography teacher, since it clearly wasn't my forte? It came down to arithmetic. The history GCSE had three textbooks. The geography GCSE had one. Finally, the entire GCSE would be available to me in a single location. I knew that in the long term this would pay off.

Ever since my own education, I knew how important it was to have course content centralised. Without textbooks, my CV would have cut off at a reprimand for stealing a Cadbury Creme Egg.

Let's rewind to the 2000s again. New Labour was at war in Iraq, Saddam Hussein had recently been executed, and now attention was being turned to the petty dictatorships of didacticism. The government decided to hamstring authoritarian teachers with the party streamer practices of keeping children entertained at all possible

---

19 Lucy Crehan, Why Textbooks Matter (11 January 2017). Available at: http://lucycrehan.com/why-textbooks-matter.
20 See https://getintoteaching.education.gov.uk/funding-and-salary/overview/funding-by-subject/funding-for-training-to-teach-geography.

times. Even an elite task force of CBBC stand-ins would've been routed – the Balamory Brigadiers or the Teletubby Troopers. Not even the Gruffalo himself would have been sufficiently fuzzy-wuzzy for the Department for Education and Skills. Never mind the fact that all these gimmicks ever do is allow teachers to trip themselves up, and that's when the fun for the students can really begin. I miss those days. Every month, it felt like we'd sent a new teacher packing, their Canadian replacements foolishly trying to yell us down in yet another adenoidal tirade.[21] Reinforcements aside, there was no War Against Terror waged on behalf of teachers, that's for sure.

I never once saw a textbook outside of my maths lessons. I have no idea why. It was as though an Educational Dark Ages had descended: the textbooks vanished from comprehensives as mysteriously as the works of Aristotle did from Europe. They had their Vandals and we had ours.

Every lesson, we were given sheets of paper – reams of the stuff. I can still see the inside of my drawstring bag to this day: several crumpled and blackening layers scrunched firmly at the bottom. If I hadn't thrown it away at the end of every half-term, I could have donated the compost to my neighbour's allotment. Unfortunately, in terms of any learning I was doing, these sheets were rather less fertile than my teachers had imagined.

I just remember the sense that I had no idea what was going on. You'd be given a worksheet in one lesson, which you were expected to look after, and then there'd be another sheet in the following lesson. How was anybody supposed to keep track? Maybe if I'd had a cork noticeboard with some pins and red string, I could have plotted the interconnections. But who wants to bother with that?

I have a number of clear memories when, having lost one of the sheets, I felt that I was permanently and irretrievably behind. Incidentally, this never happened in maths because we always

---

21 As Robert Peal notes, this actually happened: 'Many schools in London could not fill their rolls and depended on teachers in their probationary year or from overseas' (*Progressively Worse*, p. 52). I had at least four Canadian teachers during my time at Willenhall School. The most confusing aspect wasn't the transition, but why anybody would voluntarily come to Coventry. How did they know about it, for a start? It's not even on the weather map.

referred back to the same pages of the textbook. Is the situation any better today? As Lucy Crehan puts it, 'We seem to have given up on textbooks in England. TIMMS data suggest that only 10% of Maths teachers use textbooks as a basis for instruction, compared to 70% in Singapore and 90% in Finland'[22] – that is, the top-performing education systems mentioned by Tim Oates.

Skip forward to my professional years. As I say elsewhere in this book, what's good for the goose is good for the gander, and I believe that just as managing the cognitive load on pupils is important, so is it necessary for our teachers.[23] When I had the geography textbook, I felt the assurance of having the entire GCSE in my hands at all times – the kind of assurance a vicar would probably have once fully acquainted with the Bible. You don't see church leaders scrabbling around in a bookcase for Ezekiel or wondering where they left the Book of Revelations as they desperately print off a last-minute PDF copy before sermon time. No. There is value in having everything in one place.

I want to briefly consider some of the arguments against textbooks, if only to give myself the pleasure of clay pigeon shooting. One of the best books on memory, *Make It Stick* by Peter Brown, Mark McDaniel, and Henry Roediger, reports the findings of Kerr and Booth (1978), or what I call 'the bean bag study'.[24] In the study, two groups of 8-year-olds were trained to throw bean bags into a bucket that was three feet away. The first group practised solely with buckets three feet away from them, whereas the second group practised with buckets that were two and four feet away from them, but never three feet away. Interestingly, the second group – the ones who had varied their practice – were much better than the group who only practised with the three-foot bucket.

---

22 Crehan, Why Textbooks Matter. It should also be noted that textbook use is not another one of those Finnish fairy stories. 'In the period of rapid improvement in educational outcomes Finland used state-controlled textbooks to encourage and regulate the movement to a fully comprehensive system': Oates, Finnish Fairy Stories, p. 3.
23 McCrea, *Memorable Teaching*, pp. 47–50.
24 Brown et al., *Make It Stick*, p. 46; see also Robert Kerr and Bernard Booth, Specific and Varied Practice of Motor Skill, *Perceptual and Motor Skills*, 46(2) (1978): 395–401.

There is a sense in which simply using the textbook all of the time could be the equivalent to repetitively drilling the three-foot bucket throw, but only *if you do not vary the ways in which you interact with the content*. For instance, if I examined a textbook spread, I could say, 'Right, this is the propositional knowledge my pupils must know.' In terms of them recalling this knowledge, I could use quizzes, word-fill activities, varied drills, and interrogative elaboration based on this single domain. The bean bag study applies to tasks, not textbooks.

I believe that it is important to vary our teaching, not the resources. Teaching is like ballroom dancing, and resources are like a carpet upon which we trot out a quickstep. You can never learn to dance properly if you do not vary your techniques. But you can never even learn to stand up straight if the carpet is persistently pulled out from under you. If you do plan on varying the resources, ensure that you are doing it either for the purposes of interleaving or that you make it clear that the textbook is the true fount of all knowledge. I talk mostly for myself, but I know it is true for others too: having a semi-irrational belief in the omnipotence of the textbook makes it easier to retain the knowledge within.

The final complaint I have against textbook worriers is this. In *The Learning Rainforest*, Tom Sherrington quotes a curriculum from a conservative school in the United States.[25] The school describes how it is important to use textbooks because they offer 'vetted material', and that's when it struck me: textbooks are one of the few ways we can impose quality control on the resources we produce in our schools. Although Sherrington himself was not in favour of the curriculum he shows in the book, he nevertheless looks back fondly on the 'Mackean' of his own schooldays: 'a glorious large-format textbook … All the knowledge you needed was in there.'[26]

---

25 I know that by presenting the progressive and conservative curricula, Sherrington was attempting to show bias on both sides. The phrase just struck me as an important one. Personally, I'm not sure why textbooks fall on a political spectrum. They're useful. It reminds me of *Gulliver's Travels* where 'eleven thousand persons have, at several times, suffered death rather than submit to break their eggs at the smaller end'. See Sherrington, *The Learning Rainforest*, p. 51; and Jonathan Swift, *Gulliver's Travels* (London: Penguin, 2012 [1726]), p. 46.
26 Sherrington, *The Learning Rainforest*, p. 23.

Still, I wonder why so many commentators avoid the topic of vetted, high-quality, instructional textbooks. We know, for instance, that the French move away from teaching knowledge 'inadvertently set up a large-scale experiment on the effect of a specific, content-based curriculum at the elementary level. The results were dramatic. Between 1987 and 2007, achievement levels decreased sharply. The drop was greatest among the neediest students.'[27] We can't teach content on a whim. Dylan Wiliam argues that the solution must: align with testing,[28] standardise the curriculum,[29] empower teachers with weak subject knowledge,[30] and be available in physical space rather than the digital ether.[31] How do we ensure all of this? Try this gap-fill: T_XT_ _ _ K_ (E, B, O, O, S).

Think about it. Just because you've made something, doesn't mean that it's good. I've made some incredibly questionable resources, including a geography enrichment sheet where I'd put in the 'Go Outdoors' column: 'Children in Kenya walk on average three miles a day to secure fresh drinking water. This is approximately the distance from the KFC to town and back. Meet up with a friend and make the trip.' Never mind that this was during the Beast from the East cold wave of 2018, with black ice quilting the roads so that not even an Olympic bobsleigh team could have made it to town and back. Hardly an authentic Kenyan experience.

Textbook authors are paid to spend years working on these resources. They have a lot more time than you or I do. As a teacher, I have already devoted my life to this profession, and yet I still barely

---

27 Natalie Wexler, *The Knowledge Gap: The Hidden Cause of America's Broken Education System – and How to Fix It* (New York: Penguin, 2019), loc. 674.

28 'The pass rate for the mathematics assessment rose from 27 percent to 40 percent – a 50 percent increase in the pass rate just by ensuring good alignment between what is taught and what is tested': Dylan Wiliam, *Creating the Schools Our Children Need: Why What We Are Doing Now Won't Help* (West Palm Beach, FL: Learning Sciences International, 2018), loc. 3236–3265.

29 'What perhaps is most interesting is why teachers weren't teaching the necessary content … they thought changing what they taught to align with the content of the test would be teaching to the test, which they believed was inappropriate': Wiliam, *Creating the Schools Our Children Need*, loc. 3329.

30 'Given the weak subject knowledge of some American teachers, it seems unlikely that the average teacher could produce better instructional materials each day than the best textbook writers': Wiliam, *Creating the Schools Our Children Need*, loc. 3269.

31 'The physical experience of reading a book may be better for developing long-term memory': Wiliam, *Creating the Schools Our Children Need*, loc. 3283.

have the time to run a Twitter account, let alone produce the resource equivalent of a textbook. I'm only writing *ASBO Teacher* because I'm in lockdown. Of course, many textbooks are far from perfect, but 'imperfect' isn't equal to 'garbage'. And they're a sight better than anything teachers can concoct outside of meetings, marking, and planning.

Sometimes, colleagues storm into the office, textbook in hand, venting about how terrible and badly organised it all is, but I see through it. It's just an arrogant teacher notion they have that anything they have made is by default better than whatever anyone else has made – it's resource chauvinism. I'm often stunned when I'm presented with some 'awesome resource' on the group chat and it looks more like something thrown together on a ZX Spectrum using an obscure Soviet predecessor to Microsoft Word. 'Pah,' I'd think. 'How shit is that?' before noticing that the Geogglebox television guide Mary sent through was actually my own invention.[32] Oops. The textbook is obviously better. That's why it was published. And meanwhile, you can't even flog your Magical Mystery Monarchs card sort for £1.99 on the *TES* website.

In sum, my advice is, don't be afraid to reach for the textbook. And if your colleagues criticise you – remember, they're just jealous.

ON PRINTING: WHY GEOGRAPHY TEACHERS ARE HYPOCRITES

Paper accounts for roughly 25% of landfill waste and, as of September, we'd produced 298 million tons of paper in 2020 alone.[33] For scale, the heaviest building in the world is only 0.7 million tons.[34] When it's not recycled, paper produces methane, a greenhouse gas four times more potent than carbon dioxide. Yet

---

32 An extremely cunning pun on the word 'geography' and the television show *Gogglebox*.

33 See https://www.theworldcounts.com/stories/Paper-Waste-Facts.

34 James Bartolacci, The Tallest, Heaviest, and Most Eccentric Buildings on Earth, *Architizer* (26 July 2020). Available at: https://architizer.com/blog/inspiration/stories/guinness-world-record-day.

geography teachers, the self-appointed custodians of climate change in academia, are printing more than ever.

First off, I want to say that some teachers are eco-warriors. They are content to go into a lesson with nothing but a board pen and teach. These eco-warriors find whatever workarounds they can to avoid printing. They will use textbooks if the pupils need to read something, and if they do print out some material, it is on one sheet of A4 (maybe double-sided, if absolutely necessary). The Pride of Britain Awards need a new category for these individuals.

Why would any teacher ever need to print more than one sheet of double-sided A4? At the bottom, you could have your questions or whatever direct activities related to text (DARTs) you prefer. My contention is that printaholic teachers are the opposite of eco-warriors. They have scant regard for the people using their lessons, the children suffering them, or the forests so casually plundered for their card sort on the social, economic and political causes of deforestation.

For instance, some teachers think it's important for pupils to read four-page articles during the lesson. Some quantum physicists believe that there are an infinite number of parallel universes, but I still cannot conceive of one in which this would ever be necessary. If pupils have read a succinct page that encompasses the learning objectives, relevant content, and key vocabulary, what use is the other three pages of waffle? Perhaps I'm getting ahead of myself. Quigley notes that 'it is important that pupils read extended texts if they are to grow more sensitive to text structures'.[35] I agree. What do we do? See the previous section for some subtle hints.

Avoidance of textbooks only brings us back to the problem of resource chauvinism: remember, just because you created something, doesn't mean that it's good. Even the Hunchback of Notre Dame probably had a mother who loved him.

Printing is not only problematic in terms of the environment and the standardisation of resources; it is an inherently stress-inducing

---

35 Alex Quigley, *Closing the Reading Gap* (Abingdon and New York: Routledge, 2020), p. 136.

activity. In schools, multitasking interferes with learning; in the workplace it lowers productivity; and, finally, there is not even any scientific evidence that women are any better at it than men.

As a trainee teacher, I used to print like the Amazon rainforest was going out of fashion. I also remember why I was printing. In all honesty, it was because standing in front of thirty pupils is difficult and I wanted to buffer myself against direct interaction. Like an endangered tribesman, I was bombarding them with DARTs so that I could stall for time if the lesson went wrong.

There is a scientific basis for this: it's an offshoot of the placebo effect, what the moral psychologist Jonathan Haidt has termed 'self-placebbing'.[36] By printing, I am dosing myself with a kind of sugar pill that will fortify me against the emotional maladies of directly interfacing with the class I am teaching. The naughtier the class, the longer I would spend at the printer.

But, enough about the problems, here is the solution. For reading material – OK, print. But there is no task that is worth printing out. Providing pupils are thinking about the content, that is enough. Printing will actually limit their thinking, since they will not have to contain any information inside their brain, but rather, they will have it easily accessible on a sheet of paper. It's like telephone numbers – does anybody remember them anymore? No. Why? Because they are on our phones and we never have to dial them. Pupils need to 'dial the number' of information in order to retain it. Printing will negate this desirable difficulty.

IF IT LOOKS CRAP, IT IS CRAP

There is nothing worse than being forced to stare for nearly an hour at a PowerPoint that is garish, cluttered, and ugly. As teachers, sometimes we worry so much about throwing the baby out with the bathwater that we treat our PowerPoints like vast washbasins, attempting to squeeze into them the educational equivalent of an

---

36 See Sutherland, *Alchemy*, p. 228.

entire maternity ward. All this will allow you to do is (a) confuse the children, (b) confuse yourself, and (c) make an unsightly PowerPoint.

How should a PowerPoint look? Firstly, there should be hardly any words on it. You need a few bullet points – five at the most. If you're setting a task, position one question in the corner, and that's it. This will give your PowerPoint the clear, spacious, and minimalist look that will make learning less daunting for many of your pupils.

There are psychological reasons for keeping writing sparse. Human beings are not multitaskers. By all means text and drive if you want to. Just don't be surprised when your car bonnet turns into a lamp-post sandwich. If pupils are reading from the board, they are not listening to you. If they are listening to you, they are not reading from the board. Which is more important? By having the Complete Works of Shakespeare up on a projector screen, you're asking not just for a car crash of a lesson, but for the intellectual equivalent of a multi-car pile-up. When pupils listen to you, they are keeping their eyes on the road, so to speak.

The design principle 'form follows function' is all very well if you enjoy looking at faceless, concrete tower blocks. But is it not also the case that function can just as well follow form? Look at a Ferrari. Those sleek curves, rear spoilers, and raised wheel arches serve a purpose. What makes it appear beautiful also renders it one of the most aerodynamic cars you can buy.

Having less text on your PowerPoint ensures that your teaching is similarly streamlined. You are not a computer. There is an upper limit on what you can think about during a lesson. Pupil A might ask you how many colours there are in a rainbow; pupil B might throw a bag of Skittles at pupil C; and pupil D might declare that he will fight anybody who says that leprechauns don't exist. This sort of disruption puts you on the back foot, and if you meanwhile find yourself scanning for when Hamlet talks about slings and arrows, you're already drowning in a sea of troubles.

However, it's not just the problem of TMT, or too much text. Ugly pictures, colour schemes, and Comic Sans are just as bad.[37] I am a realist, and as much as I love Shakespeare, sometimes the story is to be sold not told. Your PowerPoint is your marketing tool, you are the salesman, and the kids care far more about McDonald's than Macbeth and Donalbain. Nor am I suggesting that you spruce up your PowerPoint by adding in vacuous images or emojis. Remember, the best marketing tool is simplicity. A good diagnostic for this is to try and imagine Steve Jobs standing in front of it. If you're unfamiliar with them, look up his PowerPoints online and see how yours compare.

For each slide of a PowerPoint, I would set the following criteria. If it is a picture slide: show, at most, two pictures. If it is a slide with text on it: no more the single sentence stating the task and five bullet points, if you need them. Finally, another kind of slide that works very well is a diagram, such as a flow chart, which will allow you to show causal relations and supplement your own questioning: the text in each box should be no more than one word long. This means that pupils will not be trying to decode written language while you are speaking. Whenever you're thinking about the amount of information on a slide, remember that working memory can only contain around four chunks of new material at a given time.[38] The only exception to the above is showing a quiz on the board for retrieval practice – I advise capping these at around six to eight questions.

The final point is subjective: make the PowerPoint look good. Really look at it and ask yourself, 'Would I feel comfortable framing this PowerPoint slide and hanging it on my living room wall?' If the answer is no, then it's junk.

---

37 As for whether Comic Sans is helpful for dyslexic readers, dyslexia researcher Professor Maggie Snowling of Oxford University says the following: 'I don't know of any serious work on this issue.' See *TES*, Does Comic Sans Help Dyslexic Learners? (21 January 2018). Available at: https://www.tes.com/news/does-comic-sans-help-dyslexic-learners.
38 Didau and Rose, *What Every Teacher Needs to Know About Psychology*, p. 37.

POWERPOINTS AND RESOURCES: THE LAUREL AND HARDY RULE

Any PowerPoint you create should be simple. The resources that accompany your lesson can be larger: you can use one or two sheets of reading material or a textbook, if you see fit.

This is the Laurel and Hardy rule. Your PowerPoint is slender like Stan Laurel; your resources can afford to be a little chunkier like Oliver Hardy. The PowerPoint is not the resource, just as you would not expect Hardy to squeeze into one of Laurel's suits. They both have their part to play and these parts are to remain separate.

The reason for this rule is fairly simple. When pupils are reading they need the utmost focus, so any interference is liable to distract them. If the resource is on the desk, they don't have to look across an entire classroom to squint at whatever is written on the board. And if they do have to look at the PowerPoint, they will not have to concentrate on it for any sustained period of time.

If, for whatever reason, you decide to make your pupils read *The Decline and Fall of the Roman Empire* on the interactive whiteboard, you will find your lesson swiftly sacked. We are social creatures. If I see my mate – smirking and nodding at me to instigate some kind of mischief – well, I'd be rude not to, wouldn't I? By contrast, if you thunk down the six mammoth volumes of Gibbon's classic work on the desk in front of me, obviously I'm still going to wind up messing about. Remember the Laurel and Hardy rule – Hardy's BMI was almost certainly within the 20 to 30 range, and no higher.

The trick is to give your pupil a resource that is not too little and not too large. One or two pages is more than sufficient to cover any required background knowledge, new vocabulary, and exam skills that a lesson could demand. If it is not, then your sequence of lessons is moving too swiftly. Remember, Rosenshine's principles demand that new information should be introduced gradually.[39] You also have to model, guide practice, and check understanding, often

---

39 Sherrington, *Rosenshine's Principles in Action*, pp. 15–17.

in the same lesson.[40] This means that there will be lessons when you are trying to squeeze in many elements of the teaching sequence. And if you are trying to shoehorn more than one or two pages of reading into your lesson as well, then you'll lose out on time for modelling, practising, and questioning effectively. Bad lesson, hombre.

Going back to *The Decline and Fall*, if I wanted pupils to study this, I would introduce excerpts corresponding to a given theme. For instance, there was an Emperor named Constantine who saw the symbol of Christ in the sky on the day of a crucial battle. The pupils do not need to read the twelve discrete parts of the book that deal with this topic to understand it. I can easily present it in a coherent series of excerpts. The pupils will then focus on these sheets and will be less prone to distraction, since they are looking in one place.

Where do I go from here? Well, we need to consider the paradox of the vocabulary gap. And we can use pupil D (for disadvantaged) as an example. Pupil D lacks the relevant background knowledge to comprehend a text. Furthermore, he cannot remedy his lack of knowledge by reading a text, since he cannot comprehend texts. So, whence will he derive this knowledge? That has to come from you.

Firstly, I think we ought not to think too much about reading skills or strategies, since pupils are not the only ones at risk of cognitive overload. We need to grasp that the skill of reading is built up from many thousands of pieces of knowledge, like a mosaic. When we are teaching, we are fixing the small tiles of knowledge into an over-all shape, and this is why a well-sequenced curriculum is important. Didau says that (a) reading is composed of thousands of individual

---

40 It is important to note that Didau and Sherrington state that not all of
    Rosenshine's Principles or Didau's teaching sequence have to occur in the same
    lesson, but I am generalising from my experience in state schools, where it is an
    inevitability that some lessons will require all elements of the teaching sequence
    to be crammed together. This could be because some students are behind or
    have been absent for long periods, or the class is behaviourally challenging. For
    more see: David Didau, Great Teaching Happens in Cycles, *The Learning Spy*
    (24 June 2013). Available at: https://learningspy.co.uk/featured/great-teaching-
    happens-in-cycles; and Sherrington, *Rosenshine's Principles in Action*, p. 50:
    'it would not be reasonable or sensible to see each of [Rosenshine's Principles]
    being modelled during any given one-off lesson'.

pieces of knowledge, (b) the more we learn, the more automatised the highly complex process of reading becomes,[41] and (c) if we want disadvantaged pupils to perform well, we should not be 'so concerned with teaching procedural knowledge (skills) that [we] forget to teach new propositional knowledge (facts)'.[42] My advice? Focus on knowledge.

Securing knowledge is where the PowerPoint can assist, and it is where the double act begins to hot up and jive into a ballroom swing. (Forget the Laurel and Hardy analogy for now; I don't want you gesticulating with rage as you hurtle down a staircase.) Here is an example. The pupils are to learn about the Emperor Constantine, so I put on the board … a picture. That's it. I could have a picture of the symbol of Christ or I could have a picture of the Battle of the Milvian Bridge, where Constantine embarked on becoming sole Emperor. Will this be enough? Yes.

Some teachers are aspiring cotton-candy vendors with the amount of fluff they produce, but really all that matters is that I tell a story, outline key vocabulary as I go, and keep the story open to the participation of the pupils I am teaching.

TEACHING FOR MASTERY IN ESSAY-BASED SUBJECTS: A QUICK AND DIRTY GUIDE

Mark McCourt recommends a mastery-based progression system that is built on the following foundational assumption: 'learning is the bringing-about of some change in the long-term memory'.[43] From here, McCourt helpfully distinguishes 'attainment', or the 'point that a pupil has reached in the learning discipline', from

---

41 Didau, *The Secret of Literacy*, p. 98.
42 Didau, *The Secret of Literacy*, p. 35. 'Kids identified as having "high verbal skills" remembered a *bit more* than kids with "low verbal skills" … But that effect is tiny compared to the effect of knowledge of soccer': Daniel Willingham, *The Reading Mind: A Cognitive Approach to Understanding How the Mind Reads* (San Francisco, CA: Jossey-Bass, 2017), p. 230; my emphasis. This suggests that teaching domain-specific knowledge should be the overriding concern in every kind of instruction, as opposed to the explicit instruction of literacy or reading skills.
43 McCourt, *Teaching for Mastery*, p. 42.

'ability', which is an 'index of the learning rate'.[44] Not all knowledge-able pupils are high-ability and neither are gifted students necessarily high-attainers.

Next, McCourt elaborates on the meaning of mastery. Our current model is a conveyor-belt system where pupils are hastened through content that they may or may not have understood.[45] In my experi-ence, this is often because heads of department are pressured by senior leadership to keep classes in lockstep. The solution? SLT need to shift their focus from coverage to actual learning. It's all very well inputting into a spreadsheet that Year 10 studied rivers on 3 November, but it's meaningless if pupils associate interlocking spurs with cowboys or alluvium with cans of Coca-Cola. For McCourt, pupils are quizzed until they understand at least 80% of the propo-sitional knowledge from one topic (e.g. 'What is a meander?') before moving on. The 'study of a novel idea takes as long as it takes', meanwhile 80% of each learning episode is comprised of no-stakes quizzing of the three previous topics, and pupils under-take this outside of lesson time.[46] Eventually, students move from propositional knowledge to a fluency that allows 'far transfer' between contexts.

These ideas are valid and plausible, but more radical than McCourt supposes. They're similar to what already happens in Chinese math-ematics lessons, in a process Lucy Crehan describes as 'ping pong' style teaching: 'you do, I do, you do, I do. Students don't work for extended periods of time on independent work in class (apart from in their "study lessons"), but they do a huge amount of practice on each topic as part of their homework. The textbooks guide this, offering progressively more difficult questions for the students to tackle.'[47] The education systems of China, Japan, and South Korea approximate mastery very closely. If you want to know what a suc-cessful mastery system looks like, watch the video where South Korean high-school students sit the Welsh GCSE maths exam, com-plete it in fifteen minutes, and unanimously conclude that it was

44 McCourt, *Teaching for Mastery*, p. 44.
45 McCourt, *Teaching for Mastery*, p. 43.
46 McCourt, *Teaching for Mastery*, p. 110.
47 Crehan, *Cleverlands*, p. 181.

'really easy'.[48] Our anaemic attempts at mastery, such as lesson prep sheets or flip learning, where pupils thrash out a worksheet on the Monday morning bus to school, are amateurish by comparison.

I agree with McCourt. If we could implement mastery, it would be a silver bullet for our most gore-slathered educational werewolves: pupil disadvantage, gender disparities, and our PISA international test scores. To do it, however, we would need a culture shift, one in which pupils took more responsibility for their own learning and where parents placed a higher value on educational attainment.

The former would be resolved by teaching knowledge and thereby securing pupils a stake in their own education. Knowledge isn't power, it's property. By contrast, skills are the collateralised debt obligations of the educational system. It's as if, for decades, we've repackaged pupils whose understanding is subprime at best, expecting them to grow up to raise educationally solvent children. British parenting isn't bad, but the mindset we'd need for mastery is described here by Amy Chua: 'To get good at anything you have to work, and children on their own never want to work, which is why it is crucial to override their preferences.'[49] Meanwhile, in the UK, we think it tantamount to Chinese water torture to unplug the Xbox for half an hour.

The 2011 reception of Battle Hymn of the Tiger Mother tells a poignant story. Reviewers use adjectives like 'pushy', 'neurotic', and 'controversial', while even those in favour observe that the prescriptions run 'counter to the doctrine of Western parenting'.[50] Another review from The Independent sheds light on this, contrasting 'high-pressure "Chinese" parenting' with our 'feel-good [Western]

---

48 BBC News, South Korean Students Finish Welsh Maths GCSE Paper in 15 Minutes (28 November 2015). Available at: https://www.bbc.co.uk/news/av/uk-wales-38115296/south-korean-students-finish-welsh-gcse-maths-paper-in-15-minutes.

49 Amy Chua, Battle Hymn of the Tiger Mother (New York: Penguin, 2011), p. 27.

50 Dominic Lawson, Chinese Mothers ... A Lesson to Us All, The Independent (11 January 2011). Available at: https://www.independent.co.uk/voices/commentators/dominic-lawson/dominic-lawson-chinese-mothers-a-lesson-to-us-all-2181165.html.

culture'.[51] Perhaps if we could reconcile ourselves to the counterintuitive notion that mastery might be 'fun', we'd stand a chance of wholesale implementation. Until then, we must cherry-pick its most nourishing crops without overburdening teachers' baskets.

Since this book is more of a manual for dealing with the status quo than a manifesto for change, I want to think about how teachers can best implement mastery right now. I will be looking into this for the remainder of this chapter.

First off, McCourt's book is rooted heavily in mathematics. One chapter, at 142 pages, is less of a 'mathematical diversion' and more of an odyssey comprising over half of the book. That McCourt grounds his book so firmly in subject knowledge is admirable – more authors should be doing it – but domain-specificity limits its application to the essay-based subjects, such as English and the humanities.

Mathematics is a hierarchical discipline. The most advanced ideas in maths and the fundamental branches of science, such as physics, are dependent on prior assumptions with a strict logical progression. In maths, if you can work out the area of a triangle, you can compute the area of a square; once you can solve those problems, you can proceed into volumes of three-dimensional solids, and then into the Einsteinian concepts, such as gravity being a curvature of space-time. You cannot learn gravity without learning geometry. For this reason, mastery works well since pupils can sit quizzes and progress to the next level – a level in which they'll recruit knowledge from the previous 'rung' of their instruction.

By contrast, English would be considered non-hierarchical. We don't have to commence a study of literature with the *Epic of Gilgamesh* from the Third Dynasty of Ur (*c.*2100 BC). It might inform our notion that some stories are as old as written language itself, such as the flood myth which occurs in Ancient Mesopotamia just as it occurs a thousand or so years later in the Book of Genesis. But by no means is it prerequisite. When I studied English literature at A level, I read

---

51 Boyd Tonkin, Battle Hymn of the Tiger Mother by Amy Chua, *The Independent* (17 February 2012). Available at: https://www.independent.co.uk/arts-entertainment/books/reviews/battle-hymn-of-the-tiger-mother-by-amy-chua-6988528.html.

mostly Victorian literature, primarily works by Jane Austen, Charles Dickens, and Thomas Hardy. In the final chapter of *Tess of the d'Urbervilles*, where Tess is executed for murdering her rapist and tormentor, Alec d'Urberville, the narrator concludes as follows: '"Justice" was done, and the President of the Immortals, in Aeschylean phrase, had ended his sport with Tess.'[52] I don't need to have read the ancient Greek playwright Aeschylus to understand this sentence. Clearly, Tess's downfall was predetermined, as is the case with many of Hardy's protagonists. There are no rungs on the ladders of literature – the structure is more like a climbing frame; it is therefore illogical to speak of a single route to progression.

How would we 'do' mastery within our departments? First off, we would have to specify the propositional knowledge we want pupils to know. It's a mammoth task, so different members of staff should compile quizzes for different topics. We should accept that arts and the humanities are non-hierarchical, and that the propositional knowledge we choose will, by dint of the subject, be arbitrary. There should be no arguments, therefore, about what to include and what to leave out. This will only waste time. Each person decides on the relevant knowledge for their topic, which should overlap at least partially with the national curriculum and GCSE specification. For the sake of simplicity and the environment, each quiz should be on one side of A4, comprised of challenging multiple-choice questions along with short-answer questions. Once our departments have a common body of quizzes, heads of department can schedule timescales for testing, since although McCourt advocates non-stakes quizzing at home, this is unrealistic given our current culture (especially in disadvantaged urban areas).

When mastery moves beyond knowledge recall and into the territory of writing actual essays, it becomes an issue of qualitative assessment. The knowledge-recall tests will be very reliable since we will know exactly what pupils know or don't know. However, as Daisy Christodoulou notes, 'it is very hard to mark writing reliably'.[53] Her solution is to use 'comparative judgement', which is where markers simply compare two pieces of writing and say which one is

52 Thomas Hardy, *Tess of the d'Urbervilles* (London: Collector's Library, 2003 [1891]), p. 552.
53 Christodoulou, *Making Good Progress?*, p. 65.

better: 'Then they look at another pair and decide which one of the two is better, and so on. Each marker makes a series of perhaps 50 or 100 of these judgements which are relatively quick and easy to make.'[54] This technique would be consistent with the finding of behavioural psychologist Daniel Kahneman: 'what you see is all there is' (or WYSIATI). According to Kahneman, 'You cannot help dealing with the limited information you have as if it were all there is to know.'[55] We know that working memory is limited and that retrieval strength for knowledge which isn't repeatedly recalled is quite low. To my mind, this suggests that the side-by-side comparative judgement approach of Christodoulou is an optimal one.

In my experience, this is how GCSE examinations are marked currently. Exam boards outsource marking to teachers who sit at their computers and judge between various handwritten answers to questions such as, 'Explain why there was opposition in Germany to the Treaty of Versailles (1919)'. Miss Wilson will say that the answer is excellent; they made fourteen good points and deserve a level 8. However, Mrs Clemenceau is liable to start kicking off. The answer is in serious need of reconstruction and is a level 4 at best. Things get heated and Mr Lloyd-George calms everybody down by insisting that clause 231 of the mark scheme states that the candidate's answer falls into the level 6 bracket. Since it is the average, Miss Wilson will begrudgingly give the candidate a level 6. More often, though, teachers agree that 'This answer isn't as good as the previous; it can't possibly be a level 5.' In terms of mastery, then, I see no reason not to take up Christodoulou's suggestion since the side-by-side nature of the judgement will perhaps lead to greater rigour than we currently have for both ordinary school assessments and externally assessed GCSEs.

The one qualification I will make is that, when deploying the comparative technique you should do so alone. In the example above, the teachers openly dispute the grades, but often what happens is that people agree with the first option given. Just as pupils are at risk of social loafing, so are teachers. We don't want social considerations of whether or not we feel comfortable openly disagreeing

---

54 Christodoulou, *Making Good Progress?*, pp. 186–187.
55 Kahneman, *Thinking, Fast and Slow*, p. 201.

with a colleague to interfere with our assessment of a piece of writing. Objectivity in the quality model is strained enough as it is.

If the members of your department are at odds with one another, you can implement a low resolution kind of mastery for yourself. Create a set of A4 quizzes on upcoming topics and then alter them very slightly. As McCourt recommends, try to give pupils multiple exposures to these over spaced intervals. They may complain that they've done it before. If so, shrug and say, in that case, they should score 100%. Make it clear to your classes that mastery involves reconciling yourself to perpetual insufficiency. As McCourt puts it, 'What a sad state of affairs it would be if, one day, one simply closed the lid of the piano and said, "well, that's the piano finished!"' [56] Remember, not only is the journey the reward, but the journey never ends.

SUBJECT KNOWLEDGE: CREATING MENTAL RESOURCES WITH FLASHCARDS

Studies into the Dunning–Kruger effect suggest that a 'majority of people tend to overestimate their abilities'.[57] On television, the cognitive bias is most often signalled by the buzzers on *Britain's Got Talent*, dry-heaving judges on *Bake Off*, or *Strictly's* savage dressing-downs of its already scantily clad contestants. In real life, however, there aren't any such cues available to us, and often we're not only ignorant but ignorant of our own ignorance.

One of the broader themes of this book is that what's good for the goose is good for the gander – in other words, research-based educational methods that work on our pupils are also useful for teachers endeavouring to improve their own subject knowledge. And that's why I'm recommending one of the only gimmicks you'll find in this book: flashcards for professional use.

Although I've discussed retrieval practice in 'Planning on Paper', that's the sort of thing you do in school during your working day and

---

56 McCourt, *Teaching for Mastery*, p. 43.
57 Busch and Watson, *The Science of Learning*, p. 18.

to tackle last-minute occurrences. Flashcards equip you with durable subject knowledge – the equivalent of fireproofing your home rather than wading into an inferno with a fire blanket.

Why flashcards? Flashcards are great because they satisfy all evidence-based criteria for durable learning. Firstly, recall that 'intelligence is the simple accrual and tuning of many small units of knowledge that in total produces complex cognition'.[58] By using flashcards, we have a single repository for the small units that we are going to need to recall. Why not just read? Well, the problem is that it is difficult to target the knowledge you're going to need to teach effectively when it is 'baked into' the finished product of written prose. Teaching is like baking a cake. Although eating cakes (reading) may inform your preference for ones that don't taste like kitty litter, it is not particularly instructive in the process of making cakes. With flashcards, we have the ingredients and recipes of the lesson to hand, which is better than trying to reverse-engineer a soufflé that's bound to fall flat.

Secondly, we know that retrieval is superior to re-exposure and that 'posing your students questions about a topic is more powerful than presenting that topic again'.[59] Remember, as I said in 'On Printing', there is a reason we forget telephone numbers. By contrast, more experienced teachers are more knowledgeable because teaching itself is a form of retrieval practice. You are standing in front of a class reciting knowledge from memory – 'dialling the number' of information, so to speak.

You might argue that teaching is a complex skill, and that having facts to hand is about as useful as donating shingles to the Salvation Army. But this is to ignore how knowledge works. I've used the analogy of knowledge being like the tiles of a mosaic previously in this chapter, but that was to make a point about the whole being larger than the sum of its parts. The real analogy is the substrate of intelligence itself: the neuron. One single neuron can have as many

---

58 Christodoulou, *Seven Myths About Education*, p. 20.
59 Mccrea, *Memorable Teaching*, p. 80.

as 100,000 inputs,[60] and you have 86 billion neurons.[61] Where a chunk of knowledge is retained in the memory, it can communicate with other memories; if what you've read stays static in the book, it is effectively mute, though some residue may linger in passive memory. In the bicameral legislature of the mind, rehearsed memories are MPs that deliberate in decision-making, whereas implicit memories become the slumbering residents of the House of Lords. The more you practise retrieval, the better. As William James observed about learning something only once: 'a thing thus learned can form but few associations'.[62]

In terms of problem-solving, Tom Sherrington stresses the importance of learning information because it 'makes it easier to be successful with problem-solving as less space in short-term memory is needed'.[63] I would argue that classroom management requires the full capacity of your working memory, which means you need a subject knowledge that borders on automatic. Remember when you were first learning to drive – you probably couldn't even turn the windscreen wipers on without nearly flattening a letter box and turning Archie the Labrador into a scatter rug. You practised this skill so extensively that it became automatic. Similarly, if you're standing in a lesson stumped by the question of whether Pythagoras invented pi, then you're not going to notice Ismael inscribing two adjacent circles and a long oblong into the desk, or Billy wondering what the squeal of a hippopotamus has to do with triangles.

We can thwart the Dunning–Kruger effect by remembering that Shakespeare was probably being ironic when he said we were

---

60 'The branching of the dendrites can be extensive, in some cases sufficient to receive as many as 100,000 inputs on a single neuron': Bruce Alberts, *Essential Cell Biology*, 3rd edn (New York: Garland Science, 2009), p. 409
61 Frederico A. Azevedo, Ludmila R. Carvalho, Lea T. Grinberg, José M. Farfel, Renata E. Ferretti, Renata E. Leite, Wilson J. Filho, Roberto Lent, and Suzana Herculano-Houzel, Equal Numbers of Neuronal and Nonneuronal Cells Make the Human Brain an Isometrically Scaled-Up Primate Brain, *Journal of Comparative Neurology*, 513(5) (2009): 532–541. DOI: 10.1002/cne.21974.
62 William James, *Talks to Teachers on Psychology; And to Students on Some of Life's Ideals* (New York: Henry Holt and Company, 1899), p. 129; quoted in Benedict Carey, *How We Learn: Throw Out the Rule Book and Unlock Your Brain's Potential* (London: Macmillan, 2014), p. 79.
63 Sherrington, *Rosenshine's Principles in Action*, p. 37.

'noble in reason' and 'infinite in faculty'.[64] On man being a 'piece of work', he wasn't far wrong.

HOW TO MAKE FLASHCARDS FOR PROFESSIONAL USE

First off, size matters. Flashcards should be no larger than credit cards. Here's why. In *Memorable Teaching* and *Rosenshine's Principles in Action*, both Peps Mccrea and Tom Sherrington have attempted to create a workable 'manifesto', if you like, for best practice. In both, they note the importance of 'presenting new material in small steps' in order to regulate the load placed on working memory.[65] When flashcards are big, they're unwieldy. Although you want retrieval to be difficult enough to satisfy Robert Bjork's concept of 'desirable difficulty', you don't want using them to become stressful.[66] As Daniel Willingham says, 'moderate challenge' is most effective.[67] So keep them small. Flashcards are meant to subtract from your workload.

Next, write the topic name on one side and the three to four chunks of knowledge you want to remember on the other; for example, one for 'erosion' in GCSE geography might have abrasion, attrition, hydraulic action, and solution on the other side. Bullet points are optional. You could also put a quote on the other side. It may sound strange – mainly because the process of forgetting is so mysterious (as you'd expect) – but the existence of one fact will strengthen other facts and prevent their decay. When you have enough of them, they form a schema, defined as a 'cohesive, repeatable action sequence possessing component actions that are tightly interconnected and governed by a core meaning'.[68] If the Matthew effect means that the knowledge-rich get richer,[69] then schemas are like banks that are too big to fail, even in the midst of recession. You'll never forget how to ride a bicycle, but you'll probably have

64 William Shakespeare, *Hamlet*, Act II, sc. ii, ll. 324–325.
65 Mccrea, *Memorable Teaching*, p. 47; and Sherrington, *Rosenshine's Principles in Action*, p. 6.
66 See Carey, *How We Learn*, p. 82.
67 Willingham, *Why Don't Students Like School?*, p. 19.
68 McCourt, *Teaching for Mastery*, p. 277.
69 Didau, *Making Kids Cleverer*, ch. 4.

forgotten that Theresa May was once prime minister until you see her on *I'm a Celeb* in a couple of years. This is because you haven't studied the government in enough detail to have the thousands of mutually reinforcing neuronal signals that constitute a strong and stable schema.

When it comes to retrieving the knowledge, you need to use spacing. Think: it's not like Neanderthals and early hominids ever had to cram for a test. When it came to hunting, either Ug would be trod on by a mammoth or he'd have dinner for a month. There was no BBC Bitesize for the consumption of megafauna. The best survival mechanism for early humans would have been to take in the salient information from their surroundings and to forget what they didn't need. The world today is vastly different from that of our ancestors. We have a lot more intellectual clutter than they had in caveman days. So, we have to be clever about repurposing our Neolithic neurons to bagging the modern mammoth that is cultural capital.

This is how it works: I might revise the topic of rivers, since that is the upcoming topic for my GCSE classes. If it's the half-term, I can practise retrieving how an ox-bow lake forms. Then, since it is the first time I've used the flashcard, I might practise it again the next day, and then again several days later. According to Carpenter et al., the optimal spacing interval is as follows: no days (first recall), three days, eight days, twelve days, and, finally, twenty-seven days.[70]

Once you've become fluent with your flashcards, it's time to vary your practice. Knowledge that you learn is stubbornly rooted to its domain. For instance, if I've learned the topic of climate change, it might be difficult for me to make synoptic links between that topic and, let's say, desertification. I might be able to make links on the surface, but it will be a struggle to transfer my knowledge of salt-resistant crops in combating climate change to the plight of Bangladeshi farmers whose soils are degraded by salinisation (becoming saltier). In subjects such as maths, McCourt talks about

---

70 Shana K. Carpenter, Nicholas J. Cepeda, Doug Rohrer, Sean H. K. Kang, and Harold Pashler, Using Spacing to Enhance Diverse Forms of Learning: Review of Recent Research and Implications for Instruction, *Educational Psychology Review*, 24 (2012), 369–378, quoted in Busch and Watson, *The Science of Learning*, p. 4.

the need to 'utilise a variety of contexts to maximise learning'.[71] That means I might mix my climate change and desertification flashcards together. Furthermore, I'll randomise them every time I use them, so that I'm always practising with a novel sequence.

Why not use a website for this? Because people learn less from screens than from physical materials such as pads, paper, and flashcards. The 'implicit feel of where you are in a physical book' – or set of flashcards – 'turns out to be more important than we realized'.[72] No one is entirely sure why paper still edges screens in terms of retention. Perhaps it recruits both spatial and linguistic memory, thereby forming a more complete schema overall. Whatever the reason, websites don't cut it.

My final tip is to refine what you know. In terms of recall from flashcards, try to write what they have on their flipside on a pad. When you've written down what you think the flashcard says, check it, and then correct any mistakes in a different colour pen. If you've really messed up, do it again straight away. When you're able to successfully recall it, you can then begin lengthening the retrieval intervals.

---

71 McCourt, *Teaching for Mastery*, p. 248.
72 'The physical experience of reading a book may be better for developing long-term memory': Wiliam, *Creating the Schools Our Children Need*, loc. 3283. See also Ferris Jabr, The Reading Brain in the Digital Age: The Science of Paper versus Screens, *Scientific American* (11 April 2015). Available at: https://www.scientificamerican.com/article/reading-paper-screens.

Chapter 8

NARRATIVES IN THE CLASSROOM

Stories. They communicate meaning. I could sell you a kettle by saying it has a one-and-a-half-litre capacity, 360-no-scope technology, and a whistle feature. Or I could ask, 'Have you ever waited so long for a kettle to boil that you've forgotten about it? Annoying, huh. This kettle has a 'keep-warm' setting with a whistle that alerts you to the fact that, "*Hey*, you wanted a coffee, remember?"' The questioning, the participatory thought process, the personification of the kettle – that's what this section is about. I explain how to use narratives to control and regulate engagement, while also looking into the confusion surrounding teacher-led practice. At the end, I offer an alternative to stories: the analogy. 'Ever tried telling fairy tales about an ionic compound? Annoying, huh.' Analogies are far better for factual, scientific, or numerical topics.

NO SUCH THING AS A BORING TOPIC

We've all had a colleague who complains to us about *that* topic. We all know the one. It comes in many different guises: from coastal erosion to glacial landforms in geography, to the Reformation and marriage alliances of early-modern European history. The Boring Topic has as many different incarnations as Satan himself.

But a topic has no concrete reality. In coastal erosion, for instance, there is a certain vocabulary: 'abrasion' and 'attrition' to give two examples. There are certain relationships between the words in our vocabulary: a cliff will be eroded by abrasion. These words and relationships constitute the entirety of the topic. Providing you deliver this set of propositional knowledge, you can configure the elements into whatever narrative you please. Complaining about a topic for being boring is like blaming Lego for your own architectural insufficiencies.

Why might I decide that coastal erosion is a boring topic? When I first started teaching it, one of the few beaches I had ever been to was Weston-super-Mud. You never actually made it to the sea because of the signs saying 'danger of death', referring to the water-logged sediment that had the consistency of quicksand. It meant that every time I ever spoke about beaches in lessons, it was the intellectual equivalent of scraping the last few slivers of margarine out of a barren tub, and consequently my pupils were not very engaged. 'I went to Weston-super-Mare once. You could almost see the sea if you squinted hard enough.' Who could blame them?

I knew that it was my fault and had little to do with the topic. I had planned for my first lesson on coastal erosion with little more than a cursory glance at the textbook, a hastily conceived PowerPoint, and a delivery that was premature at best. Unless you take infantile screaming to be the sign of successful delivery, as many doctors do, in which case I was very successful indeed.

I taught coastal erosion four or five more times over the course of the year, and as I repeatedly came back to the topic, something strange happened. Each time I planned the lesson, I would research a little more and my skeletal knowledge of the topic would flesh out a bit. Then, I was caught off-guard when Mr Lemsip was off sick, and I had to teach the lesson spontaneously.

12.57pm and I am ready to get terrorised. There seems to be no way around it. The kids are swarming the corridors, looking in through the windows at Mr Elliott the abattoir sheep. 'Every battle is won or lost before it is fought,' Sun Tzu said.[1] If that's the case, my current plight makes Dunkirk look victorious by comparison. By 1.07pm, I had taken the register, uncapped my board pen, and begun gesturing – hoping the words would follow.

The words did follow as, incredibly, I proceeded to narrate the story of being taken to the beach one day when I was 9. We had stopped off at a gift shop near Bridlington, I placed the desired spade and castle-bucket on the counter, and we were off again. When I did get to the beach, I thought, what the hell is this? It's just a bunch of rocks. I sat on it in disbelief, shifted three fist-sized rocks into my

---

1   Paraphrased from Sun Tzu, *The Art of War*, ch. 1.

bucket, and tipped it upside down. They all just fell on the floor again.

The kids found it hilarious, and so I asked them, warming to the theme of mock indignation, why on earth this beach was just a pile of rocks? The questioning on shingle beaches followed on really nicely from this little story. I also used a technique I call 'creating emotional urgency'. When discussing constructive and destructive waves, I drew stick figures of myself and pupil A on the whiteboard. I said that myself and pupil A were setting up rival beach resorts where people could drink mocktails. We discussed erosional problems through the lens of this absurd, imaginary scenario, and it was far more engaging.

How do I feel about coastal erosion today? Now I know the topic so well that I can interleave the key vocabulary and relationships into whatever stories I feel are relevant. Together, the vocabulary, relationships, and storylines are a potent admixture that makes the pupils feel confident about the topic.

WHY TEACHER-LED QUESTIONING IS OPTIMAL

There is no reason why you can't spend an entire lesson purely on teacher-led questioning, providing you can keep it interesting. Many initial teacher training providers make the blanket statement that teacher talk is wrong and should be appended to the seven deadly sins. They have perhaps only failed in this endeavour because 'eight deadly sins' isn't sufficiently alliterative for the English teachers who swell the ranks of SLT.

In teaching coastal erosion, I might ask, 'What are the five kinds of coastal erosion?' and I'd then likely hallucinate crickets chirping and tumbleweeds rolling. If this is your first lesson on coastal erosion, then this is a bad question. The pupils don't know anything yet.

How, then, do I impart this fundamental knowledge? There are two valid options. Firstly, I could give them an activity where they could read about the different kinds of coastal erosion, maybe with DARTs.

However, in doing this, I would not be generating much buy-in for a topic that most pupils will predict to be a boring one.

The second option would be that I could use Socratic questioning. For instance, I may ask the following question that seems only tenuously related: 'Do coastlines change shape?' One pupil will mention something about water wearing down rocks. I could then say, 'What does erosion mean?' and the pupil will pluck this low-hanging fruit to determine it means when rocks are worn away.

The chain of questioning will proceed almost like a story, some of the questions being deliberately made into leading questions, allowing me to craft a narrative.

Teacher: How could a fluid like water possibly *wear away* something as solid as a rock? [open]

Pupil A: Because it happens over a long period of time.

Teacher: And when we think about seawater, will it purely be water that is *eroding* the rocks? Pupil B, what do you think? [leading]. [Notice how I'm using 'wear away' and 'erode' interchangeably. Don't merely define a key term once; for unfamiliar terms, continually establish synonyms and do so implicitly.[2]]

Pupil B: There could be something in the seawater, like maybe plastic bottles, or oil, or something like that. [Pupil B has answered incorrectly, but we won't say that he's wrong. We'll try to repurpose our questioning so that he can redeem himself – if we don't, pupil B will lose confidence.]

Teacher: OK, but what if I said that plastics are man-made substances and erosion has happened for millions of years before human beings evolved? What about this: what happens to the material of a rock when it is eroded – does it just disappear forever? [slightly leading, slightly open]

---

2   Explicit vocabulary instruction is one technique, but I think kids find it quite tiresome to have each and every synonym explained over and over. Simply using terms interchangeably is often enough to establish synonymity. So, yes, we now have implicit vocabulary instruction as well.

Pupil C (with hand up): No, the rock will be broken down into small particles, like sand, and some parts of the rock will dissolve.

Teacher: Right, and what do you think, pupil B? If there is sand being carried in the water, and waves are brushing against rocks on the shore, what is likely to happen? [slightly leading, slightly open]

Pupil B: It will be like sandpaper.

And so on and so forth. From this tiny excerpt of questioning, I could already say to the students, 'Pupils C and B have identified abrasion and solution, which are two of the types of erosion we need to know for the exam,' and, if need be, I could draw simplified diagrams on the whiteboard.

This kind of questioning allows me to fulfil three objectives simultaneously. Firstly, if I am a new teacher, I am demonstrating to the pupils that I know my subject. Secondly, I am generating buy-in for a topic that is often maligned for being dull by creating a narrative that builds suspense with each new link in the chain of questioning. Finally, I am building confidence in the pupils. It sounds cynical, but a pupil needs to feel that a subject is 'for them', and answering questions correctly inculcates this motivation.

PARTICIPATORY PRACTICE TEACHER LED IS NOT TEACHER LECTURING

In the profession, teacher-led teaching is not to be confused with a monodirectional lecture.[3] In terms of the unholy trinity of teaching practices, lecturing is right up there with group work and discovery learning.[4]

---

3   The term "explicit instruction" does not mean simply giving a lecture. Instead, it involves using carefully considered explanations, worked examples and accurate analogies alongside questioning, modelling and scaffolding, structured discussion and lots of opportunities for purposeful practice': Didau, *Making Kids Cleverer*, p. 309.
4   Teacher led does not mean 'advocating mono-directional lectures being perpetrated on children': Didau, *What If Everything You Knew About Education Was Wrong?*, p. 323.

So, what do we mean by teacher-led practice? It all comes down to narrative. You are not paid to stand up in front of a class and list a dry catalogue of details, take token questions before setting a task, and then berate pupils for not knowing their stuff.

Rosenshine's principles tell us that human beings cannot simply download large quantities of verbal, written, or numerical information into their brains.[5] We can barely get everything we need from the supermarket without a list, we struggle to remember the names of colleagues we worked with for years, and what about that book you were telling a friend they simply 'must read', before your mouth hung voicelessly open as you excitedly attempted to recall the plot for them: 'I'm not doing it justice; you just have to read it for yourself.' There's even a name for that last bias: it's called the illusion of explanatory depth.[6] If you don't believe in it, try right now to explain to a colleague how a toilet works.

Where does a narrative come in? I like to think of a narrative as like a Subway sandwich. Ever try getting a kid to eat vegetables? Not easy. But take them to Subway and they'll confidently demand that the sandwich artist give them lettuce, cucumber, jalapeño, olive, tomato, and, hell, why not load her up with everything you got? Except gherkin. Leave those. The sandwich provides a vehicle that ties together the components you would not eat on their own, creating a symphony of flavours. As absurd as the job description 'sandwich artist' may be, there are a few crumbs of truth to it. Apple Genius is still going a bit far though.

The narrative is the delivery vehicle for discrete facts that would be meaningless on their own. For instance, if I know that Britain was invaded in 1066, I might shrug or pretend to be interested with as little sarcasm as possible. If, however, you tell me the story of the Godwinson family: how they clambered up the greasy pole of monarchical power, the friendly relationship between Harold Godwinson and William the Conqueror, and the shadow cast by promises of power and mixed messages; then, if you tell me that the

---

5   'Presenting too much material at once may confuse students because their short-term memory will be unable to process it': Sherrington, *Rosenshine's Principles in Action*, p. 63.
6   Steven Pinker, *Enlightenment Now: The Case for Reason, Science, Humanism, and Progress* (London: Penguin, 2019), p. 380.

Vikings had ruled England and how various Scandinavian kings had also set their sights on Britain; and how, in 1066, these competing tempests issued from a pressure system of powers to result in a perfect storm for poor Harold Godwinson, whose eye was shish-kebabbed by a Norman arrow in 1066; if you tell me this story, the detail of the Norman Conquest of 1066 is invested with importance and I will commit it to memory.

Still, there is the question of the delivery. Do I just stand in front of the class and simply deliver this sermon? Does a Subway sandwich deliver itself to your digestive system in a single bite? No.

I would tell the story of Harold Godwinson and I would ask the opinions of pupils: 'Do you think he deserved the throne?' I might proceed to ask about William the Conqueror. I will remember at all times that they do not know this subject very well, and try to leverage what they do know to help them do some heavy historical lifting. I might say something like, 'History is written by the victors – what does this mean?' One pupil will confidently tell me. I could then inform them about our primary source for the Norman Conquest: the Bayeux Tapestry. 'What does this suggest about the story?' One pupil will perhaps talk about how King Harold has been given a bad rap because the Normans made the tapestry. And so on. You can see how this narrative is vastly different from a monodirectional lecture.

I could do the same in the sciences. In teaching Einstein's theory of relativity, I would ask pupils to think about time being a dimension. 'What does this mean?' It's a vague question, but a pupil who understands the concept of dimensionality might infer that, since objects in space can be curved like a sphere or round like a doughnut, time could be similarly warped. Then I could ask, 'If time can be stretched and compressed like bubble gum, would our watches display the same time if I floated near a black hole and pupil A remained here on Earth?' In my previous lesson, I might have explained gravity and the notion that it involves the warping of physical space. By saying 'time is a dimension', I can broaden the definition of gravity to 'the warping of space-time'. 'If space is warped, how might time pass for me?' Some might say slower, some might say faster, but the point is they've been disabused of the notion of 'absolute simultaneity'.[7] Mine and pupil A's watches will read differently. I can then bring in the concept of time dilation with a few more leading questions, and there we go: we have collaboratively constructed an understanding of at least one element of Einstein's theory.

The narrative allows you to scaffold for pupils in a way that you simply cannot do with group work. On each 'floor' of the scaffold you use a 'ladder' question that links prior knowledge to new content.

DIFFERENTIATION?
I PREFER STAIRCASE QUESTIONING

The technique is simple. You use easy inference narrative questioning to instil confidence in your pupils. 'What does that mean?' I hear you gawp. It means that you couch a question so that the answer is a low-hanging fruit. Once you have mastered this low-key, unflashy, and effortless technique, differentiation can be left to wither on the vine.

Some pupils have more background knowledge than others. Pupil A could have been exposed to 32 million more words than pupil B.[8] Comprehension becomes impossible when pupils know less than 95% of the words,[9] and even if a pupil did have such a small vocabulary, it is still necessary for them to struggle in order to improve.

Now, imagine that I differentiate for the pupils who know less (through outcome, questioning, or feedback – take your pick). Not only have I presented the lower-attaining pupils with a metaphorical dunce hat, but I am now actively engaged in perpetuating the 32-million word gap. Furthermore, the emotional component of this is just as important as the academic one. In order to close the gap,

---

7   Carlo Rovelli, *Reality Is Not What It Seems: The Journey to Quantum Gravity* (London: Penguin, 2017), p. 69.
8   'From birth to 48 months, parents in professional families spoke 32 million more words to their children than parents in welfare families': Quigley, *Closing the Vocabulary Gap*, p. 4.
9   Quigley notes that Willingham suggests this figure could be an underestimate: Quigley, *Closing the Vocabulary Gap*, p. 7.

I have to build up the lower-attainers (with knowledge *and* confidence) to answer the same questions as the higher-attainers. There is only one technique I know of that is versatile enough for this.

I call it staircase questioning, and this is how it looks. 'Pupil A, can you remember what the word "appeasement" means?' Pupil A glows red with embarrassment. 'Hang on, what about this, pupil A: if I wanted a naughty class to behave, and gave them lollipops so they would be quiet, do you think this would work?' Pupil A tells me that it wouldn't work, and confidently states that this is because once pupils receive lollipops, they will misbehave again. In fact, they would be more liable to misbehave, since then they could receive more lollipops. 'OK, good, this is what I mean by "appeasement". Now, pupil A, can you tell me why appeasing Hitler was a bad idea?' Pupil A remembers that Hitler was given a territory called the … erm … something like Sudafed – 'Sudetenland' – yes, that one. 'Say it back to me.' 'The Sudetenland. Hitler was given the Sudetenland because we wanted him to be peaceful, but all he did was go on to take over other countries, such as Poland, thereby starting the Second World War.'

I could have posed my initial question to the high-attaining pupil B and the whole rigmarole of questioning would have been over there and then. Instead, I built in a number of ideas relevant to pupil A to allow him to summon the answer, and did so without the indignity of putting a white rabbit into a top-hat compartment. As Daniel Willingham states, 'both breadth and depth matter'.[10] Exposure to unfamiliar words is the breadth,[11] and you have to face up to the limitation that, as Abraham Lincoln might have said, you will not be able to define all of the words all of the time. The depth is the explicit vocabulary instruction that I exemplified with the word 'appeasement' because 'there is good evidence that teaching children new vocabulary boosts reading comprehension'.[12]

---

10 Willingham, *The Reading Mind*, p. 92.
11 'It seems like the important factors for word learning would be whether I'm exposed to new words, the frequency of that exposure, and maybe the likelihood that I pay attention to new words': Willingham, *The Reading Mind*, p. 94.
12 Willingham, *The Reading Mind*, p. 92.

The paradox is that if you avoid exposing pupils to words they don't know, they will never learn them, since they need to have seen a word frequently enough to deem it worth knowing. Inevitably, this will involve a number of lessons where the pupil sees the word and doesn't know it, until finally they ask you, 'For crying out loud, what does détente mean?' We should not be too finicky about trying to make sure all pupils understand all words at all possible times.

One final benefit to the method above is that it doesn't stigmatise anybody. Teachers are oblivious to the savagery of children. For all their railing against the iniquities of traditional teaching methods, putting children in mixed groups with differentiated worksheets is about as close as we've come to a rehabilitation of the dunce's cap. With staircase questioning, students don't know new material deeply enough to distinguish easy from difficult questions. If you're patronising, they might: 'Dylan, do you think Hitler was a *very naughty* man?' But aside from the occasional gaffe, they won't notice a thing.

CRAFTING NARRATIVES: HISTORY

According to Daniel Willingham's four Cs, a good story must contain the following: causality, conflict, complications, and character.[13] An example of this within history could be the story of smallpox vaccination.

The story tells itself because it has lots of *causes*. Smallpox was very contagious which meant that people living in cities were badly affected. Furthermore, the death rate stood at around 30%, and so many people died from the disease. To put it crudely, as long as the story has lots of things causing other things, the narrative turbine will continue turning and the pupils will keep listening.

The main *conflict* of the story is that people wanted a cure, and yet there was no cure. We know that people were trying to develop one but there were few successes. With variolation, a small sample of infected pus was taken from a smallpox patient and used to

---

13 Willingham, *Why Don't Students Like School?*, p. 67.

deliberately infect someone without the disease (usually children). We may as well try to cure ourselves of coronavirus by inhaling hand sanitiser or injecting people with Toilet Duck.[14] Although variolation may have reduced smallpox mortality slightly, it could only be practised in small towns and villages, due to the infection rate of the disease.

The *complications* revolved around Edward Jenner and his discovery of vaccination. Once he had proven that vaccination was superior to variolation, he still had to run clinical trials, and many doctors had an interest in continuing to practise variolation (which was not banned until 1840). Jenner was the lone genius pitted against a 'confederacy of dunces'.[15]

Finally, the *character* of Jenner is more complex than many other historical figures. For instance, we know that Jenner worked tirelessly to test his hypothesis, thereby assuaging the fears of the public. However, we also know that he deliberately infected a small boy named James Phipps with both cowpox and smallpox, and that he could not have been certain the boy would survive. Jenner is interesting, therefore, in that he is not a one-dimensional figure, but rather a public-spirited utilitarian who distributed his vaccine throughout Europe, free of charge, and yet thought that the means of endangering a small boy could justify this noble end.

This is just one of the many stories available to us in history. The more obvious one is that of Hitler, which can be simplified as follows:

1 Causes: the Treaty of Versailles, the Great Depression.

2 Conflict: the Treaty of Versailles and wanting a strong nation.

3 Complications: (a) Hitler believed that a Jewish-Bolshevist conspiracy was sabotaging him, (b) France and Britain were

---

14 Gino Spocchia, 'Under No Circumstances Administer into Human Body': Dettol Tells People Not to Follow Trump's 'Dangerous' Recommendation, *The Independent* (24 April 2020). Available at: https://www.independent.co.uk/news/world/americas/us-politics/trump-coronavirus-disinfectant-injection-dettol-response-uk-a9481786.html.

15 Jonathan Swift, Thoughts on Various Subjects, Moral and Diverting (1706). Available at: http://self.gutenberg.org/articles/eng/Thoughts_on_Various_Subjects,_Moral_and_Divertinghttp://self.gutenberg.org/articles/eng/Thoughts_on_Various_Subjects,_Moral_and_Diverting.

appeasing him, which forestalled an invasion of the Western Powers, and (c) his supply lines on the Eastern Front were overextended.

4   Character: Hitler was one of the most fierce, determined, and monomaniacal dictators of all time. Yet, like Jenner, neither was he one-dimensional. He had fought bravely in the First World War. He also had a rags-to-riches story that, if not for the wars and genocides, might have been vaguely inspiring. Finally, there is the idea that Hitler was some kind of mastermind, and yet Ian Kershaw points out that during Operation Barbarossa he sat in his Eagle's Nest HQ, watching *King Kong* on repeat while gobbling opioids like Pez Candies.[16]

You can tell these stories in lessons and secure pupil engagement fairly easily. One of the best things about history is that the narrative components are all there like prefab housing, and if you want to teach them, just organise your story according to the four Cs.

Just remember that in telling your stories, it is important to avoid TMI (too much information) or what I call shaggy dog stories. My dad used to tell me these growing up, and they would usually involve him speaking to seventeen different passers-by while en route to the chippy, capped off with the M. Night Shyamalan denouement that they'd run out of curry sauce. Information in stories is best served in small portions.

CRAFTING NARRATIVES: GEOGRAPHY

Telling stories in geography is more difficult than it is in history, which arrives like IKEA furniture, all boxed up in a blue and yellow bag, components ready for assembly, and the word *berättelse* written on top, which in Swedish can mean either story or history. As for geography, no profitable synonyms here. *Geografi* has only one translation: geography.

---

16   In *Hitler* (London: Penguin, 2008), Ian Kershaw says that Hitler spent his evenings 'relaxing by watching a film (one of his favourites was *King Kong*)' (p. 293) and that 'The increased numbers of pills and injections provided every day by Dr Morell – ninety varieties in all during the war and twenty-eight different pills each day – could not prevent the physical deterioration' (p. 782).

I agree with the Swedes: I don't think storytelling applies well to geography or similar subjects like maths and science. In history and English, almost every topic can tick off causation, conflict, complications, and character. However, most physical topics in geography don't have any characters and some topics are nothing more than a catalogue of dry physical processes.

In this case, I advocate something simple and intuitive for narrative excellence in geography, and that is to create your own personal stories. For these stories to work, you have to break the fourth wall and create emotional urgency through questioning.

If I were teaching the topic of sustainability, for instance, here is how I would do it. 'So one day, back in 2009, I went to the supermarket, and, you know me, I'm a real eco-warrior.' (The character in this story is me, and I would describe the role as an ironically self-deprecating one.) 'Anyway, I went to get some milk … and there was a pile of pillows in the dairy aisle.' The pupils will be struck by this, since it is a moment of conflict. Why are there pillows in the refrigerators? That can't be very hygienic. And why is sir even talking about it – has he lost the plot? I've not lost the plot; I'm manipulating the thread of it very well, tautening and slackening it at key moments. 'There were pillows, and upon closer inspection, I could read the labels. Green labels with "semi-skimmed", and dark-blue ones that said "whole milk". The milk was in bags!'

The pupils will go crazy for this part of the story – I don't know why. Maybe it has to do with me shouting that the milk is in bags, since I am breaking the fourth wall. Anyway, one pupil will ask, 'How can you have milk in bags – won't it pour out of the little holes in the bottom?' And then I would explain that I don't mean carrier bags, and then the pupils would get the gist. 'Right, so can anybody tell me why we would have milk bags like this?' And the pupils themselves would talk to me about plastics, about the risk posed to marine life, and how future generations depend on us curbing the usage of plastic. If need be, I can drop in a few stirring anecdotes about how the bags used to fall off the shelves and explode, making the aisle look like it'd been visited by an incontinent dairy cow. It's sure to make the pupils laugh, but also consider how sustainability can often mean inconvenience.

With geography, therefore – since there are no Winston Churchills or Otto von Bismarcks – it is important to tell personal, relatable stories that star you as the protagonist. That said, they always have to relate to the topic. And they must be quite sparse in information (remember: avoid the shaggy dog narrative). You need to ration the informational content so that (a) you don't cognitively overload pupils and (b) so the pupils are making medium-difficulty inferences throughout the story.

What is a medium-difficulty inference? It means that at key cliff-hanger moments of a story, pupils will be thinking, 'What comes next?' If you have told them a very complicated story about deserts and salinisation, without introducing these concepts gradually, the pupils will not care what comes next. It will be too difficult.[17] Furthermore, when you pose questions in the midst of your narrative, it will be like putting a seashell to your ear: whistling emptiness.

There is another technique I use which involves either playing devil's advocate or setting up straw men. For instance, when talking about Heathrow's third runway, I'll explain how I don't think it's fair that a bunch of tie-dyed tree-huggers can dictate the course of British transport. Obviously, pupils will challenge this ludicrous statement, while others may argue that the protesters need a holiday.

It's fine for me to enter into viewpoints I don't really hold. It takes the conflict prescribed by Willingham out of the spoken narrative and into the classroom itself, setting myself up as the antagonist and giving the pupils the starring role in a pantomime drama. It's better than class debates since the pressures of peer group conformity mean that pupils are unlikely to openly disagree with each other.[18] The teacher, being outside of the pupil peer group, can happily circumvent these social norms. It often involves making a contentious statement – for example, 'Climate change is a hoax' – and then having the pupils justify their opposition to your point. The illusion

---

17 'Recall that problems (such as crossword puzzles) are interesting if they are neither too difficult nor too easy. Stories demand these medium-difficulty inferences': Willingham, *Why Don't Students Like School?*, p. 52.
18 'In numerous studies, a subject in a group answers some question, finds out after that – oh no! – everyone else disagrees, and can then change their answer': Sapolsky, *Behave*, p. 459.

of explanatory depth will make it difficult for them at first, but as Peps Mccrea suggests, it is important to 'expedite elaboration'.[19]

Remember earlier when you couldn't explain the toilet? It works like this. You pull a handle. The flush valve opens. Water pours in from the cistern. The refill tube fills it back up again until the float ball reaches a certain point. To expedite your elaboration, I could give you vocabulary cues: handle, flush valve, cistern, refill tube, float ball. I could change the order of these cues to increase the difficulty or render some blank to wean you off of them. Finally, I would have you telling the story instead of me.

ANALOGY MAGPIES: HOW ANALOGIES CAN BE MORE USEFUL THAN NARRATIVES

The latest truism in the heady and exhilarating twin galaxies of ITT and CPD is this: a well-sequenced narrative curriculum should serve as the centre of gravity for everything else. Do I disagree with this? No. It makes sense only from an SLT point of view. Leadership want to have every teacher singing from the same hymn sheet and children need to learn the same content.

Obviously, a narrative is important insofar as it is, as cognitive psychologist Daniel Willingham says, 'psychologically privileged'.[20] People tend to remember much of what they hear when it is in the form of a story. However, the problem with deploying narratives is that pupils won't always find them interesting. Some stories are long and very cumbersome. Think back to what happened in Europe after the fall of the Roman Empire, for instance. The continent was overrun with innumerable tribes – Goths, Vandals, Alans, Franks, and Lombards.[21] Every man and his dog, basically. We call this time the Dark Ages, not because we don't know what happened but

---

19 Mccrea, *Memorable Teaching*, pp. 57–64. Mccrea also recommends priming pupils with relevant material as well as the use of mnemonics.
20 Willingham, *Why Don't Students Like School?*, p. 66.
21 Hywel Williams, *Emperor of the West: Charlemagne and the Carolingian Empire* (London: Quercus, 2010), p. 17.

because every time we try to read about it, we swiftly find ourselves in bed with the curtains drawn.

What would be a better way of teaching difficult material like this? And how are you ensuring that what you say is creating the permanent change in long-term memory that constitutes learning?[22] Personally, I would use analogies instead. An analogy is a mode of explanation based on the similarity of a new piece of information to something you already know. According to Steven Pinker, the 'use of analogy in reasoning … is widely considered a key to what makes us smart'.[23]

For instance, in explaining gravity to their students, some teachers use the analogy of a bowling ball and trampoline. Gravity is the curvature of space-time, and so the sun, at the centre of our solar system, is like the bowling ball that weighs down the material of the trampoline. Why do planets orbit the sun? Imagine you rolled a tennis ball at an angle to the bowling ball – it would roll in a spiral towards the centre. This is very similar to the orbit of a planet.[24] A more competent science teacher than myself could extend this analogy to explain why our planet doesn't spiral in towards the sun. It is an enlightening image. The value of analogies has proven itself in the evidence-based community and, indeed, the brain is 'hardwired' for making them.[25]

My favourite thing about analogies is the ease with which you can collect them. When I hear a teacher explain a tsunami by conjuring the image of a rocked bathtub (the claw-footed kind that will grasp more tenaciously at the imagination), or an explanation of a

---

22 Willingham states that he has a problem with Kirschner's definition since it does not specify 'what long-term memory is', but that is like criticising a hairdryer because it isn't plugged in. It works well as a pithy definition predicated on the shared assumptions of cognitive psychology. See Daniel Willingham, On the Definition of Learning … (26 June 2017). Available at: http://www. danielwillingham.com/daniel-willingham-science-and-education-blog/on-the-definition-of-learning.

23 Pinker, *The Blank Slate*, p. 106.

24 Walter Isaacson, *Einstein: His Life and Universe* (London: Simon & Schuster, 2008). This analogy, along with the memorable images of Einstein riding a light beam and the notion of gravity as equivalent to an enclosed elevator accelerating up through space, appear in chapter 1.

25 Sherrington, *The Learning Rainforest*, p. 193; and Didau, *Making Kids Cleverer*, ch. 5.

waterfall's plunge pool as like a washing machine on spin cycle – these images are so crisp and memorable that I know I have to steal and use them right away. And there we go, copyright Mr Elliott.

Analogies are also useful because, if you are armed with enough of them, they can serve you in a variety of different lessons, whereas a narrative is usually bound to one topic alone. It's like the difference between chain mail and a suit of armour. Every analogy you collect can be linked to another. Furthermore, the chain mail allows you to move more freely and adapt better to unforeseen circumstances.

If somebody asked me last minute to teach a lesson on continental drift, I could do this without a lesson plan – easy! I would explain that the Earth has layers, with a thick, gooey centre like a Cadbury Creme Egg. I'd talk about how the Earth's crust is fractured into pieces we call tectonic plates – like a hard-boiled egg you just dropped on the floor. Finally, I could bring in various analogies from the sciences to explain convection currents: why hot lava rises to the surface (hot-air balloons) and how the plates move as though on conveyor belts.

At every stage of the lesson, I'd add in a link to the chain mail, thereby securing the learning and protecting myself from getting terrorised. Furthermore, I could use the hot-air balloon analogy in a completely unrelated lesson – perhaps to explain how hot air rises within the vortex of a hurricane. I could not do this with a narrative.

Imagine this instead. Pretend I've planned a narrative lesson on continental drift. I would start at the beginning when the German meteorologist Alfred Wegener published his paper back in 1911 … annnd you're back in the room. I'm sure the topic could be fashioned into a more interesting narrative, but this will take time and effort, and you will not be certain of the results. The narrative is, at times, a clunky and unwieldy suit of armour that constrains movement and isn't versatile at all.

How can we get the most out of analogies? In Japan, the curriculum is comprised of many different elements, and in order to revise it, they observe the different elements *within the classroom*.[26] If the teachers decide on a new curriculum, they do not just randomly clatter it out on a computer keyboard and then send it off bleary-eyed to the boss who has emailed at 9pm on a Sunday. Instead, every element of their scheme is subject to a kind of natural selection, and they would dispatch any dodos after careful consideration.

For instance, if I were going to plan the continental drift scheme for the curriculum, I would have several facts and analogies numbered on the scheme. My hard-boiled egg analogy could be one. Then, on a rainy Tuesday morning, several of my colleagues might file in to watch me teach. They might see confusion on little Reagan's face when I talk about plate tectonics. I then explain that it's like a hard-boiled egg you just dropped on the floor, and he gets it. At that point, my colleagues can put a green tick in the box next to '1.3. Hard-Boiled Egg Analogy' on the scheme. By contrast, when they saw that my Creme Egg analogy was evidently laid by a dodo, they put a red cross next to '1.2. Questionable Creme Egg Image'. The Earth has a solid core, my colleagues point out, whereas a Creme Egg doesn't. This could give rise to misconceptions – we're better off without it.

This does not have to be a whole-school policy. If you were to make this kind of document within your department or among a couple of colleagues, I know that it would have a lot more value than any amount of narrative curriculum sequencing that goes on behind teachers' closed doors.

But what about if a narrative is observed to work in the classroom? This is all well and good, but the problem here is that we cannot isolate which part of the narrative succeeded and therefore we have no information. Analogies are similar to genes since we can pinpoint causal relations and engineer future lessons: this analogy made pupils laugh, this one elicited understanding, and this was a piece of garbage.

---

26 Crehan, *Cleverlands*, p. 88.

Chapter 9

EXTENUATING CIRCUMSTANCES: THE NAUGHTIEST CLASSES AND COVERS

There will be occasions in your career when you are given the worst class imaginable. These kids will be a cut above your ordinary naughties. An elite unit of wily veterans, they've torpedoed their tutors, laid siege to supply, and fortified themselves against further instruction. This chapter is for the rank-and-file teachers who've been lumbered with the sink group. Why these exist, I'm not sure. It can be either bottom-set maths, the tutor group you've taken over from Mr Scarper, or even the 'mixed-ability' geography class. 'Sir, are we bottom set?' 'For the tenth time, no.' 'I don't know, sir. Something tells me this is bottom set.' 'Is it the peeling wallpaper?' 'You thought Ayia Napa and Ibiza were the same place, sir.' 'Yes, but in a sense they kind of are, aren't they?' I also examine cover lessons. As the name suggests, knowing how to boss covers allows you to paper over the cracks of improperly planned lessons. Besides, you will be asked to do them – and who wants to get terrorised?

HOW TO TAKE ON THE NAUGHTIEST CLASS IN SCHOOL – AND WIN (STAGE 1)

Your first lesson with the naughtiest class. Pupils are chewing absent-mindedly. They are talking to each other, not because they are particularly interested in conversation, but merely to put up an auditory blockade against you.

The room you are teaching this class in is going to be a dingy one. As hopeless as an abattoir, with some kind of tarnished display from the New Labour years and a projector so small that if it were in a pub there would be complaints to the landlord. Strangely, whenever the

naughty class leaves, the room is subtly transformed. The colours of the display bleed back into life and what you could swear were nicotine stains have faded from the walls. The classroom itself is broader, the whiteboard looks more pristine, and the display would not look out of place in an Odeon cinema.

The naughty class seems, through some kind of quantum principle, to alter the very nature of objective reality, making life very grim indeed. How, then, can you beat them?

Firstly, use the Hundred Flowers technique (see page 177) to establish your seating plan. If they complain that they are kept standing as you make up your mind, so much the better. This is your class. You own it. If you ripped up the floor tiles, you'd find your name etched into the concrete. As Phil Beadle puts it, 'Here the kid is testing their will against yours. If you back down at this point you are handing over the keys to the kingdom to the instruments of darkness.'[1] While Beadle is talking about detentions, I would generalise this rule. The will of a pupil should never override that of the teacher. If they need something and you can tell, respond. But never *relent*.

If you haven't established that only one person may speak at a time, pupils are liable to interrupt one another. If you fail to maintain your monopoly, they will re-establish their supply lines, routing you with paper aeroplane raids and the tactical distribution of chewing gum. If a pupil talks, you talk over them, and you make it clear using the language of authority how serious an offence this is.

This leads into my most commonplace strategy: making a mountain out of a molehill. Only for naughty classes, you ramp it to 11 on the Richter scale. The most minor instance of a pupil talking over you should stand towering on your horizon like Mount Everest, and in looking across at the class, it is likely to look like a desktop wallpaper of the Himalayan mountain range. If the class is the naughtiest of the naughty, then new snow-capped peaks will be bursting out of the ground every second.

If one pupil talks over you, here is the language you use: 'You do not have the right to hold back the learning of the pupils in this class. If

---

1 Beadle, *How to Teach*, p. 39.

you are not a part of the solution, you are part of the problem, and I will be ringing your parents. No. End of discussion.' If they question this, it's an hour; if they continue, they're isolated; and if it goes any further, it becomes an SLT matter. This may seem extreme, but once you tell them they have an hour, it usually doesn't go any further. The point is that you escalate quickly. Also, don't be too verbal about it. You're not working for the Inland Revenue, and you should not be referring them to Article 3, Subsection D of the school behaviour policy. The discipline should be delivered in short bursts that do not invite discussion and preferably are not audible to the rest of the class.

Eye contact is crucial. If you break eye contact with anyone first, you've submitted. You have to be wary of your expression while holding eye contact. By frowning, you signal aggression rather than dominance – a counterproductive strategy. The trick I've found is a blank expression, used to great effect against Hulk Jenkins and Ryan Pudsey. One way to prime yourself is to imagine you're watching television. In those moments, you're fully relaxed, with your emotions at low tide. This is the expression you need. It should be neutral since by smiling you give implicit permission for pushing boundaries. I'm not sure why this is. You'd think smiling is simply being polite and friendly. But when you have to control thirty kids, one or two will run with it like a through ball. It is better not to smile until you're established.

One of the best tricks I've learned is to always keep my eyes ahead of me. Believe it or not, you can write on the whiteboard without looking at it. Give it a go – it's easier than you think. Sometimes, pupils are just waiting for you to turn around, and then you'll be saying '3, 2, 1 … silence' yet again. If you want to grasp the full extent of the problem, try turning around suddenly when you've been writing at the whiteboard. You'll see what I mean.

My advice is twofold: never write much on the board – a directive with five short bullet points is more than enough, and practise writing on the whiteboard without looking at it. I only ever do this with extremely challenging classes; for me, it's the didactic equivalent of an around-the-world – the football trick where you whip your foot around the ball in mid-air. Bust one of those out before a game and people think you're Lionel Messi. Similarly, writing on the board without looking endows you with specious merit in the eyes of the kids. Specious or not, you need all the merit you can get.

HOW TO TAKE ON THE NAUGHTIEST CLASS IN SCHOOL — AND WIN (STAGE 2)

Here is where things start to get interesting. Although what I've described so far sounds like something more suited to the politburo of Stalinist Russia than the classroom, there is a working methodology that sits behind it. You cannot win over a class that is this naughty. You must establish yourself first.

Once you have a monopoly on speech, you can really get to work. The Hydra was a snake-like monster in Greek mythology who fought against Hercules, and who grew two heads for every one that was severed. What you have been doing so far is merely severing heads, and they are in the process of growing back. If you lose your momentum you are going to be severely terrorised, and then you'll probably wind up doing something undignified like begging a passing caretaker to intervene.

Going back to the Greek myth, Hercules manages to defeat the Hydra only with the help of his cousin, who scorched the bleeding stumps to stop them regenerating. Imagine that you had told a pupil to be quiet, they had begrudgingly done so, but then you saw the tell-tale signs of imminent regeneration: eyes rolling, a slouching posture, and a shirt that untucks every time you turn around. This pupil is going to come back twice as naughty, and soon, so here is what you do.

Keep the pupil after class. Wait until every other pupil has gone. He apologises. Should you let him go then? No. The fact that he thought behaving like that in a lesson was appropriate means you should take *at least* the amount of time he wasted. If it were me, I'd give him an hour, collect him myself, and give him a lot of work to do.

Notice here that no punishment was mentioned until the end of the lesson. This is why the Little Red Book is so crucial. It allows you to keep track of transgressions without the *j'accuse* of overt challenge.

There are several behaviour management strategies that advocate the exact opposite to what I propose. Bill Rogers argues that you should pause direction when being disrupted,[2] presumably to allow pupils to suddenly behold a vision of the Virgin Mary and tearfully recant. I suppose I could implement take-up time as well, waiting a patient forty-five minutes while pupil A contemplates not stabbing pupil B with a compass, or partial agreement ('Yes, pupil A, I can see why you would stab pupil B with a compass, but maybe now is not the appropriate time'). I do agree with Bill Rogers insofar as I use take-up time myself, only it comes in the form of an hour's detention after school every day until there is respect, compliance, and sensible behaviour. I also agree with his policy of 'forced choices': 'Either do twenty minutes of work now, pupil A, or apologise to pupil B and do ten minutes.' My preferred phraseology is this: 'You have *two choices* – one and none.'

Remember, this strategy is just about those vital first few lessons where you have to flip the script on a naughty class. You will not be able to sustain it indefinitely, and nor would you want to. In the provisional government that is you taking over this class, you need firm edicts, since the pupils are all unabashed Trotskyists lobbying for permanent revolution. The firm edicts you need are clear, defined, and obtainable deadlines for work. The work you put on the board should be so simple (not easy; simple) that a dog could understand it, and there should be a predefined word, line, or page limit. If they have not written five lines for the final task, they're staying. If they have done two and three-quarters of the three pages you requested, they're staying.

Once you have done all of this, you have won. Just keep a hair trigger on those hour detentions.

---

2   Killian, My 5 Favourite On-the-Spot Behaviour Management Strategies.

HOW TO TAKE ON A COVER LESSON — AND WIN

In all of the annals of history, from the Huguenot persecutions of Catholic France through to Dr Frankenstein's creation of a patchwork-corpse monster driven into exile by torch-wielding villagers, never has a figure been so routinely terrorised as the humble supply teacher.

Whether you're a supply or an ordinary teacher, you'll be expected to teach covers. As a teaching assistant I routinely covered lessons, despite having no qualifications whatsoever. If we fail to dissect the gouged and suppurating carcass of supply, we will never inoculate ourselves against the affliction of inflicted covers.

Is it even possible to win in a cover lesson? The pupils will sense immediately that you don't have any subject knowledge. They will also be able to infer that, since you're not their usual teacher, you are by definition a 'supply'. Some schools even helpfully provide supply teachers with green lanyards, rather like UN Peacekeeping troops are equipped with Smurf-coloured helmets and rifles with red plastic caps on the ends.

In one passage from *On the Edge*, Charlie Carroll captures what supply teachers must deal with:

'Right, girls,' I said. 'What I need you to do is …'

'I'm doing it!' erupted one of them, Tracey. 'God! Just fuck off, will you?'

'I can't have you talking to me like that,' I said, calmly. 'Please go and stand outside, and I'll be out in a minute to discuss this with you.'

She clapped her hands, hoorayed, and rushed out of the door. When I checked a moment or two later, she had vanished, taking the opportunity to go for a 20-minute walk around the school.[3]

The psychology you need to master for these situations is like nothing you're told in formal settings. If you state a rule, stick to it and

---

3 Carroll, *On the Edge*, loc. 332.

never back down. Phil Beadle is one of the few prepared to enter into this uncomfortable territory:

> Much like gangland Los Angeles, the classroom is a region where the person prepared to go the furthest wins. It is like the drug dealer who is prepared to dispense summary and brutal justice to his competitors who eventually runs the town; equally, the spoils of victory are available to the teacher who shows that they have no limits.[4]

Is it politically correct to say this? Not really. Should teachers be like drug dealers, then? Not unless you're slightly nerdy and consider knowledge an intoxicant. Anyway, true teachers will be slanging that K all day long, brudda. But do you remember the doors from *Monsters, Inc.*? The ones on rails that give you access to any home in the world. If we had doors to the best classrooms in the country … what Beadle describes is what we'd see. Little unassuming Irish ladies with the classroom presence of Scarface with an AK-47. Balding older gentlemen with empires of learning far broader than any of Al Capone's bootlegger rackets. And, gangsters aside, if you want to see any real monsters, read Carroll instead.

MARKETING, BODY LANGUAGE, AND RITUAL

Profess an expertise in the subject you're covering. Let's say it's a maths lesson. I don't care if you flunked your maths GCSE with a U, you need to pretend otherwise. Whenever I take a maths cover, I want kids to think I'm in Mensa – the High IQ Society, even though it would take me about a working week and several cans of Red Bull to solve a Barney the Dinosaur sudoku puzzle.

Even if a pupil had a copy of my GCSE maths transcript, and noticed I had a U in the subject, I would tell them the U stood for 'unknown variable', due to my unprecedentedly high score. If they told me that x was the proper notation, I'd say, 'Yeah, but only for treasure maps.' You get the point. I will profess to be an expert, even if that means telling the occasional white lie. For the record, I just scraped a C in maths GCSE, which I suppose, if I went to the Job Centre,

---

4 Beadle, *How to Teach*, p. 18.

would make me something of an expert – at least as far as Einstein's theory of relativity is concerned.

Now, you don't have to tell a white lie, but you need to imply that you're an expert. The moment they know that they don't have their regular teacher, they're already primed to misbehave. I'd imagine the psychology is like that of Ivan Pavlov's dog. Pavlov rang a bell every time he fed his dogs, and one day decided to ring the bell without feeding them, instead measuring the amount of saliva they produced. These were the heady days before the RSPCA put a stop to things like torturing animals with bells and putting dog spit in beakers. What Pavlov had discovered was a 'conditioned stimulus'.[5] The dogs had heard the bell and they thought they were getting their meal. Similarly, when the kids see their changed timetable at 8.45am, that's another conditioned stimulus, only instead of saliva they'll produce fidget spinners and leaky biros. You need to bluff enough expertise to override their knee-jerk (or pen-leak) response.

If you're squeamish about dishonesty, just market yourself differently. During a PE cover, I once explained that I was a regional boxing champion and boasted of my fabled ability to deliver a 'left, right, good night'. Did they need to know that this occurred in Year 6? Or that the 'region' was my back garden with three of my best friends, one of whom was partially sighted? Not at all. But from then on, the cover lesson got a hell of a lot easier.

I think it's also important to never profess your ignorance, and projecting overconfidence can allow you to offset whatever it is you don't know. To avoid being caught short, here's what to do. One time I had to cover a Year 7 maths lesson. God knows what a transformation is or why anybody would ever want to do one. Anyway, when I realised the subject of the lesson, I had to improvise. I told the class that transformations was my *favourite* topic. But since they had done it the lesson before, I needed a volunteer to come up and demonstrate what the class had learned. In fact, I needed several volunteers to come up, one at a time, to explain the nature of transformation for as long a time as would be necessary for a 26-year-old history/geography teacher to be able to grasp it. This took a short while.

---

5   Sapolsky, *Behave*, p. 34.

Eventually, I understood, and proceeded to look into the work-sheets left to me by Miss Benylin. I got to work. I puffed up my chest and said, 'Right then, we all know what we're doing, so let's get on with it.' I pointed to three children who became my worksheet capos, ensuring that everybody had a sheet.

Now, this is another important tip for bossing a cover lesson: move as little as possible. I don't know why – maybe it's similar to certain reptiles that can only sense prey when it's mobile. My advice is to sit on top of the teacher desk so that you are both elevated and relaxed. Either way, the more you get up when the kids are on task, the more restless you seem, and the more possibilities you create for subtle eye-flashes between comrades or some kind of smirking disruption.

Body language is key. Robert Sapolsky notes our ingenuity for detecting rank: 'forty milliseconds is all we need to reliably distinguish between a dominant face (with direct gaze) and a subordinate one (with averted gaze and lowered eyebrows)'.[6] When you do walk around the classroom, you have to keep your back very straight while scanning the work pupils are doing.

When you check on a pupil's work, try not to be too positive, and instead point to the correct answers and raise your thumb at them. This is called 'tactical grumpiness', and it allows you to signal high expectations by being 'hard to please, sceptical of excuses, and exceptionally sparing with praise'.[7]

If you notice that some pupils have got question 7 wrong, don't correct the misconception at the table. Instead, turn their attention to the whiteboard and outline how to tackle question 7 for the whole class, relying on answers from pupils where possible. Face the class while you are doing so.

Remember, these techniques apply only to supply and cover lessons, and in no way should they constitute ordinary teaching. The point is that you have very little subject knowledge and these strategies will at least allow you to avoid being terrorised.

---

6   Sapolsky, *Behave*, p. 432.
7   Didau and Rose, *What Every Teacher Needs to Know About Psychology*, p. 129.

You may be wondering: why is this so important? It's because teaching is all about your reputation. If you cover a maths lesson and get terrorised, word will spread. What if Dylan was just allowed to take the nib off his pen, streak his palms dark blue, and smear them all over the table to fashion an inkblot that looks less like a butterfly and more like your P45? How do you think he'll behave the next time you have the pleasure of teaching him? What's more, how do you think his friends will behave and his friends' friends? The domino effect applies as much to kids as to communist dictatorships.

Your mystique is very important too. What I mean by this is that you want to reveal as little of your intentions as possible. If you say too much, you're a waffler. If you're too polite, you're a pushover. And please remember that in the extreme circumstances of a cover lesson, the pressure against you is much higher than it would be normally.

An example of creating a mystique comes from that same Year 7 maths cover. I sat at the desk where I had three piles of worksheets. The pupils would come and collect a worksheet, and when they'd finished they would bring it back to me. This sounds counterintuitive but having them expend the effort of coming over to you will actually make them look upon you more favourably. Remember the Benjamin Franklin effect: it simply means that other people respect us more when they perform a task for us, and not vice versa.

By the end, the pupils were queuing at the desk to see me. It was like working at the Post Office. I would sign each sheet and then present the pupil with another: 'You've completed Article D, Subsection B, now fill out *this* for me.' I've used this technique in a number of covers, and I call it the DMV Approach – a reference to the Department of Motor Vehicles in the United States where customers queue for hours at a time.

What is the point of this rigmarole? It turns ordinary behaviour into a ritual, and as much as I satirise the many sacralised practices within teaching – the AfL deity, for instance – there is something to be said for having the children do this. Besides, if you don't have your own rituals, you can be sure the kids will have some of their own, including that perennial favourite: human sacrifice for learning (HSfL).

WHAT IF THE CLASS IS EXTREMELY NAUGHTY?

There are many instances where it will be impossible to cultivate a mystique, since the children will barge in through the doors as unceremoniously as a SWAT team at an opium den, with the added disadvantage of being too young to pay for the damages. You'll be standing there writing the learning objectives on the whiteboard, and the pupils will be in, volleying questions at you in a rapid machine-gun patter: 'When's your birthday?' 'How old are you?' 'Are you a form tutor?'

Pupils are obsessed with teachers' birthdays. And what I will say is this: do not answer the question. It's a trap – I love the way all pupils have settled on this question as the lowest common denominator for determining if you're a professional or not. When did the Naughties Against Teachers Union send out the newsletter? If you answer it, you've strayed into the realm of the personal, and not even the combined intellects of *DIY SOS* and *Scrapheap Challenge* would be able to salvage the ink-spattered ruin of a classroom left behind.

Clearly, this type of class is going to be handful. However, if you know the class is naughty in advance of the lesson, you may still have a chance. What you have to do is swot up on the subject you're teaching, even if you're not a specialist, and try to come up with analogies and narratives in advance. For instance, I had to teach a science class on the topic of waves, so I procured the textbook that Mr Beecham had left in his classroom for me. Luckily, I knew something about waves from geography, since transverse and longitudinal waves feature in the detection of earthquakes. If there is any way you can link the cover lesson to a topic you already teach, do so, since otherwise there is probably not enough time to swot up sufficiently.

In terms of the structure of the lesson, you need to plan something quickly, so here's what I would do. Start the lesson with a quiz that relates to their previous lesson. Then find a video on YouTube. The Goldilocks length is around fifteen minutes – but remember: although the art of supply is mostly about stalling for time, pupils cannot physically endure long videos. When it comes to YouTube, their eyes are bigger than their stomachs, and if you do try to show an hour-long video, the room will quickly be strewn with rubbish.

Now, even if you don't know much, you are going to have to do some questioning. The idea that you can do a lesson without questioning is as naive as trying to run a nightclub lavatory without the attendant who sprays CK One in your eyes. No question and answer? You're just a chancer. You *should* ask high-quality questions when you know your subject, but if you don't, try this.

Let's take a subject I know nothing about. Hair and beauty. To start off a lesson on this topic, I will quiz them on the previous lesson during which they learned about the intricacies of acrylic nails, then show them a twenty-minute Victoria Beckham make-up tutorial, and finally ask them, 'How does mascara make you feel?'

It sounds like satire, doesn't it? But if you can ask a question that gives emotional resonance to a topic, the pupils will respond and you can keep going indefinitely. Again, in this case, the aim is simply not to get terrorised – you're not teaching a proper lesson. The questions would continue like this: 'Is make-up empowering?' 'What do you think of people who don't wear make-up – are they stuck up?' 'Do you think Instagram is distorting our beauty standards?' 'Can you make any links between make-up and modern LGBT campaigns?'

Now, I haven't done any research on this topic (difficult to believe, I know), but if I were to ask these questions in a classroom, they would come off perfectly. You might think, 'That sounds a bit arrogant – how can you be so sure?' It's the same as the postman knowing to watch out for the yappy little Pomeranian at number 23. He's been there before. So just trust me: *commit and it will work.* Check that last question as well: 'make links'. Ask any question with the phrase 'make links' in it and you're bound to succeed. In history, for instance: 'Can you make any links between _____ [random historical topic 1] and _____ [random historical topic 2]?' Fill in the gaps with anything you like, it's bound to work: the First World War and the Second World War; Emperor Nero and the Opium Wars; hell, I bet even the Manhattan Project and *Cloudy with a Chance of Meatballs* would work. 'Well, just as in the Second World War, there was the race to manufacture nuclear weapons, so too does Flint

Lockwood perfect a device that can turn an Atlantic island into an enormous jelly doughnut. In the character of Flint Lockwood, we can almost hear Robert Oppenheimer's lament, "I am become Death, the destroyer of worlds." '[8]

You can't go on questioning forever, so you should finish the lesson with a short writing task. My personal favourite is to put five bullet points on the board with the instruction to 'rank and explain'. For instance, in the hair and beauty lesson, it would look like this:

- Acrylic nails
- Fake tan
- Lipstick
- Hair extensions
- Fake eyelashes

Rank these make-up products in order of importance and *explain* the order you have chosen.

The best part about this task is the word 'importance' – it can apply to anything. As such, the pupils will go on writing for a good while. It is also very easy to differentiate this task. Here's how I'd do it. One pupil, named Aleesha, might give a token raise of her hand before shouting out, 'Done,' then fold her arms in a petulant huff, and then start to disrupt – the fantasy notion of her pen exploding on its own beckoning to her like the One Ring did to Gollum.

I'd say to Aleesha, 'What did you put as most important?' She'll likely scowl back, 'Fake tan.' 'OK,' I'll respond, 'now what do you think is the least important?' She'll say, 'Lipstick, obviously.' I silently concur with this. She's lippy enough. 'Right, Aleesha, and have you said why fake tan is more important than lipstick?' and if she says 'Yeah,' I'll ask her to explain why, for instance, hair extensions might be more important than lipstick, which she has yet to do. In the chess match of the supply lesson, this is checkmate.

That's why this bullet-point task is so great. I don't think there is a single lesson you can't do it for. And guess what? It never ends.

---

8   Ray Monk, *Inside the Centre: The Life of J. Robert Oppenheimer*, Kindle edn (London: Jonathan Cape, 2012), loc. 9279.

Think about it. In terms of importance, there are probably about twenty different combinatorial possibilities of explanations (I think so, anyway; my maths is very much an unknown variable). You can just keep saying to the kids, 'Why is A more important than B?' 'Why is B more important than C?' 'Oh, look! You haven't explained why A is more important than C – chop, chop.'

This task is great in terms of stalling for time, but the unusual thing is how well it works for an ordinary lesson. In terms of Bloom's pyramid, it's technically a higher-level activity, and as a form of differentiation you can always give easier explanations to the struggling pupils.[9]

For instance, for a lesson on mitigating climate change I used the following bullet points:

- Planting trees
- International agreements
- Nuclear power
- Renewable energy
- Carbon capture

One child had said that planting trees was second most important and that nuclear power was the least important. He put his hand up to tell me he was done. I knew that his data showed he was a lower-attainer (plus, I was being observed for this lesson). I asked, 'Why might planting trees be more important than nuclear power?' Everybody knows about planting trees and nuclear power, whereas he'd have found renewable energy a lot trickier, so – hey presto: differentiation. Clearly, this was not an example of good teaching, but it did appease the Bull God of Differentiation, with the head of a bull and wings of an angel – never mind what comes out the other end. I almost beheld a vision of it swooping down from the learning pyramid, with its toy-xylophone colour scheme, and leaving me a small offering before flying off out of the window. The following

---

9   Personally, I wouldn't bother with differentiation. The policy is merely an afterglow of the catastrophic implosion of learning styles of the early 2010s. Nevertheless, it *is* enshrined in the Standards, meaning you may have to differentiate for some observations. If required, do so in the perfunctory manner outlined: see Department for Education, *Teachers' Standards*, p. 11.

lesson, when I wasn't trying to put on a showstopper lesson, I actually taught the pupil what renewable energy was.

Quick aside: this is part of the problem I have with differentiation and Bloom's taxonomy – the triangle, not the book, which hardly anyone has actually read. They incentivise teachers to use workarounds during observations that merely sweep problems under the carpet, rather than address them. As David Didau puts it, 'Teachers have felt under pressure to pretend they don't teach. On hearing that someone is planning to observe them they say, "Oh they won't want to see that, I'll have to change my plans. They won't want to see children working in silence; they'll expect some sort of show." '[10]

Moreover, the consequences of having a bad observation, as you'll remember from 'Teacher Training in Leamington', can be pretty awful. In terms of this bullet-points activity, yes, it allows me to not be disrupted in a supply lesson and also to gain a good observation, but it is also problematic. I did not address the lower-attainer's lack of knowledge in the lesson because, from an observer's standpoint, the messy business of learning isn't particularly outstanding.

The other problem is that there are many observers who know Bloom's taxonomy but not the nuances of the underlying work. The triangle itself 'does not appear anywhere in either [of Bloom's taxonomies]. The triangular representation was quite likely designed by someone as part of a presentation made to educational practitioners (e.g. teachers, administrators).'[11] Moreover, it lacks an empirical basis, since it was 'just what Bloom reckoned'.[12] Most training coordinators don't understand the taxonomy. They saw it in a PowerPoint once and that clinched it: higher-level skills over lower-level drills. This is their Manichean worldview of light versus dark. Even though the light that is 'skill' doesn't really exist, any more than a rainbow

---

10 Didau, *What If Everything You Knew About Education Was Wrong?*, p. 96.
11 Hendrick and Macpherson, *What Does This Look Like in the Classroom?*, loc. 2795.
12 Hendrick and Macpherson, *What Does This Look Like in the Classroom?*, loc. 2781.

has a physical presence. Skills are mere iridescences of particulate knowledge.[13]

Anyway, the five bullet points are a tried-and-tested tactic that will allow you to meet several objectives at once: differentiation, class-room control, and stretch and challenge (just keep asking questions).

Aside from this, the only other tactics I would recommend are con-tained within 'How to Take On the Naughtiest Class in School – and Win (Parts 1 and 2)', which will help you with the behaviour manage-ment you'll need to boss a cover. If I had to summarise this section, I'd say the following:

- Bluff about being an expert.
- Develop a mystique.
- Stories and analogies.
- Emotional questioning.
- Five bullet points task.

There's no rank and explain here: they're all equally important.

---

13 'Because thinking skills require knowledge, they don't exist generically. There's no such thing as the generic ability to be analytical or creative; you can only analyse some thing or be creative in a particular field': David Didau, Didau's Taxonomy, *The Learning Spy* (4 April 2017). Available at: https://learningspy. co.uk/featured/didaus-taxonomy.

CONCLUSION:
ARE YOU ON TEAM TEACHER?

If a Google search can tell you anything, it's that 'putting students first' is very important: 622,000,000 results is nothing to sniff at. By this criterion, putting students first is five times more important than Brexit, twelve times more important than xylophones, and sixty-two times more important than liposuction. Incidentally, it matters only a third as much as *Family Guy* and *Love Island*.

My point? Just because a phrase is ubiquitous, doesn't mean it has any value. What problem could I possibly have with the idea of putting students first? It's the same problem that retailers have with the expression 'the customer is always right'. The customer is not always right. £60 billion a year is lost to retailers through the phenomenon of 'wardrobing' – where a customer buys an outfit, wears it once, and then returns to the store for a refund.[1] Meanwhile, every time I walk around Willenhall, the estates are littered with discarded shopping trollies. How does this even happen? The nearest Sainsbury's is 3.8 miles away. Whoever pushed that trolley through parks, A-roads, and industrial estates is as mysterious to me as the Druids who pushed those first bluestones to the Salisbury Plain. The one, perhaps only, thing I can infer about that occult shopper is that what they did was definitely not 'right'.

Am I exempt? No. One summer, I bought a Bill Bryson book on Kindle, read it, and then got a refund within the seven-day return period. I didn't stop there. I did it for every book the poor bloke's ever written. That said, I'm sure Bryson would be delighted to know that I was at least 'right' for doing this – I was exercising my God-given rights as a customer!

---

1 Paul Skeldon, ASOS Leads the Way in Ending 'Wardrobing' Trend That Costs Retail £60bn a Year, Internet Retailing (10 April 2019). Available at: https://internetretailing.net/industry/industry/asos-leads-the-way-in-ending-wardrobing-trend-that-costs-retail-60bn-a-year-19443.

These phrases can be insidious, since the more we hear them, the more they're invested with an aura of truth. 'Hmm, it just sounds right!' This is called the 'mere exposure effect'.[2] It works as follows: if I wanted you to have a positive response to a meaningless word, such as 'bungawunga', I could say it to you a number of times. Once you'd heard it enough, studies suggest you'd prefer it to other similarly meaningless words, like 'differentiation'.

It's why the Conservatives have won the past six elections/referendums: they always have a simple phrase they can beat you over the head with. It was 'Labour's legacy' in 2010, 'Better together' for the Scottish independence referendum of 2014, 'Living within our means' for David Cameron in 2015, the Vote Leave campaign's 'Take back control' in 2016,[3] Theresa May's infamous 'Strong and stable leadership' of 2017, and finally, Boris Johnson's 'Get Brexit done' in 2019. If that last one is anything to go by, it is not by any inherent truth value that these slogans have succeeded. They convinced the electorate because of the mere exposure effect.

So, what's Team Teacher, then? Quite simple really. Teachers in this country are routinely terrorised by children. I think the doormat philosophy of explicitly 'putting students first' has had its day.

Uncritical child-centred ideology is leading to what I call the Sports Directification of the profession. Ever shopped at Sports Direct? Here's my advice: don't. The customer service is so bad it makes me want to bring back the feudal system. 'Yes, I'm happy to work sixteen hours a day picking wheat and rye for you, m'lord, just please don't subject me to those red-and-blue Slazenger shirts ever again.' I hear it's because they're underpaid.[4] They have my sympathies, but reacting to shoppers as if they were woodlice on an overturned log is hardly going to lift their pay scale. Once, I wanted to purchase an XXL Adidas bag I'd seen on their website. It was on the top shelf and they would have to get the ladder out. The shop assistant

---

2 Kahneman, *Thinking, Fast and Slow*, p. 66.
3 Technically not a Conservative campaign, since David Cameron backed Remain, but definitely a right-wing cause.
4 Simon Goodley, Sports Direct May Be Paying Less Than Minimum Wage, Investigation Shows, *The Guardian* (23 July 2020). Available at: https://www. theguardian.com/business/2020/jul/23/sports-direct-undercover-minimum-wage-mike-ashley.

informed me that the ones on the top shelf were the same size as those on the bottom. They weren't. Those were merely XL. I pointed this out and he reacted as if I'd said it about his mother. Besides, it's a matter of perspective: things that are further away appear smaller. Am I to suspect that this employee thinks a Big Ben in a snow globe is a life-sized representation? Another time, they threw my stop-watch at me at the till and told me they'd run out of bags. On my way out, I was accosted and accused of theft. 'Is it because I is white British?' I asked, before showing them the receipt.[5] What's happening at Sports Direct has been happening to teachers for a while.

The workload is too high, disruption is unduly stressful, and, mean-while, those in management are not helping class teachers. I invite my friends on work nights out: 'Come, it'll be a laugh,' I say. They are then witness to the spectacle of thirty teachers sitting around scowling as they listlessly put away shots of Apple Sourz. 'Why did you bring us here, Sam?' say my friends, before buggering off to somewhere less depressing. Other colleagues tell me they're look-ing to marry an heiress so they can quit the profession and go yachting around the Med, presumably playing the saxophone in all of the jazz bars between Naples and Sanremo.

As for me, I enjoy teaching. But only because I've read around the subject, which has given me a sense of having an internal locus of control. What this means is that my ability to meet the challenges of the career are within my means, thereby keeping my stress levels low.[6] This is opposed to having an external locus of control, whereby I might feel that what I do in the classroom is determined by exter-nal events such as how tough the class is, blindly following the advice of my superiors, or deciding that pupils will succeed or fail regardless of what I do (a fixed mindset approach that is bad for both pupils and practitioners).[7] It sounds bad, but if a colleague or

---

5 One of the few stores in which I would implement a 'customer is always right' policy, although I prefer the inverse formulation: 'the staff are always wrong'.

6 'The more competent someone is at something, the less likely they are to become stressed while doing it': Busch and Watson, *The Science of Learning*, p. 51. See also Didau and Rose, *What Every Teacher Needs to Know About Psychology*, p. 242.

7 'Teachers with a fixed mindset were more likely to endorse a comfort-focused approach' and 'students who heard comfort-focused [as opposed to strategy-focused words] were actually disheartened': Busch and Watson, *The Science of Learning*, p. 60.

mentor tells me to do something, I'm more than happy to ignore it. I largely go off what I read in the literature, since authors have to meet publication standards whereas so-called authorities in schools can say any old thing. If you want to know who my real mentors are, read the footnotes.

Anyway, Team Teacher works like this. As teachers, we strive to get the best results for our pupils and obviously this necessitates a certain level of well-being. Those with precarious mental health need to be supported as much as possible. However, we also understand that sometimes our pupils are against us, that some of them want to terrorise their teachers for fun, and that this is a game we must win. Teachers are not primary caregivers. No one should ever see us this way. Once pupils get their foot in the door, they're like emotional bailiffs.

In schools, we have pastoral departments and the dedicated individuals staffing them cannot be praised highly enough. As a teacher, remember that the emotional well-being of pupils is *their* territory. They are better qualified to deal with mental health issues – especially if you're a young teacher – and so I would try to leave it to them. Teachers are sovereign in the realm of academia, and this is the sphere in which we must play to win. Incidentally, where teachers do win, the students win too. Indeed, as far as teacher obligations go, I agree with the following: 'the best pastoral care for my most socio-economically challenged students is 5A*–C. Period.'[8]

If you're having heart palpitations at the thought of students being left ailing in the gutter as teachers savagely go on bar crawls during lunchtimes or smoke cigarettes behind the bicycle sheds, I wouldn't worry. In my experience, all teachers want to do well, and if your pupils are failing, so are you. If students aren't getting the best possible grades to improve their life chances, you should be ashamed of yourself. The fates of pupils and their teachers are inextricably bound together like Fiat 500s and Pandora bracelets.

---

8   David Didau, Differentiation: Are High Expectations Enough? *The Learning Spy* (12 June 2014). Available at: https://learningspy.co.uk/learning/high-expectations-enough.

This idea has a long pedigree: 'It is not from the benevolence of the butcher, the brewer, or the baker, that we expect our dinner, but from their regard for their own self-interest.'[9] Adam Smith had it right – and if you're still doubting, think about it like this. Do students actually know what's best for them? When I was in Year 10, I thought drinking Strongbow in St Margaret's Park was best for me and that smoking cigars at the back of the number 33 bus to town was perfectly acceptable (the window was open). What actually proved to be best for me was my maths teacher, Miss Moorcroft, who brooked no dissension and never once allowed me to terrorise her. By some miracle, I passed my maths GCSE, despite the extenuating circumstances of being in bed at the commencement of it and of being picked up by my French teacher to sit the remaining half. Miss Moorcroft lent me a pen.

When I sit in my department, I am always ready to support my colleagues whenever I have to, and we work together to keep kids out of the corridors. Pupils, like adults, are territorial, and once they have some measure of control over their environment they start thinking they can have whatever mad thing they like. When I'm out on that corridor, I keep telling myself that I'm on Team Teacher and this is our turf. I'm well aware that it sounds ridiculous, but the more I play to win, the more control my colleagues and I have over our environment. The pupils benefit most from us, and not them, having control over the school.

What happens when the pupils start winning and Team Teacher starts losing? I can tell you from personal experience, but it does largely depend on the catchment of the school. In wealthy areas, students will mock and disrespect their teachers, and aside from the occasional whiff of head-shaking apathy, will largely do their work. In more deprived catchments, you'll see pupils squaring up to teachers, following and abusing them as they video it all on their smartphones, along with declining levels of behaviour and achievement. Older, more experienced staff will retire to rural towns that sound vaguely fictional, like Upton Snodsbury or Ashby de la Zouch. And the head teacher will spend so much time in his office that you're half expecting him to have discovered quantum gravity by

---

9   Adam Smith, *An Inquiry into the Nature and Causes of the Wealth of Nations*, Kindle edn (Chicago, IL: Chicago University Press, 2016 [1904]), p. 10.

the time he comes out. Meanwhile, whole departments will become entirely comprised of trainee teachers and NQTs, causing you to patiently await the arrival of Alan Sugar at the staff assembly to congratulate you for having made the final cut of Junior Apprentice. Last, but not least, pupils' lives will be ruined.

When I got into the profession, people would ask me what I did for a living. You know what those British hairdressers are like. 'Yeah, I'm a teacher,' I'd say. You could just as well have said you were on the dole. Watch them try not to look too sorry for you as they change the topic back to the minutiae of hairdressing: 'So, what made you go for a 2 on the sides? I've always been more of a 3 man, myself.' Next time, I'll make my life easier and say I work at Jobcentre Plus. 'What, on the desks?' 'No, as a recipient.' 'Ooh, how exciting. Tell me, what are those application forms like? Do they really ask for your driving licence *and* passport?' But no. I'm on Team Teacher, damn it. I love and enjoy my job. It's the most difficult job in the world but the rewards are immense. Now, whenever I hear the groans and sighs, or witness the comically slanted expression of pity, I put them straight. 'Yeah, the holidays are good, but I kinda miss teaching when I'm off for so long. Attitude? Yeah, sometimes, but I have these techniques …' And then comes the clincher: 'I'm so glad I don't work in an office. I'd die of boredom. Teaching is the new Wild West and I'm right on the frontier. It feels so good to be making a difference.' The hairdresser cogitates on that before placidly going back to the shit haircut he's given me. 'Yeah,' I say. 'Building brighter futures for these kids. That's me, brudda. Anyway, have you ever heard of *Danny Dyer's Deadliest Men*?

BIBLIOGRAPHY

Alberts, Bruce (2009) *Essential Cell Biology*, 3rd edn (New York: Garland Science).

Ariely, Dan (2009) *Predictably Irrational: The Hidden Forces That Shape Our Decisions* (London: HarperCollins).

Ashman, Greg (2012) Research on Seating Arrangements, *Filling the Pail* (12 October). Available at: https://gregashman.wordpress.com/2016/10/12/research-on-seating-arrangements.

Ashman, Greg (2018a) Homework, *Filling the Pail* (26 September). Available at: https://gregashman.wordpress.com/2018/09/26/homework.

Ashman, Greg (2018b) *The Truth About Teaching: An Evidence-Informed Guide for New Teachers* (London: SAGE).

Azevedo, Frederico A., Carvalho, Ludmila R., Grinberg, Lea T., Farfel, José M., Ferretti, Renata E., Leite, Renata E., Filho, Wilson J., Lent, Roberto, and Herculano-Houzel, Suzana (2009) Equal Numbers of Neuronal and Nonneuronal Cells Make the Human Brain an Isometrically Scaled-Up Primate Brain, *Journal of Comparative Neurology*, 513(5): 532–541. DOI:10.1002/cne.21974.

Ban the Booths (2018) Moral Rights and Wrongs (16 December). Available at: https://banthebooths.co.uk/blog/rightsandwrongs.

Bartolacci, James (2020) The Tallest, Heaviest, and Most Eccentric Buildings on Earth, *Architizer* (26 July). Available at: https://architizer.com/blog/inspiration/stories/guinness-world-record-day.

BBC News (2015) South Korean Students Finish Welsh Maths GCSE Paper in 15 Minutes (28 November). Available at: https://www.bbc.co.uk/news/av/uk-wales-38115296/south-korean-students-finish-welsh-gcse-maths-paper-in-15-minutes.

Beadle, Phil (2006) Four Steps to Being Chucked on the Scrapheap, *The Guardian* (24 October). Available at: https://www.theguardian.com/education/2006/oct/24/teaching.schools.

Beadle, Phil (2010) *How to Teach* (Carmarthen: Crown House Publishing).

Bennett, Tom and Berry, Jill (2017) Behaviour. In Carl Hendrick and Robin Macpherson (eds), *What Does This Look Like in the Classroom? Bridging the Gap Between Research and Practice*, Kindle edn (Woodbridge: John Catt Educational).

Brown, Peter, McDaniel, Mark A., and Roediger III, Henry L. (2014) *Make It Stick: The Science of Successful Learning* (London: Belknap Press of Harvard University Press).

Bryson, Bill (1993) *Notes from a Small Island* (London: Transworld).

Busch, Bradley and Watson, Edward (2019) *The Science of Learning: 77 Studies That Every Teacher Needs to Know* (Abingdon and New York: Routledge).

Carey, Benedict (2014) *How We Learn: Throw Out the Rule Book and Unlock Your Brain's Potential* (London: Macmillan).

Carpenter, Shana K., Cepeda, Nicholas J., Rohrer, Doug, Kang, Sean H. K., and Pashler, Harold (2012) Using Spacing to Enhance Diverse Forms of Learning: Review of Recent Research and Implications for Instruction. *Educational Psychology Review*, 24: 369–378.

Carroll, Charlie (2010) *On the Edge: One Teacher, A Camper Van, Britain's Toughest Schools*, Kindle edn (London: Monday Books).

Christodoulou, Daisy (2014) *Seven Myths About Education* (Abingdon and New York: Routledge).

Christodoulou, Daisy (2015) Assessment: High Stakes, Low Improvement. In Robert Peal (ed.), *Changing Schools: Perspectives on Five Years of Educational Reform*, Kindle edn (Woodbridge: John Catt Educational).

Christodoulou, Daisy (2016) *Making Good Progress? The Future of Assessment for Learning* (Oxford: Oxford University Press).

Chua, Amy (2011) *Battle Hymn of the Tiger Mother* (New York: Penguin).

Coe, Robert (2013) *Improving Education: A Triumph of Hope Over Experience*. Inaugural lecture of Professor Robert Coe, Durham University, 18 June (Gateshead: Centre for Evaluation and Monitoring). Available at http://www.cem.org/attachments/publications/ImprovingEducation2013.pdf.

Cowley, Sue (2014) *Getting the Buggers to Behave* (London: Bloomsbury).

Crehan, Lucy (2016) *Cleverlands* (London: Unbound).

Crehan, Lucy (2017) Why Textbooks Matter (11 January). Available at: http://lucycrehan.com/why-textbooks-matter.

Darwin, Charles (2017 [1871]) *The Descent of Man, and Selection in Relation to Sex*, Kindle edn (New York: Createspace).

Dehaene, Stanislas (2020) *How We Learn: The New Science of Education and the Brain* (London: Penguin).

Department for Education (2011) *Teachers' Standards: Guidance for School Leaders, School Staff and Governing Bodies* (July; introduction updated June 2013). Available at: https://www.gov.uk/government/publications/teachers-standards.

Department for Education (2016) *Behaviour and Discipline in Schools* (January). Available at: https://www.gov.uk/government/publications/behaviour-and-discipline-in-schools.

Dickens, Charles (2003 [1853]) *Bleak House* (London: Penguin).

Didau, David (2013) Great Teaching Happens in Cycles, *The Learning Spy* (24 June). Available at: https://learningspy.co.uk/featured/great-teaching-happens-in-cycles.

Didau, David (2014a) An Argument for Order, *The Learning Spy* (24 October). Available at: https://learningspy.co.uk/behaviour/an-argument-for-order.

Didau, David (2014b) Differentiation: Are High Expectations Enough? *The Learning Spy* (12 June). Available at: https://learningspy.co.uk/learning/high-expectations-enough.

Didau, David (2014c) *The Secret of Literacy: Making the Implicit Explicit* (Carmarthen: Independent Thinking Press).

Didau, David (2015a) *What If Everything You Knew About Education Was Wrong?* (Carmarthen: Crown House Publishing).

Didau, David (2015b) Why I Struggle with Learning Objectives and Success Criteria, *The Learning Spy* (6 December). Available at: https://learningspy.co.uk/learning/8696/#_edn1.

Didau, David (2016) What Every Teacher Needs to Know About … Seating Plans, *The Learning Spy* (9 September). Available at: https://learningspy.co.uk/planning/every-teacher-needs-know-seating-plans.

Didau, David (2017) Didau's Taxonomy, *The Learning Spy* (4 April). Available at: https://learningspy.co.uk/featured/didaus-taxonomy.

Didau, David (2019a) The Madness of Flight Paths, *The Learning Spy* (23 March). Available at: https://learningspy.co.uk/assessment/how-do-we-know-pupils-are-marking-progress-part-1-the-problem-with-flightpaths.

Didau, David (2019b) *Making Kids Cleverer: A Manifesto for Closing the Advantage Gap* (Carmarthen: Crown House Publishing).

Didau, David and de Bruyckere, Pedro (2017) Learning Myths. In Carl Hendrick and Robin Macpherson (eds), *What Does This Look Like in the Classroom? Bridging the Gap Between Research and Practice*, Kindle edn (Woodbridge: John Catt Educational).

Didau, David and Rose, Nick (2016) *What Every Teacher Needs to Know About Psychology* (Woodbridge: John Catt Educational).

Dyer, Kathy (2019) 5 Formative Strategies to Improve Student Learning from Dylan Wiliam and NWEA, *NWEA* (14 February). Available at: https://www.nwea.org/blog/2019/5-formative-strategies-to-improve-student-learning-from-dylan-wiliam-and-nwea.

Forbes (2001) 'Because It's There' (29 October). Available at: https://www.forbes.com/global/2001/1029/060.html#397284ad2080.

Fromm, Erich (2002 [1955]) *The Sane Society* (Abingdon and New York: Routledge).

Gallo, Carmine (2010) *The Presentation Secrets of Steve Jobs: How to Be Insanely Great in Front of Any Audience* (New York: McGraw Hill).

Gonzalez, Tony (2020) Heavyweight Mike Tyson on Why He Loves Fear [video] (21 February). Available at: https://www.youtube.com/watch?v=zeRlmGTMZM8&t=2s.

Goodhart, David (2017) *The Road to Somewhere: The New Tribes Shaping British Politics* (London: Penguin).

Goodley, Simon (2020) Sports Direct May Be Paying Less Than Minimum Wage, Investigation Shows, *The Guardian* (23 July). Available at: https://www.theguardian.com/business/2020/jul/23/sports-direct-undercover-minimum-wage-mike-ashley.

Haidt, Jonathan (2015) *The Righteous Mind: Why Good People are Divided by Politics and Religion* (London: Penguin).

Haidt, Jonathan (2018) *The Coddling of the American Mind: How Good Intentions and Bad Ideas Are Setting Up a Generation for Failure* (London: Penguin).

Hammang, Angela J. (2012) The Effect of Seating Assignments on Student Achievement in the Biology Classroom. Master's thesis (July). Available at: https://www.teachertoolkit.co.uk/wp-content/uploads/2017/05/HammangA0812.pdf.

Hardy, Thomas (2003 [1891]) *Tess of the d'Urbervilles* (London: Collector's Library).

Hattie, John (2012) John Hattie: Learning Intentions and Success Criteria [video], *Stem Learning*. Available at: https://www.stem.org.uk/rxacud.

Haynes, Charlie (2015) 'I Was Put in a School Isolation Booth More Than 240 Times', *BBC News* (15 April). Available at: https://www.bbc.co.uk/news/education-47898657.

Hendrick, Carl and Macpherson, Robin (2017) *What Does This Look Like in the Classroom? Bridging the Gap Between Research and Practice*, Kindle edn (Woodbridge: John Catt Educational).

Hirsch, Jr, Eric D. (2017) *Why Knowledge Matters: Rescuing Our Children from Failed Educational Theories* (Cambridge, MA: Harvard Education Press).

Hobbes, Thomas (1979 [1651]) *Leviathan* (London: Pelican Classics).

Isaacson, Walter (2004) *Benjamin Franklin: An American Life*, Kindle edn (New York: Simon & Schuster).

Isaacson, Walter (2008) *Einstein: His Life and Universe* (London: Simon & Schuster).

Jabr, Ferris (2015) The Reading Brain in the Digital Age: The Science of Paper versus Screens, *Scientific American* (11 April). Available at: https://www.scientificamerican.com/article/reading-paper-screens.

James, William (1899) *Talks to Teachers on Psychology; And to Students on Some of Life's Ideals* (New York: Henry Holt and Company).

James, William (1918) *The Principles of Psychology* (New York: Henry Holt and Company).

Kahneman, Daniel (2012) *Thinking, Fast and Slow* (London: Penguin).

Keeley, Brian (2007) *Human Capital: How What You Know Shapes Your Life* (OECD Insights) (Paris: Organisation for Economic Co-operation and Development).

Kelbie, Paul (2004) Burberry Checks Out of Baseball Caps to Deter Hooligan Fans, *The Independent* (11 September). Available at: https://www.

independent.co.uk/news/uk/this-britain/burberry-checks-out-of-baseball-caps-to-deter-hooligan-fans-545812.html.

Kerr, Robert and Booth, Bernard (1978) Specific and Varied Practice of Motor Skill, *Perceptual and Motor Skills*, 46(2): 395–401.

Kershaw, Ian (2008) *Hitler* (London: Penguin).

Killian, Shaun (2019) My 5 Favourite On-the-Spot Behaviour Management Strategies from Bill Rogers, *Evidence-Based Teaching* (22 November). Available at: https://www.evidencebasedteaching.org.au/bill-rogers-behaviour-management.

Laplace, Pierre-Simon (1902) *A Philosophical Essay on Probabilities* (New York: John Wiley).

Lawson, Dominic (2011) Chinese Mothers … A Lesson to Us All, *The Independent* (11 January). Available at: https://www.independent.co.uk/voices/commentators/dominic-lawson/dominic-lawson-chinese-mothers-a-lesson-to-us-all-2181165.html.

Lewis, Michael (2011) *The Big Short: Inside the Doomsday Machine*, Kindle edn (London: Penguin).

McCourt, Mark (2019) *Teaching for Mastery* (Woodbridge: John Catt Educational).

Mccrea, Peps (2017) *Memorable Teaching: Leveraging Memory to Build Deep and Durable Learning in the Classroom* (London: Peps Mccrea).

Mance, Henry (2016) Britain Has Had Enough of Experts, Says Gove, *Financial Times* (3 June). Available at: https://www.ft.com/content/3be49734-29cb-11e6-83e4-abc22d5d108c.

Marx, Karl (1887) *Capital: A Critique of Political Economy* [Das Kapital] (Moscow: Progress Publishers). Available at: https://www.marxists.org/archive/marx/works/1867-c1/ch01.htm#S1.

Monk, Ray (2012) *Inside the Centre: The Life of J. Robert Oppenheimer*, Kindle edn (London: Jonathan Cape).

Moran, Michael (2018) 10 of the (Unintentionally) Funniest Quotes from *The Apprentice*, *Digital Spy* (6 November). Available at: https://www.digitalspy.com/tv/reality-tv/a869591/apprentice-quotes.

Neill, Alexander S. (1998) *Summerhill School: A New View of Childhood* (New York: St Martin's Press).

Oates, Tim (2015) Finnish Fairy Stories, *Cambridge Assessment* (April). Available at: https://www.cambridgeassessment.org.uk/Images/207376-finnish-fairy-stories-tim-oates.pdf.

Old, Andrew (2020) Isolation Booths, *Teaching Battleground* (2 January). Available at: https://teachingbattleground.wordpress.com/2020/01/02/isolation-booths.

Peal, Robert (2014) *Progressively Worse: The Burden of Bad Ideas in British Schools* (London: Civitas).

Pinker, Steven (1999) *How the Mind Works* (London: Penguin).

Pinker, Steven (2003) *The Blank Slate: The Modern Denial of Human Nature* (London: Penguin).

Pinker, Steven (2011) *The Better Angels of Our Nature: A History of Violence and Humanity* (London: Penguin).

Pinker, Steven (2019) *Enlightenment Now: The Case for Reason, Science, Humanism, and Progress* (London: Penguin).

Quigley, Alex (2018) *Closing the Vocabulary Gap* (Abingdon and New York: Routledge).

Quigley, Alex (2020) *Closing the Reading Gap* (Abingdon and New York: Routledge).

Ripley, Amanda (2013) *The Smartest Kids in the World* (New York: Simon & Schuster).

Rosenshine, Barak (2012) Principles of Instruction: Research-Based Strategies That All Teachers Should Know, *American Educator* (spring): 12–19, 39. Available at: https://www.aft.org/sites/default/files/periodicals/ Rosenshine.pdf.

Rousseau, Jean-Jacques (1921) *Emile, or Education*, tr. Barbara Foxley (London & Toronto: J.M. Dent and Sons). Available at: https://oll. libertyfund.org/titles/2256.

Rovelli, Carlo (2017) *Reality Is Not What It Seems: The Journey to Quantum Gravity* (London: Penguin).

Sapolsky, Robert (2018) *Behave: The Biology of Humans at Our Best and Worst* (London: Penguin).

Sherrington, Tom (2017) *The Learning Rainforest: Great Teaching in Real Classrooms* (Woodbridge: John Catt Educational).

Sherrington, Tom (2019) *Rosenshine's Principles in Action* (Woodbridge: John Catt Educational).

Shotton, Richard (2018) *The Choice Factory: 25 Behavioural Biases That Influence What We Buy* (Petersfield: Harriman House).

Skeldon, Paul (2019) ASOS Leads the Way in Ending 'Wardrobing' Trend That Costs Retail £60bn a Year, *Internet Retailing* (10 April). Available at: https:// internetretailing.net/industry/industry/asos-leads-the-way-in-ending-wardrobing-trend-that-costs-retail-60bn-a-year-19443.

Smith, Adam (2016 [1904]) *An Inquiry into the Nature and Causes of the Wealth of Nations*, Kindle edn (Chicago, IL: Chicago University Press).

Spocchia, Gino (2020) 'Under No Circumstances Administer into Human Body': Dettol Tells People Not to Follow Trump's 'Dangerous' Recommendation, *The Independent* (24 April). Available at: https://www. independent.co.uk/news/world/americas/us-politics/trump-coronavirus-disinfectant-injection-dettol-response-uk-a9481786.html.

Sutherland, Rory (2019) *Alchemy: The Surprising Power of Ideas That Don't Make Sense* (London: Ebury Publishing).

Swift, Jonathan (1706) *Thoughts on Various Subjects, Moral and Diverting*. Available at: http://self.gutenberg.org/articles/eng/Thoughts_on_Various_Subjects,_Moral_and_Diverting.

Swift, Jonathan (2012 [1726]) *Gulliver's Travels* (London: Penguin).

TES (2018) Does Comic Sans Help Dyslexic Learners? (21 January). Available at: https://www.tes.com/news/does-comic-sans-help-dyslexic-learners.

TheRealVinceOffer (2010) Slap Chop [video] (6 July). Available at: https://www.youtube.com/watch?v=UxGn2Egekic.

Thurman, Wallace (2008) *The Blacker the Berry* (New York: Dover Publications).

Tonkin, Boyd (2012) Battle Hymn of the Tiger Mother by Amy Chua, *The Independent* (17 February). Available at: https://www.independent.co.uk/arts-entertainment/books/reviews/battle-hymn-of-the-tiger-mother-by-amy-chua-6988528.html.

Training and Development Agency for Schools (2007) *Professional Standards for Teachers* (September). Available at: https://www.rgs.org/CMSPages/GetFile.aspx?nodeguid=8284e377-3980-4d16-8348-a6d4c75a705a&lang=en-GB.

Treadaway, Mike (2015) Why Measuring Pupil Progress Involves More Than Taking a Straight Line, *FFT Education Data Lab* (5 March). Available at: https://ffteducationdatalab.org.uk/2015/03/why-measuring-pupil-progress-involves-more-than-taking-a-straight-line.

Tzu, Sun (1910) *The Art of War*, tr. Lionel Giles (London: Luzac and Company). Available at: http://www.gutenberg.org/ebooks/132.

Vilanova, Felipe, Beria, Francielle M., Costa, Ângelo B., and Koller, Silvia H. (2017) Deindividuation: From Le Bon to the Social Identity Model of Deindividuation Effects, *Cogent Psychology*, 4(1). Article: 130810. Available at: https://doi.org/10.1080/23311908.2017.1308104.

Wegner, Daniel M., Schneider, David J., Carter, Samuel R. and White, Teri L. (1987) Paradoxical Effects of Thought Suppression, *Journal of Personality and Social Psychology*, 53(1), 5–13.

Wexler, Natalie (2019) *The Knowledge Gap: The Hidden Cause of America's Broken Education System – and How to Fix It* (New York: Penguin).

Wheldall, Kevin and Bradd, Larraine (2013) Classroom Seating Arrangements and Classroom Behaviour. In Kevin Wheldall (ed.), *Developments in Educational Psychology*, 2nd edn (Abingdon and New York: Routledge), pp. 181–195.

Wiliam, Dylan (2018) *Creating the Schools Our Children Need: Why What We Are Doing Now Won't Help* (West Palm Beach, FL: Learning Sciences International).

Wiliam, Dylan and Christodoulou, Daisy (2017) Marking, Assessment, and Feedback. In Carl Hendrick and Robin Macpherson (eds), *What Does This Look Like in the Classroom? Bridging the Gap Between Research and Practice*, Kindle edn (Woodbridge: John Catt Educational).

Williams, Hywel (2010) *Emperor of the West: Charlemagne and the Carolingian Empire* (London: Quercus).

Willingham, Daniel (2009) *Why Don't Students Like School? A Cognitive Scientist Answers Questions About How the Mind Works and What It Means for the Classroom* (San Francisco, CA: Jossey-Bass).

Willingham, Daniel (2017a) *The Reading Mind: A Cognitive Approach to Understanding How the Mind Reads* (San Francisco, CA: Jossey-Bass).

Willingham, Daniel (2017b) On the Definition of Learning … (26 June). Available at: http://www.danielwillingham.com/daniel-willingham-science-and-education-blog/on-the-definition-of-learning.

ABOUT THE AUTHOR

Samuel Elliott has been a classroom teacher since 2016. Having grown up, lived in and taught in deprived areas, Samuel possesses key insights into misbehaviour that many teachers lack. These experiences informed his approaches in his trainee and NQT years, which, combined with his research into behavioural psychology, have since given rise to a pedagogy that borrows from both traditional and progressive philosophies.

asboteacher.com
@ASBOTeacher

THE SECRET OF LITERACY
MAKING THE IMPLICIT EXPLICIT
ISBN: 978-178135127-7
DAVID DIDAU

Literacy? That's someone else's job, isn't it?

This is a book for all teachers on how to make explicit to students those things we can do implicitly. In the Teachers' Standards it states that all teachers must demonstrate an understanding of, and take responsibility for, promoting high standards of literacy, articulacy, and the correct use of standard English, whatever the teacher's specialist subject. In *The Secret of Literacy*, David Didau inspires teachers to embrace the challenge of improving students' life chances through improving their literacy.

Topics include:

- Why is literacy important?
- Oracy - improving classroom talk.
- How should we teach reading?
- How to get students to value writing.
- How written feedback and marking can support literacy.

WHAT IF EVERYTHING YOU KNEW ABOUT EDUCATION WAS WRONG?

ISBN: 978-178583157-7

DAVID DIDAU

If you feel a bit cross at the presumption of some oik daring to suggest everything you know about education might be wrong, please take it with a pinch of salt. It's just a title. Of course, you probably think a great many things that aren't wrong.

The aim of this book is to help you 'murder your darlings'. David will question your most deeply held assumptions about teaching and learning, expose them to the fiery eye of reason and see if they can still walk in a straight line after the experience. It seems reasonable to suggest that only if a theory or approach can withstand the fiercest scrutiny should it be encouraged in classrooms. David makes no apologies for this; why wouldn't you be sceptical of what you're told and what you think you know? As educated professionals, we ought to strive to assemble a more accurate, informed or at least considered understanding of the world around us.

MAKING KIDS CLEVERER
A MANIFESTO FOR CLOSING THE ADVANTAGE GAP
ISBN: 978-178583366-3
DAVID DIDAU

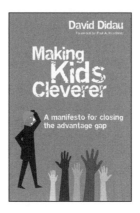

In this wide-ranging enquiry into psychology, sociology, philosophy and cognitive science, David argues that with greater access to culturally accumulated information – taught explicitly within a knowledge-rich curriculum – children are more likely to become cleverer, to think more critically and, subsequently, to live happier, healthier and more secure lives.

Furthermore, by sharing valuable insights into what children truly need to learn during their formative school years, he sets out the numerous practical ways in which policy makers and school leaders can make better choices about organising schools, and how teachers can communicate the knowledge that will make the most difference to young people as effectively and efficiently as possible.

THRIVE

IN YOUR FIRST THREE YEARS IN TEACHING

ISBN: 978-178583304-5

MARTHA BOYNE, EMILY CLEMENTS AND BEN WRIGHT

Martha, Emily and Ben are thriving teachers. In *Thrive* they share their personal experiences and demonstrate how you too can thrive during the tricky training year, the daunting NQT year and the crucial RQT year. Using their collective insights, and plenty of evidence-informed strategies and advice, they detail how you can get to grips with the classroom basics – from behaviour management and lesson planning to differentiation and providing for SEND – and effectively continue your professional development.

This book is not just a survival manual to help teachers get through their first three years in teaching. Nor is it an academic text that has been written by authors who have only a distant memory of what it takes to stand in front of a class of teenagers for the first time. *Thrive* is something very different. It gives both the aspiring and the newly qualified the support and guidance to become a thriving teacher, and has been co-authored by three recently qualified teachers who in this book invest their passion and practical knowledge to inspire and inform others who want to pursue enjoyable and rewarding careers in teaching.

TEACH LIKE NOBODY'S WATCHING
THE ESSENTIAL GUIDE TO EFFECTIVE AND EFFICIENT TEACHING

ISBN: 978-178583399-1

MARK ENSER

In *Teach Like Nobody's Watching*, Mark Enser sets out a time-efficient approach to teaching that will reduce teachers' workload and enhance their pupils' levels of engagement and attainment.

At a time when schools are crying out for more autonomy and trust, teacher and bestselling author Mark Enser asks educators the critical question 'How would you teach if nobody were watching?' and empowers them with the tools and confidence to do just that.

Mark argues that a quality education is rooted in simplicity. In this book he convincingly strips away the layers of contradictory pedagogical advice that teachers have received over the years and lends weight to the three key pillars that underpin effective, efficient teaching: the lesson, the curriculum and the school's support structure.